THE
RED-HAIRED GIRL
FROM THE BOG

The
Red-Haired Girl
From the Bog

The Landscape of
Celtic Myth and Spirit

Patricia Monaghan

New World Library
Novato, California

New World Library
14 Pamaron Way
Novato, California 94949

Front cover design by Mary Beth Salmon
Text design and typography by Tona Pearce Myers

Library of Congress Cataloging-in-Publication Data
Monaghan, Patricia.
    The red-haired girl from the bog : the landscape of Celtic myth and spirit / Patricia Monaghan.
        p.   cm.
Includes bibliographical references and index.
    ISBN 1-57731-190-6 (hardcover : alk. paper)
1. Monaghan, Patricia—Journeys—Ireland. 2. Mythology, Celtic—Ireland.
3. Goddesses, Celtic—Ireland. 4. Women, Celtic—Ireland—Folklore.
5. Ireland—Description and travel. I. Title.
    BL980.I7 .M66 2003
    299'.162—dc21   2002014317

First Printing, February 2003
ISBN 1-57731-190-6
Printed in Canada on acid-free, partially recycled paper
Distributed to the trade by Publishers Group West

10   9   8   7   6   5   4   3   2   1

To Tom Hannon and Barbara Callan,
grá agus buíochas

Contents

Chapter One

The Sacred Center

I remember the exact moment I knew I would go to Ireland. It was a cold Alaskan night, and I was talking with Sikvoan Weyahok. That was his birth name; in English he was called Howard Rock. Every Wednesday Howard held court at Tommy's Elbow Room, where I unfailingly joined him. Almost forty years my senior, he was Eskimo; although that Algonkian word for "raw fish eater" is disdained by many now, it was Howard's word for himself and for his people, the Tigaramiut of Point Hope. He had been an artist in Seattle until threats of nuclear testing near his coastal village brought him home to become a crusading newspaper editor. As one of the most politically significant thinkers of the state, he was treated with respect by Native and non-Native alike.

Howard had no children, but he sentimentally called me his grand-daughter. Perhaps that was because, at our first meeting, I fell into treating him like I treated my own grandfather, offering him attention that was both undivided and untinged by flattery. Just as I had with my grandfather, I challenged Howard when he became pompous, plied him with questions when he grew withdrawn, teased him when he turned maudlin. We were close for a dozen years. When Howard died in his mid-sixties — still so young, I now think — I was on the cusp of my first trip to Ireland.

I have only to close my eyes to see it now, the way it was then: The old mill below Thoor Ballylee, its whitewash long since dissolved away, its stones gray and rough. Nettles palisaded around its perimeter like sharp warnings. The broken millstone near the little sing-song river. The damp chill that hung about even on the brightest day.

I went to Ireland because Howard told me to. Not directly: he was far too traditional to give me explicit commands. Nevertheless, he told me to go. It happened one Wednesday night in 1970. We were sitting at his usual table halfway down the dim room at Tommy's, talking politics, as always. The Native land claims had not yet been settled, so we were probably discussing congressional strategies when Howard suddenly turned to me and asked, "You, now: Where are you from?"

There is this wonderfully oblique yet direct quality — something like what the Irish call "codding," a kind of blunt pointedness — about old-fashioned Eskimo speech. Perhaps that is why I fell into a special relationship with such a distinguished Native elder, because I recognized that kind of talk from my own grandfather, whose sidewise testing comments had been part of my childhood. Pop once commented to my roundest sister, when she complained of her weight, "Ah, but you'll be glad of it when the next Famine comes." Another time, when he was nearing ninety and his son's mother-in-law insinuated that he drank to excess, Pop inquired mildly of her teetotaling spouse, "What was he when he died? — seventy, wasn't it?"

I was reminded of Pop one evening when I showed off my new bearskin mukluks to Howard. I had stretched and tanned a hide for the traditional footwear, razored it into careful pieces, sewn the seams tightly with dental floss — that modern sinew substitute — and tied on bright multicolored yarn pom-poms. I thought my mukluks marvelous, but Howard was less impressed. Squinting down, he shook his head. "I think you forgot the claws," he said. I followed his eyes to where, yes, my feet resembled misshapen bear paws in the floppy oversized booties.

So I was used to listening beneath the surface of conversation. What was Howard asking? He knew I had grown up in Anchorage, that my parents still lived in Turnagain near the ruined clay cliffs of Earthquake Park. Clearly he wanted something other than the family address. Underlying our discussion of land claims was an unvoiced agreement about the importance of Howard's Eskimo heritage, so my own must be of interest. "Well," I offered, "I'm Irish."

Even when it wasn't March, I was proud of being Irish. I was proud of my ancestral home, that colonized land of splendid myth and bitter history whose yearning sentimental songs my family sang and whose poets I yearningly imitated. But I didn't know Kinvara from Kinsale, Kildare from Killaloe. The Ireland I imagined that I loved — so green, so beautiful — was vague, indistinct, unreal, not a place at all but a haunted haunting dream.

Howard waited, his face still, both hands around his glass. I tried again. "From Mayo. *County* Mayo," I said, retrieving what I could remember of my grandfather's stories. "From...a town..." Bohola, I would answer instantly now, but then I could not name where Pop John Gordon and Grandma Margaret Dunleavy had been born. Bohola: three syllables in a language I could not speak, meaningless because they were connected with neither memories nor stories, faces nor dreams.

The road beyond Bohola on a cloudy day. A sudden looming shape, blue-gray in the mist. A perfect pyramid that retreats, advances, retreats as the road dips and swoons. Around the mountain twists a pilgrims' path. Atop its height of eagles stands an ancient circle of stone.

Howard repeated my words. "From...a town." I could hear how ignorant it sounded.

"More like a village, I think." The word *village* has resonance in Alaska. Native people come from villages. Villages are where people know you and your family, where you know the land and its seasons and the food it provides. I had never been to Point Hope, yet when Howard's eyes grew distant at its name, I could almost see a cluster of brown houses, the sea churning gray near it in summer, thin skeins of geese overhead in spring and fall, the sun's red ball on short winter days. I thought perhaps my grandparents were from somewhere like that, a small place far from the centers of power, easy to overlook, significant because of how deeply rather than how widely it was known.

"More like a village." Howard continued to repeat my words. I had exhausted what I knew. I stared into my drink. Finally he said again, gently, "A village. In Ireland." And I could only nod.

In his subtle Tigaramiut way, Howard had asked me a profound question. How could I ever know myself if I did not know where I was from — not just the scenes of my personal memories, but the places where my ancestors had walked, where my body understood the way time unfolded its seasons on the land, where people still spoke a language whose rhythms echoed in my own? Where history had been made by people with my family names? Where the unrecorded history of ordinary loves and losses had been lived by people with features like mine? Howard knew what Carson McCullers meant when she wrote, "To know who you are, you have to have a place to come from." Not knowing where I came from, I did not know who I was or who I might ultimately become.

At that moment, sitting silent beside Howard, I knew I would go to Ireland. Howard died before I came back with my first insights into a proper response. Where am I from? Even now, I cannot fully answer that question, but it was Howard who set my feet upon the path toward understanding.

The Sky Road across from Errislannan. The full moon sheets the calm ocean with silver light. A vanilla fragrance — gorse — drifts past on a slight summer breeze. Beneath my feet, the boreen is pebbly and uneven. Somewhere on the hill, someone whistles to a dog.

"Is this your first trip home, then?" people asked me. That odd, common question. Home? Wasn't I already at home in Alaska? Yes, but no. My uprearing was there, but my heritage was not. I had only to look around me in Ireland to realize the difference; for the first time, I belonged. For more generations than I can count, people like me have worked the Irish land and fished the Irish seas. Short square bodies and strong faces are common there. I have the Dunleavy nose ("I've never really seen it on a girl," said my great-aunt Sarah, that first time over, codding me the way Pop had always done). My forehead is the same as my cousin Bridey's. I have the Gordon build. It was strange to me, that first time over, hearing my features

— which I had grown up thinking of as unique — dissected and re-assigned. And just as my face was familiar to my Irish relations, I found Ireland strangely familiar. Having grown up deeply loving a land to which I nonetheless was a newcomer, even an invader, I found myself learning to love another land just as deeply and specifically, even knowing that I was and would probably remain an exile from it.

An *exile.* That is the old word for people forced, by economics or politics, to leave Ireland. America called them immigrants; Ireland calls them exiles. Coming from a family of exiles, I was welcomed back as though it were the most natural thing to be drawn to the island where my blood ran in the veins of others. The fact that I was so strongly pulled to Gort, where I had no known family connections, instead of to Bohola, the center of the clan, was a mystery to my friends for many years. "Whyever did ye come to Gort?" fretted antiquarian Tom Hannon until he learned that my grandmother was a Daley. That relieved him greatly, since the Daleys — the Ó Daillaighs — were historically the poets of New Quay, just a few miles away. "Ah, there, Patricia," Tom exulted. "There. Now we have it. Now we have it, Patricia."

The holy well at Liscannor on a dank winter day. The slanting path slippery, the sound of the holy spring masked by pelting rain. Saint Brigit in her protective glass box. The litter of mementoes — handwritten pleas for help, rosaries, bits of damp yarn, bedraggled feathers. Ivy clutching its way up black, wet stones.

When I picture Ireland, I never see a postcard of some generic greenness. I see the Burren, Connemara, Mayo in a wet spring, the mountains of the hag. More specific yet: I see a familiar greening field, a particular thunder-stricken yew, a granite-strewn patch of bog that looks a great deal like other granite-strewn patches of bog but with a certain ineffable difference. For I know Ireland not as a single place but as a mosaic of places, each one steeped in history and myth, song and poetry.

When I meet someone Irish, whether in Ireland or in America, the conversation invariably turns to place. "Where are you from?" it begins. You name the county first, then the town; the parish, then the farm. "Oh, where?" the listener encourages, nodding as familiar names are voiced. My mother's family is from Mayo. Near Castlebar. Bohola. Carrowcastle. When someone can follow all that, you move onto family names. Gordons. Dunleavys. McHales. Deaseys. "Oh, I have a Deasey married to my cousin who lives now down the country in Wicklow." Oh, where? And so it begins again.

"Each single, enclosed locality matters and everything that happens within it is of passionate interest to those who live there," the great novelist John McGahern tells us. Ireland is the land of the *dindshenchas,* the poems of place-lore that tell the mythic meaning of hills and crossroads, dolmens and holy wells. Even today, houses in the West bear names rather than numbers. I was once asked to deliver an article from America to my friend, folklorist and singer Barbara Callan, in Connemara. "We don't have her address," the sender fretted. "We just have the words Cloon, Cleggan, Galway." That *is* her address, I explained. Cloon is the clutch of houses, Cleggan the village, Galway the county. The local postmistress would envision Cloon's heathery low hill just outside Cleggan town, just as mention of the Gordon farm at Carrowcastle, Bohola, Co. Mayo, conjures for those who know the area wide green pastures and a substantial stucco house. A stranger might find 23 Clifden Road or 125 Highway N5 more helpful, but Irish house names are not meant for strangers but for neighbors who know each twist of the road and every boulder that shadows it.

The coral strand near Ballyconneely, the dark mass of Errisbeg rising behind me. The tide is out, the rocks covered with lacy dark seaweed. Somewhere offshore, a seal barks. The endless wind fills me, lifts me, blows through me until I dissolve.

I am lucky, among Americans, in coming from a place. Growing up in Alaska, I learned the land with the kind of voluptuous intimacy the rural Irish know. I learned the summer cycle of edible berries — raspberries first, then blueberries, then low-bush cranberries — and how to recognize, even in other seasons, their favored terrains. I still keep secret the location of the best chanterelles in interior Alaska, in case I ever move back. I know the history of towns and the families connected with them, so that when I pass a certain turnoff near Delta, I see generations of the Kusz family in a flash. When I first came home to Ireland more than twenty years ago, I already possessed a rootedness that helped me recognize the power of place in the Irish spirit.

A shaded path through Páirc-na-lee. Sunlight glancing off the dark waters of Coole Lake. Wild swans, pair by pair, mounting the pale summer sky. The raucous unmelodic calls of hoodie crows in nearby trees.

The lore and love and specificity associated with Irish places grow directly from Ireland's residual paganism. "Scratch a bit at the thin topsoil of Irish Catholicism," the saying goes, "and you soon come to the solid bedrock of Irish paganism." Ireland is still what novelist Edna O'Brien calls a "pagan place." But that paganism does not conflict with a devout Catholicism that embraces and absorbs it, in a way that can seem mysterious, even heretical, elsewhere. In Ireland, Christianity arrived without lions and gladiators, survived without autos-da-fé and Inquisitions. The old ways were seamlessly bonded to the new, so that ancient rituals continued, ancient divinities became saints, ancient holy sites were maintained just as they had been for generations and generations.

Thus the goddess remains alive in Ireland even in the first years of the third millennium of the Christian era. But that sentence is inexact. For the goddess does not merely remain alive in Ireland — she *is* Ireland. "Ireland has always been a woman," says Edna O'Brien, "a womb, a cave, a cow, a Rosaleen, a sow, a bride, a harlot, and, of course, the gaunt Hag." The island still bears her ancient name: Éire, from Ériu*, an ancestral goddess whom the invading Celts met and adopted (or did she adopt them?) around 400 B.C.E. Ireland *is* the goddess. She is every field still fertile a thousand years after its first cultivation. She is every river that still floods with salmon despite millennia of fishing. She is the dancing pattern of the seasons, the fecundity of sheep and cattle, the messages written in the migratory flight of birds. She is the sun's heat stored deep in the dark bogs. She is the refreshment of pure water and of golden ale. She is living nature, and she has never been forgotten in Ireland.

This residual Irish paganism is, perforce, polytheistic, because what monotheism leaves out is the goddess. There has never been a religion that had a goddess but no god, in the way that monotheisms have gods but no goddesses. But the difference between mono- and polytheisms does not end with number and gender of divinities. As Celticist Miranda Green argues, polytheism involves a close relationship between the sacred and the profane, especially in relation to the natural world. Where monotheism imagines god as transcending nature, as separate from this world, polytheism — paganism, if you will — sees nature as holy. Every stream has its special connection with divinity and thus is pictured as a unique and individual god or goddess. As the Greeks expressed it, every tree has its dryad, every rock its oread, every ocean wave its nereid. Paradoxically, such

---

* For this and other Irish words, see the pronunciation guide at the back of the book.

polytheism often sees nature as a whole — called Gaia by the scientist James Lovelock, after the Greek goddess of earth — as divine. In Ireland, that divinity is unquestionably feminine.

This paganism remains a part of Irish life today. Celtic spirituality did not just bring together the goddess of the land with the god of the cross; it brought together a deep love of nature, the heritage of paganism, with the new social ideals of Christianity. What resulted is a Church that has always been subtly different from the Roman one. Subtly? Perhaps radically. Sometimes I fancy that the Irish have not yet heard the news that Augustine bested Pelagius. Sixteen hundred years ago, the bishop of Hippo waged a war of words on the Celtic monk who preached that the world we see and hear and touch and taste was created, just as it is, by god. Therefore, Pelagius said, we must learn to love this world, just as it is. Sex is good; why else would god have created us as sexual beings? Death has a purpose; why else would god have made us mortal? The sky, whether blue or slate, is there when we lift our heads. Water is there, clear and cool, to quench our thirst. Life is good, Pelagius said. We only have to love it, as god intended.

This was the "happy heresy" that Augustine, infuriated by his inability to control his sexual urges, set out to crush. And crush it he did; we have the African Saint Augustine, but no Celtic Saint Pelagius. Yet in Ireland, love of the natural world continued to be the baseline of spiritual experience. The passionate joy of life in a mortal body in a world of changing seasons floods Irish poetry, including that written by monks and clerics. "I have news for you," goes the first Irish poem I learned, "the stag calls, snows fall, summer goes....Cold catches birds' wings, ice covers all things, this is my news." I immediately loved — and still love — the tension between the first and final lines and the rest of the poem. News? What can be new about the commonness of life? But that anonymous poet of the ninth century reminds us of the only real news we can ever know: the glorious sensual specificity, the absolute newness, of each moment we experience in our unique and living bodies.

I have news for you: it is February in Kildare. In greening fields, lambs spring after weary ewes. On the Curragh, horses thunder past in deep morning mist. Near Athy, a lark warbles the territories of its nest. Spring has come. This is my news.

It is impossible to utterly separate goddess from nature from poetry from song in Ireland. She remains alive not only in the land but also in the words that name and define that land. No one is surprised to hear of the importance of music in Ireland, for it has been one of the island's most vital exports for years. But it is hard for my American friends to believe how important poetry is in Ireland. "Brendan Kennelly's *Book of Judas* was on the best-seller list in Dublin," I offer, knowing that a best-selling book of poetry is unimaginable this side of the water unless penned by someone celebrated for sports or murder or both. In Ireland, stores are named with lines from William Butler Yeats's poems. People recite, often in Irish, in pub and kitchen. There is a thriving industry in literary conferences, such that a friend jokes that he is looking for the last Irish poet without a designated week, to stake his claim and make his fortune.

Ireland's residual paganism and its poetic heritage have in common a recognition of the paradoxical connection of the specific and the universal. As poet Patrick Kavanagh said, there is a marked difference between parochial and provincial art. In the latter, the poet attempts to translate local reality into the language of the powerful; she directs her words from Gort to New York, as though no one in Gort matters. The parochial poet speaks in the local language to those who know its references — and thereby speaks to all our hearts, for each of us knows our own world in that kind of immediate and specific detail. Every universal epic, Kavanagh says, is ultimately local:

> *... I inclined*
> *To lose my faith in Ballyrush and Gortin*
> *Till Homer's ghost came whispering to my mind*
> *He said: I made the Iliad from such*
> *A local row. Gods make their own importance.*

The goddess, too, makes her own importance, in various local identities and guises: as the hag called the Cailleach in the Burren, as a reckless maiden in rivers like the Shannon, as the healer Brigit in Kildare and the wounded mother Macha in Ulster. But she is also one, the universal goddess, just as a woman remains herself as both colleen and cailleach. This infinitely divisible goddess lives in those infinitely numerous holy places of the landscape.

I am reminded, in considering this paradox, of the concept of *kami* in Japanese Shinto. For *kami,* although often translated as "gods" and "goddesses," means nothing so simple or personalized. The best translation of the word is "outstanding." It describes those moments and places and myths and beings in which divine presence makes itself felt. The blossoming of cherry trees, a sharp outcropping of rock, the sun bursting through clouds: these are *kami* because they remind us of the order — the divinity — into which we are born. In Ireland, similarly, the goddess is experienced as a hierophany, a breaking through, of divine power into our human consciousness, with specific natural settings and moments as the medium of communication.

Beside the ocean in west Cork, a small flat rock, almost hidden in the wind-flattened grass. In the timeless time of myth, the children of Lir once touched that rock. I bend down: coins fill every crevice, coins and tiny flowers. I have nothing else, so I sing the first song I remember: "Flowers bud in the rain, always and never the same; above, the wild geese skein."

In Ireland, the link between mundane time and space, and sacred space-time, is maintained through ritual and myth, song and poetry. Some rituals, like the annual ascension of Croagh Patrick in Mayo or the wild Puck Fair in Kerry, have been held for as long as a thousand uninterrupted years. The myths are reinforced with every recitation — reinforced even by the naming of the places in which they occurred, for Irish place-names are gateways to the mythic past. The tradition of the *dindshenchas,* the naming of significant places to evoke their myths, continues in Irish song, for there is scarcely a town that doesn't have a song mentioning its name. "Not far from Kinvara in the merry month of May..." and "While going the road to sweet Athy, a stick in me hand and a drop in me eye..." and "Bohola, whose great men are famed near and far."

Poets, too, follow the tradition, for there is power and magic in the names on the land. Raftery, the great blind bard of Galway and Mayo, once sang of his love for a woman by naming the places he looked for her: "To Lough Erne, and from Sligo to the foot of Kesh Corran, I shall take my course, I shall walk the Bog of Allen, and Cork and Bend Edar, and I shall not stand in Tuamgraney until I go to Tralee." Raftery covers the entire island with his desire, beloved woman and beloved land becoming one in his quest and his journey. This tradition holds fast among poets today. "Ballyvaughan, peat and salt, how the wind bawls across these mountains, scalds the orchids of the Burren," Eavan Boland writes, invoking and hallowing the memory of a tiny village. Even in exile, poets remember the names of Irish places. "Along a boreen of bumblebees, blackahs & fuchsia, somewhere around Dunquin," remembers Greg Delanty, "you said that

Pangaea split there first & America drifted away from Kerry & anyone standing on the crack got torn in two slowly." It is not only important, to Corkman Delanty in his Vermont home, that Ireland and America were once joined, but that he learned of this fact precisely there, beside the hedgerows of Dunquin.

What I know of Ireland, I know in this specific way. I know certain places in Ireland through the experiences I have lived in those places. I know these places in the context of living and lost people as well as history, of jokes as well as poetry, of parties as well as rituals, of heartbreak as well as myth. What I know of the goddess, what I know of magic, I learned in those places in Ireland, places from which I remain an exile even while I continue to inhabit them in my dreams.

Two paths cross in a new-growth forest near Annaghmakerrig. A buck stands there, a fallow doe behind him in the red willow herb. We all stare at each other awhile, and then my friend begins to dance. There has never been a dance as awkward or as graceful as what he offers the deer. The many-tined buck stands, stately and silent, until the dance is over. Then he turns and bounds away, the doe flashing her white tail as she follows.

Ireland is full of holy places, stone circles and solar wells and haunted glens. My experiences in some of these have been so shattering that I knew, even in the moment of being shattered, how my life would be transformed. Such a place is Newgrange, when the winter solstice sun shafts through the cave like a searching amber fire. Under that stone roof, weeping from the majesty of the moment, I knew that I would never be able fully to describe the way the world seemed to shift and alter in the piercing solar beam. Such a place is Kildare, when the holy well reflects the light of hundreds of candles while pilgrims sing ancient songs and dance with fiery torches, echoing other pilgrims whose bodies traced the same motions that will, in turn, be echoed by future pilgrims tracing the same motions.

Loughcrew on a fall afternoon, the sky swept with feather clouds. Only sheep accompany me as I wander amid the fallen stones. The grass is damp and long. I sit within the farthest circle and lean against ancient rocks. On the lower portion of one of them, my fingers find fading traces of spirals and bursting stars.

But some holy spaces seem nondescript, even a bit seedy, when one first encounters them. It is only afterward that their power becomes apparent. The first time I wandered onto the Old Bog Road in Connemara, I saw only emptiness. It was when I descended the slight hill into town that I realized how transporting that emptiness had been. The first time I visited the Brigit Vat at Liscannor, I saw only the mess of offerings and the dreary unkemptness of it all. But later, back in America, I remembered it as filled with light and song, even in the pelting rain.

American Indian scholar Vine Deloria has argued that non-Indians can only have an aesthetic appreciation for the American landscape, because we cannot appreciate "walking along a riverbank or on a bluff and realizing that their great-great-grandfathers once walked that very spot." That sense of continuity and of community is what I have felt at Newgrange, a glorious suncatcher built six thousand years ago; I have felt it at Kildare, where I placed gorse wood on a fire in the very spot Celtic priestesses and medieval Irish nuns had performed the same action. In Ireland, I know that my body comes from the bodies of others who moved across that land. Whether nondescript or astonishing, each holy place there reinforces my connection, through the body, to the past and to its wisdom.

And then there is that other, that dreadful place. I only know one place like it, in Ireland or anywhere else. It does not, as far as I know, have a name. No one has ever spoken of it. It appears on no maps. There is only the warning, in myth and song, of fairy kidnappings in its vicinity.

I have found places sacred to the goddess by listening rather than by looking. I listen for the names, finding holy wells near towns called Tubber and vestiges of sacred groves where the name Dara appears. I listen to what my elders tell me, about the myth and history hidden in the folds of the remarkably elastic Irish landscape. I also look, but I early found that maps and signposts alone would not lead me to the hallowed places. I have to use the inner eye instead: to notice the way in which a certain stone goes out of focus, then comes back more sharply than before. The way a space of glowing silence seems to open in a field on a sunny bee-buzzing day. These moments are ineffable; they elude capture, being always both more and less than what words express. But these moments have taught me about the way spirit resides in nature and in myself.

Beyond the inexpressible, there is another kind of spiritual reality that Ireland has taught me, and that is the unspeakable. Especially in the West, stories of people disappearing near specific spots are still told, warnings against the hubris that leads us to think that we are the reason that nature exists. The goddess is larger than we are; there are places — what my friend the Ulster folklorist Bob Curran calls Ireland's "dark places" —

where we encounter her in such terrifyingly inhuman shape that we never quite recover. Deloria speaks of places of revelation, where time and space as we know them cease to exist, where life takes on new dimensions. In America, their location and meaning are closely guarded secrets, and medicine people who approach them realize that they may have to pay with their lives for what they learn there. "Indians who know about these things find it extremely difficult to describe what they know," Deloria tells us. "There seems to be an abiding spirit of place that inhibits anyone from trying to explain what has been experienced there."

I open my mouth to speak. I am about to say something about that place. I am about to give it a name and a location. But time stops. The room is suddenly dark and quiet. Invisible eyes. Something listening. My eyes water. My legs shake. I grope for balance. I close my mouth. Time begins again. No one has noticed anything at all.

What I know of the goddess, what I know of the spirit, I have learned not from books but from the land. Ireland is a great teacher, for it harks back to a pre-Cartesian world where mind and body and spirit were not yet artificially divided. Similarly, nature and humanity are not separated there in the way that is so common in Western European culture. That culture defines nature as existing "out there" — in wildernesses beyond the towns. Forests are nature, farms are not. Oceans are nature, cities are not. That culture speaks of "virgin land," as though the touch of human consciousness despoils nature. But we are part of nature, not separate from it like gods. In Ireland, human consciousness and the land's consciousness have communicated for so many centuries that the land welcomes us. The road rises up to meet our feet. And it teaches us, if only we will listen.

Come with me to those places; listen to those lessons. We will travel the old way around the island, *deiseal,* an Irish word that means to circumambulate a sacred center, moving in the direction of the sun's passage. But the word connotes more than simple direction. To move *deiseal* is to live rightly, to move in the order that nature intended. And nature's order, as chaos theory reminds us, is not the rigid order of logic and theory. It is spontaneous and creative play, an intricate dance of unfolding possibilities.

Our circumambulation follows the path of the old Celtic diurnal cycle, from sunset to sunset, for the Celts counted time from darkness into light, just as they measured the year from harvest to burgeoning. We begin in stony Connacht, traverse the broad green flanks of Ulster, ride the fertile waters and cross the lush fields of Leinster, conclude on the mountain peaks of Munster. We trace as well the wheel of the year, for a calendar of ancient holidays is embedded in the landscape: Lughnasa rites on the stony Burren, fairy kidnappings at Samhain in Connemara, the winter sun's rebirth in the cave of Newgrange, Imbolc relighting of Brigit's Kildare fire, Bealtaine fires on Ériu's central hill, and Lughnasa again in the harvest festivals of Munster.

Within that sunwise circle, we ramble — an English word that the Irish have stolen to describe a kind of movement fully open to the serendipity of each instant. A man in Sligo once told me that when he was young, people went out rambling: "The route they took totally depended on which way the wind was blowing, tidbits of stories of who was visiting from outside the area, the way your feet met the path you were on. Going left or right depended on which foot your weight was on when you came to the crossroad." In the same way, we will dip into myth and history, geography and geology, friendship and passion, poetry and music. This book is my own private *dindshenchas,* my song to the Irish places I know and to their inner meanings. It is my poet's circuit, circling the island with my left shoulder to the sea, repeating the stories I learned in my travels.

But however far afield we ramble, we never lose sight of the center. Irish tradition explains that paradox easily. Four of the great ancient provinces — Leinster, Munster, Connacht, and Ulster — were associated with a direction in the outer world. *The Settling of the Manor of Tara* tells us that each direction had a quality: "wisdom in the west, battle in the north, prosperity in the east, music in the south." But the Irish word for province means "one fifth," for a fifth province — Míde, the center — existed not in the physical realm but in the magical and symbolic one. To the ancient Irish, the five directions were north, south, east, west, and the center. All are relative to the speaker, for the center is "here" — wherever we stand, orienting ourselves to our world, centers of a compass whose center is everywhere. But the center being everywhere is not the same as the center being nowhere — far from it. The center is not outside us. It is within our innumerable, individual, unique, and irreplaceable hearts.

I have news for you: the holy well bubbles from the ground. The wind flows like water over the bog. The stone circles rivet sky to earth. The goddess breathes the moist green air. Ireland is sacred, as all land is sacred, as we are all sacred. This is my news.

Chapter Two

Mountains of the Hag

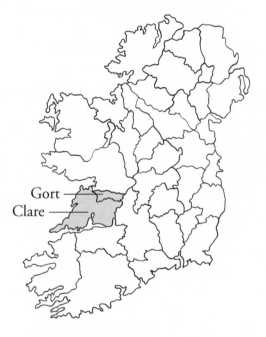

Gort
Clare

There is nowhere for me to begin but in the West. On the harsh stirring Burren, where ancient dolmens stand like portals to the sky and orchids scent the air. On Slieve Echtghe's lonely green slopes and the gray cliffed bays of the Clare coast. In the haunted woods of Coole and the bramble-crowned boreens around Kilmacduagh. For me, Ireland begins with the bouldery borderland around the little market town of Gort, for it was there that I first came to know Ireland and the feminine soul of her land.

"Gort? However did you get to *Gort?*" my Irish friends ask, knotting their brows when they learn of my connection to the undistinguished town on the Burren's edge. "Turned left at Loughrea," I shrug. It always gets a laugh and is as good an answer as any. Why Gort? Few young American women stayed alone in the West of Ireland a quarter century ago, and among them, Gort was hardly a popular destination. Doolin was, for the music; Connemara for its lonely vastness; Galway city for its rowdy Salthill pubs. But Gort boasts neither picturesque scenery nor fashionable nightlife. In British comedian Tony Hawks's phrase, Gort looks just like it sounds. Gort is to Galway what Podunk is to Idaho.

However *did* I get to Gort? Not through the dartboard method I suggest to other Americans, although my journey did have something of that random quality. When asked for a list of Ireland's must-see sights, I suggest getting a map of the country and a dart, perhaps one borrowed from an American bar popular with the Irish. Pin the map to the wall, I say, step back ten paces, and throw the dart at the map. Then pack your bags and head for whatever village the dart pierces. Find a bed-and-breakfast and tuck in for the duration. Befriend any willing locals, ramble the countryside, frequent the pubs, eavesdrop on the gossip. You will learn more about Ireland that way, I assure the aspiring tourist, than with any if-it's-Tuesday-it-must-be-Clifden package. For Ireland is not a single place but a mosaic of innumerable pieces, each fascinating in its own way, not one identical to another.

Today Gort remains my special piece of Ireland's mosaic, decades after I first came over. There are places in Ireland I love more, but none where I feel more at home. Not only in the town itself, but also in the lands around it and in the villages strewn across its baronies: Kinvara, to whose deep harbor the tall-masted Galway hookers return each August; Ballinderreen, scarcely a crossroads but with your choice of two pubs; Kilnaboy of the famous bawdy goddess; Feakle, high in the mountains of the hag; Liscannor, where a spiral pattern is still walked around the holy well; Roo, no longer even on the map but once the region's richest village; Ballyvaughan on the Burren's ocean edge and Carron deep in its rocky recesses. Each of these names evokes memories of days spent rambling the countryside, evenings spent in the company of friends, countless hours spent learning the lore of the land.

However *did* I get to Gort? I came that first summer, decades ago, challenged by the man who called himself my Eskimo grandfather to find my home place, the Mayo town from which my grandparents hailed. South

Galway is not east Mayo — nowhere near — but I was an Alaskan girl, and space in Alaska is measured in hours rather than miles. When I touched down at Shannon ready to see my grandparents' village, I had already written ahead to the cousins. Having met scores of Americans in Ireland trying to trace their roots with only surnames and perhaps a county to go on ("My grandfather was a Flaherty, from — Galway I think?"), I recognize my luck in having addresses, even descriptions, of my relations before ever I set foot on Irish soil. The Gordons kept in touch, despite the sixty-five years between Pop's emigration and his first trip back. Just after his eightieth birthday, a decade before my own first expedition there, Pop returned to Bohola to renew family bonds and, while he was about it, to blow on the coals of a few family feuds. My Irish grandfather thus opened the door for the trip my Eskimo grandfather inspired.

Pop never stopped being Irish. When he died, more than eighty years away from Mayo, he still spoke with an unmistakable brogue. In New York, where we lived during my early childhood, Pop instructed us to say "Irish-American" when asked our nationality. We learned countless Irish songs — mostly drinking, some rebel — that we sang as we jolted up the then-unpaved Alcan Highway to our new home. No Irish community welcomed us in Alaska, but I never lost my sense of myself as a hyphenated American. When I studied literature in graduate school, it seemed natural to gravitate toward Irish writers. Indeed, I remember over-fervently pointing out to one professor that everyone on his Major British Writers seminar syllabus — Edmund Spenser, Jonathan Swift, George Bernard Shaw, William Butler Yeats, Gerard Manley Hopkins, James Joyce, Samuel Beckett — was either Irish or had lived in Ireland. Intellectually insecure and thus easily offended, the man repaid my jingoism by persecuting me that entire semester. But I did not back down, as the title of my paper on "British" comic poetry shows: "When the Irish Smile," it taunted, "They Bare Their Teeth."

Thus, as I examined tourist brochures and studied maps for what I was already calling "my first trip to Ireland," I discovered a goal beyond meeting the family Pop had left at the century's turning. I wanted to see the places of which I had read, places so precisely limned by Ireland's writers that, like the image of Point Hope behind Howard's closed eyelids, I could almost see them. At first I thought of doing a complete literary tour, but I soon realized that lifetimes of peregrinations would not suffice. Every region, every county, almost every village has a writer or two connected with it. Clare has Brian Merriman; Galway, Anthony Raftery; dear old dirty Dublin has Joyce and Gogarty and O'Casey. There is no place in Ireland that a writer had not cherished or loathed — sometimes both at once.

I decided to specialize. Although I admired many Irish writers, there was only one I loved without reservation. For years, I had read Yeats's poetry from the tattered brown volume given me by my favorite professor. So I decided to visit the places Yeats had made familiar: the demesne of Coole with its beautiful, mysterious wild swans; Kiltartan Cross, home of the Irish airman who foresaw his death somewhere among the clouds above; the stately home of Lissadell with its great windows opening to the south. Ben Bulben and Glen-Car, Dooney Rock and Raftery's cellar, lonely Echtghe of streams, the Seven Woods, the lake isle of Innisfree. I began to annotate my map with the places of which Yeats sang.

It did not take me long to discover that my grandparents' Mayo village lay conveniently between the two places that figure prominently in Yeats's work. Galway is the next county to Mayo, which in turn borders Sligo; little over a hundred miles separates the furthest points. As my itinerary became clear, I noticed a town near two vital sites. Gort is adjacent both to Yeats's tower home at Ballylee and to Coole Park, demesne of Lady Augusta Gregory, founder of the Abbey Theater and Yeats's artistic patron (perhaps more accurately, matron). Gort it would be! I would find lodgings in that little Galway town from which I would take day trips to Mayo and Sligo.

I shake my head now at my ignorance. Distance in Ireland is not like distance in America. When friends are making their first trip over, I like to offer them an unfolded sheet of paper. "Now this is America," I tell them. Then I wad the paper up into a tight little ball. "Now this is Ireland: same size, only smaller." A hundred miles in Connacht is a long, long way, much longer than in Indiana. Gort is nowhere near Bohola. You have to go through Ardrahan and Kilcolgan and Clarinbridge, then through that interminable series of roundabouts near Oranmore, up past Claregalway and Claremorris and Tuam, through the pilgrim congestion of Knock, then turn left at Kiltimaugh. Oh, you could be up and back in a day if you had a car, but whyever would ye?

Whyever indeed. Besides, that first trip over, I did not have a car; I had a Rambler bus/rail pass. And service was neither fast nor direct between my destinations. After finding a cheap, no-mod-cons room above a pub on

Gort's main street, I jumped the bus to Galway City and asked for the next connection to Bohola. The attendant shook his head, "Ah, but you don't want to go to Bohola." Yes, in fact I did. "No," he assured me smoothly, "you do not. It's hard to get to, and there's nothing there." He returned to his paperwork without offering further assistance. I took the printed schedules back to Gort and puzzled it out for myself.

I did get to Mayo, and then beyond to Sligo, but only once, and that toward the end of my stay. The rest of the time, I hung around Gort. Tom Hannon from Roo, Gort's antiquarian, eventually theorized that blood instinct compelled me to remain near the ancient center of the Ó Daillaighs, my paternal grandmother Daley's clan. Proof was near to hand: had not the Ó Daillaighs held their annual gathering over on the Flaggy Shore in the very month I first appeared on the local scene? The fact that I had no prior knowledge of the "Burren Bards" was inconsequential. Blood will out.

Not only had I never heard of the Ó Daillaighs, I knew virtually nothing about the Daleys, not even their county of origin. "The Daleys have *always* been from New Jersey," my grandmother Elizabeth proclaimed as her daughter Reggie researched our family history. "Oh, right," snapped my aunt. "Of course. We're Indian. Daley is a famous Native American name." Elizabeth stuck to her story, more from ignorance than intransigence. Her family kept silent about life before America, a strategy common to those who wished to extinguish memories of poverty and pain. Undeterred by the drying up of my family stream in New Jersey, Tom rooted through an astonishing assemblage of photocopies, newspaper clippings, and notes written in his spidery hand to find material on the Ó Daillaigh bards.

Thus I came to learn about my alleged ancestors. There was Cearbhaill, who stole away the beautiful Eibhlin á Ruin from another man, posing as a harper at their wedding and proclaiming his love in a tender song over which Handel sighed in envy. And Angus the satirist, who stirred up constant trouble among the West Clare overlords with his biting quatrains. There was Donnchadh Mór, who inspired Dante; Gofraidh Fionn the fair-haired, the passionate religious poet; Angus MacDara, who wrote Ireland's most rousing war chant. And my favorite, the wild Muireadhac, the "irritable genius": insulted by an ill-dressed tax collector at Lissadell — *lios Ó Daillaigh,* the fort of the Daleys — he brained the scoundrel, was forced to flee to Scotland, and ended up famous for his poetry on both sides of the Irish Sea.

I am happy to claim these hotheads and romantics as my forebears — I'm a bit of a romantic hothead myself — although I remain unconvinced that it was ancestral blood that kept me in Gort. Nevertheless I stayed. Weeks passed without my catching that bus to Mayo and Sligo. Mornings I wrote Yeats-haunted ballads, afternoons I rambled the countryside. And evenings I drank in local lore along with my pints at Máire's pub, where I found an odd friendly home with my publican landlady and her somewhat ragtag assortment of patrons. The back door of the long, dim pub opened right into the kitchen, so that family and business life melded together seamlessly. The black-and-white twins, Sharon and Gráinne — the first dark and intense, the other a sunny redhead — served pints beside their sturdy mother, who knew all gossip worth sharing and had an Ó Daillaigh-like disdain for attempted overregulation of struggling publicans.

I think in retrospect that it was neither the poetry of Yeats nor that of the Burren bards that kept me stalled in Gort. Nor was it the boisterous action at Máire's, where I witnessed plenty of singsongs and occasional fights and even, one time, a hedgehog set loose by Freddy the Frenchman. No, Gort held me because of the glimpse it afforded into the importance of place in Ireland. I don't mean place in the abstract, but place in the exhaustingly specific. Every night in the pub, I was quizzed on where I had spent the day. Then the storytelling would begin, providing narrative context for what I had seen on my rambles. Sometimes I learned of recent events, as when Ardrahan was defined as where Michael Slattery's sheep — hoisting themselves through a narrow gap in the stone wall of borrowed pasturage — had escaped to ravage whole fields of cabbages. More often, reference was to an older tale, as when my visit to Ballylee's disappearing river brought to mind blind Raftery's love for fair Mary Hynes two centuries earlier, or when my exploration of Kilmacduagh recalled ancient king Guaire's dinner disappearing skyward when he prayerfully offered to share it. Thus was I taught — gradually, merrily — how inseparable are place and story in Ireland.

Had I used the dartboard method to plan my trip, would anything have been different? Had my dart pierced Garryowen or Glengariff, had I gone there and boarded above a pub for a few months, would I have discovered a similarly dense aggregate of history and gossip, poetry and mystery?

Without question. That I found it in Gort is not surprising, for that is where I was looking. Yet Garryowen or Glengariff might not have called me back time and again, as Gort has. For just as place and story are inseparable in Ireland, neither can be separated from the goddess, for she is the full mosaic of which these places are the distinct, individual pieces.

This multiplicity of goddesses can be traced to the earliest written records. *The Book of Invasions* tells us that not one but three ruling goddesses greeted the Celts as they stepped onto Ireland's shore. To Fódla, Banba, and Ériu — each in turn — the Celts promised that if she did not hinder their settlement, they would name the island after her. Although invaders are typically cavalier about such promises, the Celts faced an uncomfortable future if they betrayed the majority of their welcoming committee. Which of these intimidatingly powerful goddesses would they disappoint, and what excuse could they give? To cover the Celtic rear, it was decided that because Ériu's pledge had been spoken by the bard Amairgin and because the words of a poet can never be reversed, the land would be called Éire. That decision remains in force, but queenship of the country is held just as firmly by Ériu's whispered sisters and by scores of other goddesses, fairy queens, heroines, and other figures of feminine power who evoke and express the qualities of Ireland's varied landscapes. And among that numinous assembly one stands out, one to whom I have felt compelled to return again and again: the goddess of the stark Burren hills and the slopes of watery Echtghe.

※※※※※

I did not know her when I first arrived. Settling into my dim third-floor room above the pub, I fancied myself conversant with, even fluent in, Ireland's goddess heritage. Had I not studied Celtic mythology, the better to understand my favorite poets? I had read of brilliant Brigit and wild Medb and strong-willed Síonann, figures recent enough that their myths and symbols, feasts and rituals, had been duly recorded. But even the most voracious reading could not have prepared me for the goddess I would encounter, one of such immense antiquity that her rites and liturgies were never written down, at least not in script we can read today. To encounter that soulful goddess — she who stares out to sea from the western Cliffs and who shadows the land from mountain heights in the east — I had to travel to her land, because more than any other Irish goddess, she *is* that land.

She is the Cailleach, the old one, the hag, the witch, the rock-faced crone, the giantess of vast years and even vaster power. In the Irish Triads, she stands as a synonym for antiquity: "Three great ages: age of the yew, age of the eagle, age of the Cailleach." Elder sister of Irish goddesses — Yeats called her "the Mother of the Gods herself" — the hag flourished so long ago that we know nothing of her people: not their date of arrival in Ireland, not their race, continent of origin, language, or religion. We do not know how long their culture existed or why it ended. Did epidemic or starvation lay waste the hag's tribe? Were they crowded off the land by later arrivals? Did conquerors exterminate or assimilate them? All we know for certain is that new goddesses, brought by new settlers, so thoroughly supplanted the Old One that there are no holy places in Ireland where her rituals are still kept.

And yet she survives. That she does so is testimony to a remarkable feature of Irish culture: the tenacity with which people cling to topographical names. What's in a place-name? A great deal, I learned that first summer as I drifted about a countryside awash in names. Most were in Irish — as I quickly learned to call the language of my grandparents rather than "Gaelic," Welsh for "untamed" and a word rather like that Attic coinage for people who barked (*"bar-bar"*) their own languages rather than speaking civilized Greek. From the moment I disembarked in Gort, I felt engulfed by names. My map labeled counties, towns, cities, rivers, mountains, islands, and peninsulas, but the torrent did not stop there, for Ireland also has provinces, baronies, townlands, parishes, quarters, and demesnes. The mob at Máire's knew even more: names of crossroads, wells, boulders, big old trees, waterfalls, river bends, gaps in mountain ranges, sections of forest. Names defined physical characteristics, provided historical context, evoked myth and poetry. Every slight rise, every indistinct section of bog, had its own name — sometimes more than one. Swimming in that sea of names, I learned that their function was not to provide me navigational assistance but to anchor the present to the past. Beneath the surface of today's Ireland, all earlier Irelands remain, as tantalizingly close as the submerged fairy cities that float beneath the waves of the Burren's lakes.

Amid this flood of place-names, those that evoke goddesses are consistent in one regard. Archaeologist Helen Lanigan Wood has established that while a hill fort (*rath*), church (*kil*), or other human site is rarely named after a goddess, natural features — like a mountain (*slieve* or *knock*) or lake (*lough*) — invariably are. The more prominent a natural feature, the more ancient its name. Worship of the Cailleach may thus date to those primordial Irish who, some six thousand years ago, entered a nameless land. They were not Celts; the word *Cailleach* derives from a lost non-Celtic tongue, most likely that of her original worshipers. The tribe of the hag named whatever caught their eyes, leaving the leftovers to later settlers. Layer upon layer, like sedimentary limestone, names accumulated on the Irish landscape. The Cailleach is bedrock, or near enough, her name on the highest mountains evidence of her great antiquity.

Sometime in the dim past, those who worshiped the hag saw her in the land — saw the land *as* their goddess — and cemented that connection through place-names. Although uncounted years have passed since the hag's religion died away, she lives on in the region around Gort. We see her silhouette on Ceann na Cailleach, "Hag's Head," the most southerly of the Cliffs of Moher. Her personal name, Mal, appears in a nearby town, Miltown Malby. The hag's body forms Slieve Echtghe, the "mountains of the awful one." She stands tall upon the stony heights of Slievecallan and Knockycallanan, both of which mean "hag mountain"; she rests in the gentle valley of Glennagalliach, "hag's glen." The unyielding Irish conservatism regarding place-names has kept alive an unimaginably ancient harvest goddess whose aged appearance belies her enormous vigor and prodigious sexual vitality. Like the Burren that hides orchids in its gray stone crevices, the Cailleach hides the power of youth within her great age.

But how, knowing nothing of her people or their rituals, can we describe the hag's character with such assurance? Because wherever we find the Cailleach's name, we also find folktales about her, "fragmentary recollections . . . degenerated from myth," as John Kelleher calls them. Place-names provoke storytelling, as the mob at Máire's taught me, and what is true today was doubtless true in the past. Imagine this scene: walking the trail above the Cliffs, a mother points out the hag's face to her child. "Who *is* she?" the child wants to know. The mother spins a yarn about the Cailleach, one she learned from her mother. Delighted, the child begs for more. And so another story is unwound, then another. When might such a scene have occurred? A hundred years ago? A thousand? Five thousand?

I myself saw the Cailleach at that very spot, when Tom Hannon took me on a winter solstice expedition in search of the hag. It had been a decade since Tom and I had first raised pints, that first time over when I discovered in him a teacher of the old ways. On a return visit when I convinced Tom to show me some of his favorite sites around the Burren, he told me he would come to Máire's — still my home-from-home in Gort — promptly at sunrise.

The sun rises late on Irish December mornings; it was half-nine before the light was strong enough to draw us from Máire's warm kitchen. A slow drive in icy rain under a low slate sky brought us to the ocean's edge. There, dwarfed by a timeless treeless landscape, we gazed down nearly a thousand feet to foam-flecked black waves. Shouting the Cailleach's name above the roar of storm and sea, Tom pointed out her face on the farthest of the Cliffs of Moher, tracing it with lifted arm. As he did, I felt the shadow of ages upon us, as tangible as the cold rain on our cheeks. How many others, over how many centuries, had made that same gesture, invoked that same ancient name?

⌗⌗⌗⌗⌗

The cluster of places incorporating the Cailleach's name is less obvious a monument than Brigit's gray stone statue on the Kildare square or Medb's massive tumulus that gathers clouds above Sligo town. She exists in another way, too, for Ireland's regional goddesses call forth human avatars, historical women whose biographies become assimilated into their own myths, like streams joining a great river. Brigit's healing wisdom was made manifest in the great abbess who bore her name; Medb reincarnated herself in fiery-haired Maud Gonne and her friend, the revolutionary warrior Constance Markiewicz; the Cailleach wore many guises, as many as the countless old women who embodied her wisdom.

These hags are mostly nameless, their memory barely traceable in folklore. As we learn from Seán O'Sullivan's 1930s handbook for apprentice folklorists, mention of old women provoked the following standard questions, revealingly full of associations: "Are the hags regarded as being very old and wise and possessed of supernatural powers? Were they looked upon as supernatural beings? Had they unusually great wisdom? Could they cause sudden storms and sickness?" Countless anonymous crones merged with the Cailleach, renewing her ancient legend even as they became submerged in the archetypal sea.

But one haggish woman from the Gort area retained an undiluted individuality: Biddy Early, the White Witch of Clare. I learned of her that first year, when I used Yeats's poetry as a gazetteer for my rambles. Biddy Early appears in the section called "The Shadowy Waters," wherein Yeats describes the famous Seven Woods of Coole. Reciting the poem to myself, I paced the paths, learning to distinguish Shan-walla from Kyle-dortha, sunny Kyle-na-no from dim Páirc-na-carraig, Páirc-na-lee from magical Páirc-na-tarav. My favorite was the curiously named Inchy Wood, of which Yeats wrote:

> Dim Inchy Wood, that hides badger and fox
> and marten-cat, and borders that old wood
> Wise Biddy Early called the wicked wood.

Yeats's words are so smoothly beautiful that it is easy to miss an odd inexactitude, one that becomes more baffling the more intimately you know the Seven Woods. What was this place called the wicked wood? I tramped around Coole looking for it, only to realize that Inchy borders several of the other woodlands. Was one of them the wicked wood? If so, which? Or was there an eighth woodland, unnamed by the poet? Was it within or outside Coole's boundaries? And whatever did the name mean? My wanderings provided no answer. I scoured Yeats's *Celtic Twilight* and Lady Gregory's folklore collection to no avail; neither mentioned the wicked wood.

The poem pointed to "wise Biddy Early" as the source of the phrase. Born Bridget O'Connor on the slopes of Slieve Echtghe late in the eighteenth century, red-haired Biddy moved down to Feakle, married, bore a child, and lived there until she died. She might have passed an ordinary anonymous life save for the fact that, sometime in her youth, Biddy showed a special courtesy to the fairy people. For that kindness, they offered her a little gift. It did not look like much — just a blue glass bottle — but the fairy object endowed its owner with gifts of farsight and prophecy.

No one knows exactly what Biddy saw when she peered into the blue bottle. Some believed clouds formed miniature pictures; others claimed a tiny man pantomimed answers; Burren folklorist Thomas Westropp was told the bottle contained a single soaked shamrock that performed interpretive dance. However Biddy gained her answers, they were stunningly accurate. Soon she was the region's most famous personage, a combination of doctor, criminologist, prophet, and therapist who could diagnose illnesses, uncover dishonesty, foretell love's likelihood — and tell you how to relieve your woes as well. Those seeking Biddy's aid clogged the hilly roads to Feakle, traveling by foot or cart or horseback from as far away as Connemara. They threw down bedrolls on the stony ground or rented a neighbor's cot for a few pence. There was no cost for the healing itself; the fairies had forbidden Biddy to charge for services. So grateful clients brought gifts, often in bottles and jugs. The availability of free poteen made Biddy Early's cottage a popular destination even for those with no urgent need for healing.

Other than running an unlicensed pub — I like to imagine a nineteenth-century version of Máire's, complete with tale spinning and singsongs far into the night — Biddy seems to have led a morally unobjectionable life. Nonetheless, her magical powers attracted rumor and innuendo. Where, insinuated a certain faction, did that blue bottle originate? With the fairy folk, or somewhere darker? This faction consisted mainly of the local clergy, who saw Biddy as a competitor for souls and wallets. Biddy responded by calling down curses on them — minor ones, like snaring their horses in mud with rider still attached, but curses nonetheless. Otherwise she worked hard, healing colicky babes and prolapsed ewes, rooting out scoundrels, warning against one enterprise and encouraging another. Her personal life was similarly full. She had four or five husbands, the last a man who came for healing and never left. She agreed to treat him in return for a wedding; the fairies apparently did not disallow this particular fee-for-service arrangement. Oh, yes, and another thing: her last groom was Biddy's junior by sixty years.

Twenty years after Biddy Early's death, Lady Gregory predicted she would soon become entirely a figure of legend. But Gregory's own work, together with that of Yeats and Westropp, forestalled that; today no one doubts Biddy's historicity, despite the tendency of wild tales to attach themselves to her name. In handwritten folkloric documents at the Ennis library, you learn little of Biddy's everyday routine but many versions of where Biddy got the blue bottle, what she did with it, and where it was hidden after she died. Such posthumous fame would have unsettled Biddy, who tended to grow angry at invasions of her privacy. One telling incident, recorded from the Bradford farmer Mr. Minogue, describes a man who named his horse Biddy Early. When Biddy courteously requested that he find another name, the man just as courteously agreed. The next time she met the pair, the witch learned the horse's new name — Biddy. She looked deeply into her blue bottle, and the horse fell over dead. (My apologies, Missus, if I have myself given offense by speaking of you!)

Despite Biddy's discomfort with publicity, she receives more rather than less as time goes by. A brewpub in Inagh is named after her, and new books trumpet her reputation. There was even a foiled attempt at creating a commercial Biddy Early center. I say foiled, rather than failed, because if you credit local gossip, the White Witch herself prevented the project. "Above in Feakle" as they say in Gort, Biddy's cottage still stands, a roofless ruin. In the 1990s, dollar-and-punt-hungry developers began restoration work with the aim of opening a witch-kitsch shop. Disaster struck: workers were injured, relatives died, and funds evaporated. The project was abandoned. If Biddy did not herself wreak the havoc, I have been assured, she had a hand in it. "She was a good woman in her day, she only wanted to be left in peace, shouldn't she be given her rights?" offered a friend from near Crusheen.

Oh, yes, what about the wicked wood? That mysterious passage in Yeats led me to Biddy Early, but there the trickle of information disappeared like water down Raftery's cellar. Either Biddy kept secret the location of the wicked wood, or no one had ever recorded it. No matter: I had discovered my first avatar of the Cailleach and had experienced for the first time the power of the archetypal hag. And those rambles around Coole seeded in me a deep connection to the countryside. It is easier to explain why I return to Gort than why I first went there. I may have arrived by serendipity, but I go back by choice, drawn by the magic of the Cailleach and by the beauty of her land.

I have seen it in every season, from gray summer to green winter. Time changes the hag's cliff-face only imperceptibly, but my human friends manifest its passage clearly. Tom Hannon, in the prime of life when first we met, is now stiff with age. Angela Coen, the weaver whose Galway shawl I wear, was taken by cancer in midlife and lies beneath the stones of Kilmacduagh. Dark Sharon, one of Máire's twins, was killed one morning when a lorry driver lost control on a Clare roundabout. Like Burren orchids, human lives bloom and fade. If I live long enough to wear the hag's face, I must endure more such losses. As my life's journey brings me closer to the Cailleach, she whispers to me ever more urgently. And so, hoping to understand her secrets, I journey again and again to her land.

⚌⚌⚌⚌⚌

Its eastern and northern boundaries are formed by the mountains where Biddy Early lived. Slieve Echtghe or Aughty, named for an obscure goddess called the "awful one," makes a great arc from Ardrahan down to

Lough Derg, through the parish once called Tuam Aughty, now known as Feakle. Within that mountainous half-moon nestles silver Lough Graney, named for the Cailleach's sunny younger self. Westward lies the country's heart, in the gray stony Burren that poet Emily Lawless called the "soul of fierce Clare, wild west of all our west" and memoirist Nuala O'Faolain, "landscape of stone and wide blue air." It is in the Burren that we find the greatest concentration of sites named for the hag, the most legends about her, and a land carved in the stark features of her image.

Extending over several hundred square miles of northwest Clare, the Burren can be oddly invisible. There is no "welcome to the Burren" sign, no fence or gatehouse to mark its boundaries; indeed, there is some contention about precisely where the Burren starts and ends. Its distinctive fissured limestone terraces reach the sea near Kinvara, home of the king after whom Gort is named: *Gort inse Guaire,* the fields of Guaire. Follow the coast road to friendly Ballyvaughan, skirt the Flaggy Shore where my Ó Daillaigh ancestors hosted their poetic assemblies, then turn south toward music-filled Doolin, and you will be in the Burren the whole way. Embracing the villages of Kilnaboy and Kilfenora, Corofin and Carron, and the famous spa town of Lisdoonvarna, the area's gentle green valleys and stark rock mountains provide rich fodder for arguments about what exactly is Burren, what not.

Between the Burren and Slieve Echtghe rolls open farmland into which occasional stony fingers stretch. But even where the rock seems to peter out, the Burren is invisibly present, for beneath the fields around Gort lies an intricate karst landscape of deep caves and tunnels. Rivers disappear into great rock cellars, only to reappear a few miles closer to the sea; winter lakes called turloughs fill and empty with the changing seasons. Coole Lake itself is part of a series of turloughs that, in the rainy 1990s, flooded to such an historic extreme that you could sail from Inchy Wood straight out into the Atlantic. Water — ocean and stream, lake and river — reveals the shape of the hag's landscape but it is rock, above and below ground, that defines it.

I have often shaken my head at the irony that I first came to the Burren because of an Eskimo named Rock. The very name of the land — from the Irish *Bhoireann* — means "rock" or "rock place." Rock is the hag's prime element, her stony spine. This not a mere figure of speech, for Burren rock is not igneous — ejected from the earth's core during some ancient cataclysm — but carboniferous, created from the skeletons of once-living beings. Four million years ago, a shallow sea covered what is now the Burren. Over immeasurable eons, billions of sea creatures died, their bodies drifting down to the ocean's bed. Sand and mud buried their remains, and the water's enormous weight pressed the combination into limestone.

Layer upon layer, like names on the Irish landscape, the Burren composed itself beneath that great ancient ocean. A million years passed, then another million, before the sea retreated. Rain sculpted the newly lifted land, slipping through porous stone to carve out caverns and tunnels, gullies and grykes. Glaciers sandpapered the land, then melted northward, leaving fertile till in which great trees rooted themselves. Bears claimed residence in the Burren's caves, and giant deer roamed its climax forest of pine and yew. Thousands of millennia passed before the first humans camped on the ocean shores. Soon after, the sound of the ax rang through the hag's country. One tree at a time, one acre at a time, the great dark forests were laid waste. With the trees gone, the wind took charge, sweeping topsoil from the Burren's hills to expose the primeval seabed. Limestone pavements and glacier-sown wildflowers are ancient features of the land, but its barrenness is comparatively new, only a few millennia old.

The hag is an appropriate goddess for such a landscape for, like the Cailleach, the Burren is hard to appreciate from a distance. Today we understand a land's beauty predominantly through our visual sense, but except for the Cliffs of Moher, the Burren is severely unphotogenic. As Kinvara artist Ann Korff has pointed out, our definition of scenery, unduly inflamed by eighteenth-century landscape painting, demands sublime vistas like the Ring of Kerry or the Bens of Connemara. But the Burren is the antithesis of the picturesque. I have taken hundreds of photographs of the Burren, not one of which captures its monochrome vastness, rock pavements stretching toward rock mountains up which climb rock walls. A close-up of a single orchid nestled in a gryke, one of those long fissures that vee into the limestone, can hint at the Burren's stern drama and secret delicacy. But anything larger fails. Gazing into my viewfinder, I convince myself that this shot will, finally, catch the Burren's grandeur. When the film comes back, I find just another blur of indistinct grayness.

Photographs record an instant, but the Burren is a landscape of epochs. As such, it takes time to appreciate, time most visitors do not allow. Hordes are disgorged daily at dolmens; they mill about for a bit; then they're off to Galway city, muttering about "having come all this way to see a bunch of rocks." Such visitors might agree with Cromwell's general who called the Burren "a savage land, yielding neither water enough to drown a man, nor tree to hang him, nor soil enough to bury him." Savage? Any old woman can seem that way to those too rushed to appreciate her. The Burren does not startle you with its beauty. But beauty is there — orchids in stone — and because of, not despite, the limestone wrinkles.

Regardless of its visual severity, or perhaps because of it, the Burren is Ireland's most sensuous landscape. Touch, smell, hearing are teased to attention by wind and weather, rock and flowers. In summer the rains fall softly warm, in winter sharply chill; breezes stroke me sweetly or press against me, hard and strong; ocean waves lick at my feet, and tiny holy wells sprinkle my hands. And I can never, not for an instant, forget — even when I do not lay hands upon it — the hard tactility of the rock. Yeats called it "cold Clare rock," but when I touch it, it is always warmer than I expect, for the Burren holds heat like an enormous solar battery. Pocked and striated and tattooed, the Burren is like the body of a great barnacled whale, inscribed with ocean hieroglyphs we read not with eyes but with fingers.

Scent, too, awakens. Burren grass pierces the air with greenness. Rooted in the nourishing warmth of limestone, the far-from-barren Burren provides Ireland's richest pasturage. "The rugged rocks abound / but sweet and green / the grass between / as grows on Irish ground," goes the song I have heard so many times in Doolin's pubs. The fourteenth-century *Caithreim Thoirdhealbhaign* described the Burren as a "hilly gray expanse of jagged peaks and slippery steeps, a country nevertheless flowing with milk and yielding luscious grass." *Petra fertilis,* the "fertile rock," the monks of Corcomroe called their cherished contradictory Burren. Between that ruined abbey and the village of Carron stands Ireland's only wild-flower perfumery, where the improbably lush Burren blooms are distilled into mythically named scents. In stone fissures and pockets, Mediterranean flowers — orchids and maidenhair fern — flourish beside arctic plants I recognize from girlhood, mountain avens and Siberian primrose, whose first seeds were sown in the Ice Age. On a spring day, Burren air intoxi-cates with mingled scents.

And ah, the Burren's sounds. Westropp called it a place of "unde-scribed sounds . . . the noise of the wind in the rocks and bushes, the strange prattle of streams in crannies deep down in the rocks." My Ó Daillaigh forebears employed the poetic device they called the "catalog of beloved sounds" to evoke their homeland. I, too, have recorded in my heart a Burren symphony. Its winds are never silent: sighing in the foyer of Liscannor's holy well, shrieking like a banshee across Hag's Head, groaning in the branches of Coole's ancient rock-breaking yews. The ocean drums on the stony coast; rain tambourines the limestone pavements. Uncountable brassy birds cry out, puffins on the Cliffs and ducks on Coole Lake and peacocks at a little farm near Lough Cutra. And — most beloved of all — the voices of my friends swell in a chorus: Brendan reciting Yeats above Coole Lake, Anna murmuring over tea, Máire clucking comfortingly, Jessie crooning silly songs to her dogs, Tom spinning tales endlessly and effortlessly.

Not only are the senses enlivened by the stark Burren beauty, but the spirit is stirred as well. As we attend to subtle shifts in wind and weather, as we follow the slow movement of clouds over sea, as we watch the setting sun delicately bronze the gray rock, we fall into a trance of reflection. Early Christian monks were drawn to the Burren, and with good reason, for no landscape among Ireland's *dyserts,* its deserts of the soul, more fully invites us to ponder temporality. Its flowers form a natural clock; the blooming of the first gentians is met with the tender Irish prayer, *go mbheirimidh beo ar an taim seo arís,* "May we be alive at this time next year." Time is the song of the Burren. Primeval oceans echo inaudibly in its sediment; ancient glacial rivers resound silently in its ravines. Humanity's remains — dolmens on stone pavements, cairns on hilltops, ruined abbeys in cradling valleys — seem mute by comparison. The tempo of the Burren is not human but geologic. Eon by eon, century by century, tide by tide, the Burren composes and recomposes itself.

The Burren turns all but the most adamantly shallow toward profundity; temporal reflections lead naturally to graver thoughts. Thus it seems at first glance appropriate that the land's matron, its harvest queen, is dubbed a goddess of death. The logic seems impeccable: the Cailleach is old, therefore she will soon die. But this facile interpretation bears closer scrutiny, for what has age to do with death? People — like birds and bears, harebells and hazels — die when they die. The Cailleach's worshipers saw infants fail in their first hour, young women felled by childbirth and young men by war, strong elders stricken with sudden fatal illnesses. The same is true today, however much we may delude ourselves that only the aged stand at death's door. When an elderly person passes, grief is rarely contaminated by outrage. But when a girl is "taken before her time," when a middle-aged man does not "live out his allotted years," the bereaved cast about for something to blame, somewhere to vent their fury at this break in the "natural order of things." But what is natural about death is its inevitability, not its timing. Who would have predicted that Tom Hannon, waving an already-arthritic arm for a pint, would outlive by so many decades young Sharon who filled his glass?

Rather than a grim reminder of the reaper, the Old One is a symbol of survival — merry and spry, strong and hard, enduring as rock. The most provocative image of this victorious Cailleach is found right at the heart of the Burren, in a village near Hag's Head where an ancient Christian convent succeeded an even-more-ancient pagan sanctuary. The abbess there, according to local legend, was Inghean Bhaoith; her church was called Kil-Inghean-Bhaoith, later corrupted into Kilnaboy — a name that, although the convent has long since vanished, still applies to the town. The once populous religious center is now sparsely tenanted. Only the occasional local auto wends along the cow-crowded roads. Even more rarely, a vehicle bearing the name of another county than "An Clár" or "Gaillimh" — Clare or Galway — pulls into the wee car park near the crossroads. Outsiders in Kilnaboy? Rest assured they come in search of the region's most famous hag.

She is easy to find. On a little steep hill beside the road, a roofless stone church stands open to rain and wind. A latch secures a black metal gate in the churchyard wall; beyond, new-mounded graves crowd against sunken older ones. Walk around the ruin to the right, then turn and gaze upwards, perhaps twenty feet over your head, to a space above the arched doorway. Give your eyes a moment to adjust to stone grayness, then you will see her. Worn by wind and time, the granite relief is still bold enough to reveal a woman who, you cannot help but notice, is stark naked. Her posture is just as bold: she does a bawdy dance, holding open her legs to display her vulva. She appears to be laughing.

The sculpture is called Inghean Bhaoith, just as the early abbess was. But why should this naked self-exposing hag sport a nun's name? And such an odd one, for Inghean Bhaoith — "daughter of madness" — is hardly a name suggestive of sanctity. Did Burren nuns once moonlight as bawdy dancers? Or was some subtle resemblance between nun and namesake detected by observant locals? ("Holy Mother o' God, Séamus, don't that nekkid hag there remind you of our sainted abbess?") No: the name must have passed from hag to nun, rather than vice versa. Perhaps there was no "abbess" at all, the word a euphemism for the goddess of the locality. Or, if a nun named Inghean Bhaoith actually existed, she may have assumed the goddess's name when she took command of a pre-Christian holy place and sought to associate herself with its prestige.

Most of the camera-toting outsiders — tourists? pilgrims? — arrive ignorant of the Kilnaboy hag's proper name. They call her Sheela-na-gig, an untranslated and possibly untranslatable term recorded in the 1840s from a Tipperary farmer describing a similar sculpture, now the generic for self-exposing stone hags. Scores of Sheelas have been found in churches and other holy places throughout Ireland. While a few remain in situ, most have been carted away to Dublin's National Museum, which occasionally lets the lewd ladies reveal themselves to the public but usually restricts their display to archaeologists, whose research has not answered the question of the bawdy sculptures' origin. Some call them Celtic, others pre-Celtic. As long as the Sheela's cultural genesis remains a subject of debate, we can only guess at her intended meaning.

But there is no question about what we see: a hag assuming various odd postures that force us to look her right in the thigh. In some instances, Sheela — a world-class contortionist — reaches hands around legs to stretch her vulva into a circle the size of her head. In others, as at Kilnaboy, she squats and spreads. (Great *craic,* that Sheela.) She is, incongruously, both young and old. Some Sheelas are skeletal above the waist, flush with life below; sometimes the hag's breasts are sunken and shriveled, her hips round and firm. She is shown frontally; she grins hugely. And when the Sheela smiles, she bares her bum; she is always naked, always displaying her sex. Squeamish scholars call her a symbol of women's reproductive power. But the hag is unmistakably past menopause; her posture cannot conceivably indicate desire for impregnation. Call it a stance of power or a posture of sexual invitation; call it yoni yoga or vulva vaudeville. We may not know what the original sculptors intended her to mean, but we can certainly say this: Sheela-na-gig is one old woman who does more than just wear purple.

My friend Fiona Marron, whose grand unsettling paintings of the hag include several based on Inghean Bhaoith, links the Sheela-na-gig with the Cailleach, arguing that both represent the same transgressive, transformative feminine energy. Earlier Irish, too, probably connected the figures, but such easy association ceased with the coming of Christianity when, like Biddy Early, the hag confronted a clergy that feared her power. By imprisoning her in church walls, the patriarchs simultaneously exalted and dishonored the wild hag. They also attempted to circumscribe the Old One's freedom by tossing a nun's veil on her gray head and concocting a suitably restrained hagiography. Saint Cailleach? Why not? The famous "Lament of the Hag of Beare" is the alleged memoir of a Cailleach who found in the convent a solution to her dissolution. But the hag seems unashamed of her past:

I do not deem it ill
That a white veil be on my head;
Time was when cloths of every hue
Bedecked my head as we drank good wine . . .

I had my day with kings
Drinking mead and wine:
To-day I drink whey-water
Among shrivelled old hags.

The only known attempt to canonize the hag failed utterly. The poet could not prevent his "nun" from boasting of her seven consecutive maidenheads and the seven sturdy husbands she had outlived. The hag even hinted that her future held not chastity but an eighth virginity: "The time is at hand that shall renew me."

Her recycled hymen would not be maintained like some holy relic. No, the Cailleach's renewal served one purpose, and one purpose only: to permit the thrill of another deflowering. Age did nothing to depress the Old One's sexual appetite. And her chance of satisfying that appetite was undiminished by an appearance that was, frankly, loathsome. The kindest thing we can say about the Cailleach is that she looked her age. Her few remaining teeth were red, her hair stringy and white. Her wrinkled skin was black and blue, her clothing gray and shabby. A fourteenth-century Burren writer described her as having "a blue face, green teeth, rough hair, bent nails, lumpy forehead, eyes like red berries, large blue-green nose, wide nostrils from which flowed a stream of snot, a turned-up beard on her upper lip." Yeah, and so? The lips beneath her lower beard were flush with lust, which is all that mattered to the hag.

The Cailleach liked to offer free land to any man who could match her strength and stamina. Taken in by the Old One's obvious age and apparent frailty, many died trying to match her pace. In putting strenuous demands upon her lovers, the hag is not alone among Irish goddesses. References to men literally dying to satisfy women's sexual desires can be found in texts as early as the *Book of Invasions*. There, we learn that Ireland's first settler, Cesair, arrived in a boat that was inadequately provisioned, having only three men to fifty women. Delighted to set foot — well, actually, more intimate parts of their anatomy — on solid land after their arduous journey, the crew got busy:

Lightly they lay and pleasured
In the green grass of that guileless place.
Ladhra was the first to die;
He perished of an embrace.

In short order, only one man was left standing, — err, swimming, because Fintan turned himself into a salmon to escape the women's advances. The others expired exhausted — but happy, one hopes — in attempts to satisfy the women.

But better to die servicing the hag than to steal what she would gleefully give, we learn from the *dindshenchas*. Once upon a time, the story goes, there were five brothers who were named (aptly, as you will see) Proud, Rash, Evil, Foolish, and Thick. Camping on the Burren one night, the brothers were roasting game over a fire when a leprous hag limped up and begged a morsel. "Beautiful is the hag's eye," Proud leered, then dragged the Old One away so that his brothers would not witness his actions — not that any had spoken a word of restraint or raised an eyebrow in concern.

Behind a rock, Proud assaulted the hag. She may have looked frail, but the Cailleach quickly overpowered Proud and bound him with magical chains. She then limped back to the fire and again begged for food. Asked where Proud had gone, the Old One answered that he had hidden in shame over mistreating such a pathetic creature. The men — who were indeed rash, evil, foolish, and thick, to say nothing of proud — ignored the warning. One by one, they tried to rape the hag; one by one, she overpowered them, until she had them all tied together in her magic chains. (Remember this hag, for we shall meet up with her again up north in Ulster.)

Respectful lovers who matched the Cailleach's vigor were amply, indeed handsomely, rewarded. Of the many tales about the hag's treatment of her favorites, the one I like best tells of Niall of the Nine Hostages and his brothers. Once, so the story goes, noble Niall entered the forest with his brothers. They were all renowned hunters, but that day luck turned against them. The woods were unaccountably silent; even the squirrels had disappeared. As the day wore on, the brothers grew more and more tired, more and more hungry, more and more thirsty.

They found a shady glen in which rose a sweet-water well. The parched brothers ran toward it, then stopped short. For like most mythic places, the well had a guardian — in this case, an especially revolting hag. Picture her, now, if you will: rheumy pale eyes, massive wen on a bulbous red nose, nose hairs drooping into a moustache, corkscrew beard on sunken chin, goitery throat, pink scalp beneath thin white locks, shrill quavering voice, breasts hanging below waist.

The Cailleach offered the lads all the water they could drink. She asked only one small thing as payment. Nothing, really: a kiss, just a kiss. She puckered her wrinkled lips, wiping off the drool with a shaky hand, and awaited the first suitor. Overcome with revulsion, Niall's brothers backed away as one. But Niall was as wise as he was handsome. He took the hag in his arms and gave her, not a quick pursed-up peck, but a deep lingering kiss into which he fell as though into a trance. Niall felt his manhood stir. His hands, as though possessing a will of their own, reached beneath the hag's clothing while his own dropped away. Finding the Cailleach's own wet well, Niall drank deeply. He made love to her passionately and intently, joyously and vigorously.

And, when both were satiated, Niall found his partner no longer a wizened hag but a glowing young woman who offered him sweet water and a rich kingdom as well. The ancient hag was none other than the bountiful goddess of the land, source of all wealth and power. When Niall swooningly asked her name, she said simply, "Sovereignty."

⁂

Whenever I hear this marvelous tale, I envision it occurring on the Burren's edge, right near Hag's Head, at a place I have known for decades: the holy well at Liscannor. The association may seem eccentric, for the story is set in forest depths, while only a few trees shade Liscannor. Neither notably large nor unusually situated, the Liscannor "vat" is not particularly picturesque or historic. Unlike Sligo's Tobernault, the holy well is not esteemed as Ireland's most beautiful, or its most famous, as Kildare's Tober Bríde can claim. Nonetheless, when I hear of the Cailleach's well, Liscannor rises unbidden before my inner eye.

Since first entering its precinct with Tom on that long-ago solstice expedition, I have returned to Liscannor too many times to count. I walk the traditional pattern, ritually spiraling three times up and down the slippery hill. I place a few coins in the dinged metal donation box before entering the small stucco well house. There, the clutter invariably overwhelms me: statues, rosaries, scribbled prayers on cardboard, baby pictures, soft drink cans scratched with pleading messages. The offerings are crammed on narrow shelves, suspended from low roof beams, tied to rafters. Holy cards, broken crutches, hand-painted portraits of saints, scraps of clothing. Urgency and pain and hope crowd the dim narrow room. Bits of yarn, reed poppets, unopened envelopes, canes, steel crucifixes, feathers. A ceramic labyrinth plaque. A peace symbol button. An empty mint carton.

At the end of the long foyer, a roofless square opens onto the hillside. Water trickles down from its deep source, blackening the rocks before filling a pool where coins glitter. My own offering makes a little splash as I perform a Celtic ritual now become a Christian devotion. Standing before the trickling spring, I sense uncountable spirits of earlier pilgrims, each the center of a singular life's drama. Sick in soul or body, each knelt as I do, dipping water from the dark sacred pool and whispering a prayer for better times. Afterward I linger over the handwritten notes of recent visitors: mothers of desperately ill children, bereft spouses, jobless fathers, cancer warriors. Years ago I read a message that haunts me still, from someone who, having lost a number of loved ones at once, could barely finish a sentence for grief. Each time I visit Liscannor, I send forth another prayer for that unknown person whose pain so touched my own.

Most prayers at Liscannor are addressed to Saint Brigit, for the shrine bears the name Dabhach Bríde, "Brigit's Vat." For many years the lower ritual circle centered on two identical decrepit statues, each in its own fogged-glass protective box. "Saints Brigit of the phone box," I called them, for they appear to be involved in that peculiarly rural Irish penitential practice, placing a long-distance call. Renovation has since restricted the number of saints to one; the clouded glass is gone as well. A decade ago the shrine was quiet on Imbolc, only a few devotees turning out to walk the pattern. Now hundreds visit the well on Saint Brigit's day.

Association of Liscannor with Imbolc, however, is relatively recent. The well was traditionally visited six months later, on the harvest feast of Lughnasa. Calendar alterations mean that the feast's date varies from late July through mid-August; in Liscannor, the rites centered on "Garland Sunday" around August 15. North in Mayo, where tens of thousands still pray their way up pyramidal Croagh Patrick, the feast was fully Christianized. Not so on the Burren. Unmarried folk ascended Slievecallan, "hag hill," to snatch seasonal pleasures, while at the well near Hag's Head — site of what the great folklorist Máire MacNeill called "one of the most strongly lasting survivals of Lughnasa" — celebrants imbibed sacred water, then danced and sang the night away. "In bygone days," MacNeill records, "the peopled slope was fitfully lit by candles, and tradition fondly asserts that, however wild the night, the candles were unquenchable." Quite quenchable, by contrast, were those suspiciously pagany rituals, which guttered out in mid-century; High Mass is all the Lughnasa Liscannor sees today. But memory of the well's original matron is not so easily extinguished. Personal association is not the only reason I envision Niall's amorous adventure occurring at Liscannor, for its festival reveals which goddess was honored there.

Lughnasa marked the beginning of a season that extended to Samhain on November 1 — a season ruled by the Cailleach who, in bygone days, was omnipresent across Ireland. A tied sheaf called "the Cailleach" stood at the center of each field, toward which harvesters cut the grain. Small animals — frogs, corncrakes, partridges, and especially hares, the hag's animal — fled before flails and scythes into that central sheaf. When the field was nearly mown, the workers set up a din, shouting and clanging tools together to "put the hare out of the corn," as folklorist Kevin Danaher attests. Frightened away from the Cailleach, the animals scurried to an unharvested field. Thus the harvesters drove the hag's animals before them as they cut down, again and again, the Old One herself. Because the last stalk cut in a region was an especially potent reservoir of hag power, great care was taken with the ceremony. Depending upon the region, lots were drawn, or blindfolded women took up scythes, or the youngest worker was assigned the deed. This final cutting of the Cailleach was a moment of great power and equivalent danger. Her freed energy brought healing, but were the rite botched, a bitter winter resulted.

Once cut, the Cailleach sheaf was treated reverently. Dressed as an old woman or plaited into a cross, it hung in house or barn until replaced by the next year's sheaf. In many areas, the Cailleach sheaf provided material for spring's Brigit crosses — the same hag-into-virgin motif we encountered in our tale of Niall visiting the well. Here we peer into the deep heart of the Cailleach, for her power derives from this ability to revirgin herself. Some writers, like Barbara Walker who identifies her with Hindu Kali, proclaim the Cailleach ruler of death, offering her connection with harvest as incontrovertible proof. But plants die in that season, not humans. The U.S. Department of Vital Statistics reports that even today, more people die as spring approaches than they do in autumn. Before food became plentiful year-round, this pattern was stronger; even in lean years, there was more food after harvest than before. Once the cows were driven in — booleyed, from *bó,* the Irish for cow — from the hills and the hay saved, communities enjoyed a period of full-bellied leisure. The Cailleach's season was a time not of privation but of abundance.

I have never witnessed the ritual of the Cailleach sheaf, but a few decades ago, I helped harvest a field near Ardrahan in the traditional way. As in my grandfather's time, we raked in a steady rhythm, our movements patterned into an exhausting exhilarating dance. That day shines in my memory. I can still name the divisions of the raked hay: sop, bart, tram, cock, rick. I recall the heady fragrances, the sting of sweat in my eyes, the pain in my blistering hands, the occasional whistle of a corncrake breaking our panting silence. The hard monotonous labor altered my consciousness until time dissolved into one lingering evening, and space pooled within our field's stony boundaries. Paradoxically, it is the specifics of that particular ordinary day and that particular unremarkable hayfield that I hold fixed in memory. As did Paddy Kavanagh, I found "a star-lovely art / In a dark sod. / Joy that is timeless! O heart / That knows God!"

Such timeless, boundaryless specificity — what anthropologist Clifford Geertz called "a motionless present, a vectorless now" — is Cailleach time, which moves from moon to moon, harvest to harvest. It is pagan time, rooted in the eternal return rather than the once-off redemption; it is sensuous, embodied time, singular moments lived in specific locations. In the mosaic of Irish places, such time serves as glue, storytelling as grout. Elsewhere time and place have been sundered, a process that began with the invention of mechanical clocks. Earlier timekeepers like sundials were cemented in place, but clocks made time external to the passage of sun or moon or stars above a specific bog or lake or hill. This development radically changed our lives, historians John Robinson and Geoffrey Godbey claim, making possible precise punctuality and as a result changing "the nature of work and, subsequently, the rest of life, making time scarce."

Time is not yet scarce in rural Ireland, which went from pre- to post-Industrial without stopping in the middle. There is still something called the "Irish hour" (however long it takes to do it) parallel to the "Irish mile" (however long it takes to get there). It drives tourists crazy when a destination retreats like a mirage "just a mile up the road, now," or when the band advertised for half-nine enters the pub promptly at half-ten. The old joke goes that a scholar, working on a Spanish-Irish dictionary, could find no Irish equivalent for *mañana.* He called a native Irish speaker, who explained that "there is no word in Irish that conveys quite the same level of urgency."

The Irish remain stubbornly unconstrained by objective measurement, a heritage from that time when, as Galway writer Martin Ross and her partner Edith Somerville put it, "people told time by the sun, and a half an hour either way made no difference to anyone." One night at Máire's, Tom took offense when a German farmer from Ardrahan belittled his neighbors as being unnaturally unpunctual. No, Tom argued, it is clock time that strains against nature. In an impassioned oration, Tom made a startling claim: "In bygone days, hours didn't matter, even years didn't matter. No one knew their ages, Uli. A widow in middle age might marry a man the age of her grandson, Uli, without any comment whatsoever."

Speaking with the lofty certainty that religion once affected, science today claims that diminished estrogen — the word is etymologically linked to "estrus" — results in diminished eroticism. Yet testosterone, alleged source of men's sexual vigor and an etymological cousin of "testy," increases proportionately in older women. Could legends of the Cailleach's stupendous sexual energy offer as much insight as hormonal assays by biologists peering down culturally ground lenses? What is nature, what culture? In truth, we have no idea. As Simone de Beauvoir points out, "Neither history nor literature has left us any valid account of the sexuality of older women. The subject is even more taboo than the sexuality of older men." Could the lustful Cailleach encode information about the sexual potential of older women?

Armed only with the flaccid comfort of contemporary science, a vigorous older woman must puzzle out for herself what transformation into a Cailleach means. One of these seekers, the great Irish memoirist Nuala O'Faolain, took a midlife visit to the Burren that made her piercingly aware of a still-vital sexuality. Hiking over rock hills near Ballyvaughan, she felt passion coursing through her veins undiminished — nay, stronger than in her youth. "Is it that a woman's life is bracketed by two hormonal tides, and one goes out, in middle age, and she runs down the beach after it?" she pondered. In words as searing as those of the Hag of Beare, O'Faolain laments her isolation, for unlike the Cailleach, she does not remember — ah, none of us remembers — how to grow young again.

But O'Faolain intuits an answer. "It is not about sex," she muses, "it is about creation." Her insight is appropriate to the setting, for the Burren offers Ireland's only true creation myth. It is a fragmentary story, not more than a snapshot: the land was born when the Cailleach dumped out the contents of her apron. Slievecallan, Knockycallanan, Slieve Echtghe — the mountains of the hag have their genesis in that ridiculously offhand gesture of the Cailleach. Such casual creativity reminds me of the Eskimo goddess Aakuluujjusi, who made the world simply by tossing her clothes around. Creativity, these hag stories suggest, can be quite ordinary and undramatic.

These hag tales remind me, too, of what friends say about how, as they age, ordinary life becomes charged with erotic energy. "The whole world has become my lover," says one, describing in plain words what psychologist Erik Erikson theorized was the psychosexual goal of successful aging: the "generalization of sensual modes that can foster and enrich bodily and mental experience." Far from being diminished, the older woman finds her sense of vital connection — sex, creation, call it what you will — expanding, expanding, expanding. Perhaps this is why the Cailleach was always described as a giant, standing boldly astride rivers, her body towering over even the highest of her mountains.

But what about that mythic transformation, withered hag into fresh maiden? It defies reason: women grow old; they do not grow young again. Except in Irish myth. There, Cailleach and maiden change places over and over. Indeed, the protean Cailleach specializes in reversals of all sorts. She invented fall sowing, called *Coirce na bhFaoilli* or February's oats, more prolific than spring sowing. In her Burren landscape, cows are booleyed up the hills in winter and down in summer, a reverse of the usual practice. Time anthropologist Edward Leach has defined such reversals as indicating sacred time, when world-restoring rituals take place. At the juncture of sacred and profane, he argues, time flows backward and "sacred time is played in reverse, death is converted into birth." Cailleach time is a time of miracles. In a timeless ageless moment, situated in a specific endless place, Cailleach becomes maiden once again, and once again, and once again.

⊠⊠⊠⊠⊠

Lately I have turned once again to Yeats, who seemed to have all the answers when, in my dim room above Máire's, I spent my mornings imitating his ballads of tortured love. I read him differently now, no longer expecting to find truth capitalized, more willing to enjoy him as a piece of the human mosaic. I read different poems now too. "The Lake Isle of Innisfree" and "The Host of the Air," however beautiful, now hold little mystery. I turn instead to "Words for Music, Perhaps" to ponder the words of Crazy Jane. Yeats once described a drunken old woman from Loughrea as the inspiration for the most famous hag in modern literature, but Crazy Jane is bigger than any single woman, even one from Loughrea. There are echoes of Biddy Early, who like Jane had public arguments with the clergy, and of the Traveler woman of Ballylee, who like Jane lived with whatever man she chose. Most of all, Crazy Jane seems to me to embody the Cailleach, about whom stories are still told in the region where Yeats lived, stories that embed the hag in a land that bespeaks her wild soulful energy.

"Love is all / Unsatisfied / That cannot take the whole / Body and soul," Crazy Jane says, and I ponder the complexity of who takes, who gives, in love and in life. "A woman can be proud and stiff / When on love intent," says Crazy Jane, and I ponder what that curiously androgynous language implies about women's sexual potential. "Fair and foul are near of kin, / And fair needs foul," cries Jane, and I ponder the unity of opposites, the maiden hidden within the hag hidden within the maiden. I ponder how acceptance can combine with strength when Crazy Jane calls herself "a road / That men pass over / My body makes no moan / But sings on." In Yeats's inspired words, I hear echoes of the stone Sheelas, of the ageless stone of the Burren, of the historical Cailleachs of the country I long ago learned to love.

Although I have never been able to answer my Eskimo grandfather's question about where I come from, with each passing year I know more fully where I am going. Like every woman, I am turning into her, into the wild creative hag who has always lived in my soul. Crazy Jane and the Sheela and the Cailleach all whisper to me the same secret: that there is more passion in a woman's heart than her body can contain. That she lives timelessly in boundless space that is, simultaneously, the specific located present. That survival means not stasis but endless renewal. And that to live fully we must learn to dance, naked and laughing and wild.

Chapter Three

THE RED-HAIRED GIRL FROM THE BOG

Connemara

"So, you were out the Old Bog Road, were you?" Frank Kelly asked. "And did you meet the red-haired girl?"

His own hair was more silver than sand, his eyes more water than sky, but otherwise my friend seemed no older than he had been when I first wandered into steep and steepled Clifden two decades past. Back then Frank had owned a pub on the square and a house around the corner. Now he and his sweet shy wife, Françoise, hosted a bed-and-breakfast above the ruined castle overlooking Clifden Bay. Sky Cottage's white-curtained breakfast room faced America, but nevertheless the sun flooded in each morning as I drank my strong sweet tea.

"The red-haired girl?"

"Ah, no, of course, but you wouldn't have met her. You'd have to be a lad, and probably in a pub — but then you had better watch out."

Is there no such thing as a direct conversation in Ireland? Never mind your desire to move on to a new place or a new subject, your need to shoot like an arrow to some important engagement. An old joke has it that the Irish never answer a question except with another question. "Never answer a question with another question? Now whoever would have told you that?" It would not be funny were it not so true, just as it is true that in Irish there are no words for our simple "yes" or "no." Indirection is an Irish way of life.

It was early fall. Everyone told me how dreadful the summer had been: sheets of rain, the sky blanketed in gloom, the hay barely saved. But it had been bright for a week. The previous day, I had driven down the coast, car dancing to Niamh Parsons and the Loose Connections, windows open to the sea air. Orange montbretias and butter-yellow gorse waved as I sped past the coral strand at Ballyconneely. At Roundstone I turned left, onto a road marked only as a faint line on the map.

On one of my first return trips to Ireland in the 1970s, when I felt smugly and confidently post-tourist, I had turned down that road, imagining it the perfect shortcut from Toombeola to Clifden. Within moments I regretted my decision, for I was on an oddly endless road across an eerily desolate bog. It reminded me uncomfortably of the time I had turned off, one moonless night near Gort, onto an unpaved wee road that led into an axle-high swamp from which I had to drive out three miles — in reverse, as there was no way to turn on the narrow track. I had learned to be wary of bog roads.

But this road was paved, though roughly so. It took only half an hour to get to Clifden, but I was on edge the whole time. It was not just the fear of sinking into a bog miles distant from help that kept my hands fisted around the steering wheel. There is an unshakeable feeling of airy remoteness — one I have since grown to love — about the Old Bog Road. You pass nothing, not boreen nor fence nor cottage, along its length. Well, that's not quite true; there are those ruined stone foundations near the bog's edge, the remains of Marconi's telegraph station. And a pile of rocks that was once, perhaps, a midway cottage. Other than that, all you see is quaking bog and shallow lakes and jutting granite, and hoodie crows soaring above wandering sheep. And wind, unceasing wind, bending the bog grass, ruffling the gray water.

When I reached it, tiny Clifden seemed a cramped crowded place. Everything jangled and clattered around me, while Roundstone Bog seemed serene and distant. Since then, I have made it a point to travel the Old Bog Road whenever I visit Connemara. Hoping to bring home some of its magic, I search for paintings and photographs of the bog in Connemara shops. But I have never found a picture that captures it, perhaps because the bog's most salient feature is invisible. What draws me there is silence: "Nothing breaks the silence in a Roundstone bog," says poet Joan McBreen, "but a curlew's cry caught in the wind." Silence draws me there, and the solitude that blows through one on even the stillest days. I have known that silence, that intense solitude, in only one other setting. On the Alaskan tundra, no tree or shrub interrupts the eye as it sweeps across the land. There on the tundra, as on the bog, I sense beneath my feet a separate and discrete world, both museum and mausoleum of the vegetative kingdom. Growth and death, death and growth, interlaced and intertwined. On the tundra, I have felt the same unmeasured antiquity as in Connemara.

Connemara: the wildest place in Connacht, the most westerly of Ireland's five traditional provinces, the province of wisdom. The syllable that begins both names is etymologically related to *ken,* the Anglo-Saxon word meaning "to know." To know is to remember deeply; to remember deeply is to be wise. When the English drove the Gaelic-speaking Irish "to hell or Connacht," they banished those they did not kill into the province of memory. Even today, the old ways — the Irish language, ancient customs, mythic characters and narratives — are alive in Connacht, and most especially in Connemara. W. Y. Evans-Wentz, the early folklorist who stalked Coole's Seven Woods with Yeats in hot pursuit of fairies, found Connemara the most Irish of places. "If anyone would know Ireland, let him wander amid the fairy dells of gentle Connemara. When there are dark days and stormy nights, let him sit beside a blazing fire of fragrant peat in a peasant's straw-thatched cottage listening to tales of Ireland's golden age — tales of gods, of heroes, of ghosts, and of fairy-folk. If he will do these things, he will know Ireland, and why its people believe in fairies."

I love Connemara in a way I love few places. I have never lived there, only visited, more times than I can count. Almost every time I go to

Ireland, I fly like an arrow to Connemara, whose changeful terrain moves me in a way I have rarely felt, and never so intensely. There is a curve on the road from Galway City, a few miles out of Oughterard, where the Maamturk Mountains suddenly heave into sight. At that moment, predictably, my throat tightens as I sense the boundary of Connemara. Coming from Mayo, on the northern road, I have not detected a similarly precise point of entry. But somewhere before Leenane on Killary Harbour, when the sun begins to play shadow tricks upon the Partry Mountains, I realize that I have passed into another state of consciousness, that an unseen veil separating me from living nature has disappeared. I do not penetrate the veil or tear it as I pass through; it simply drifts away like smoke.

I have had the same sensation where France yields to Celtic Brittany, near the mythic forest where Merlin is trapped, still alive, inside a tree by the spell of his fairy mistress, Vivienne. In both places, music suddenly fills me: thin piercing notes that make me shiver with inexpressible longing. Yeats describes this sound-that-is-no-sound in "The Host of the Air":

> *He heard, high up in the air,*
> *A piper, piping away,*
> *And never was piping so sad,*
> *And never was piping so gay.*

The silvery strains call to mind the etymology of our word *enchantment,* for music is said to signal the presence of fairy folk. The fourteenth-century author of the *Voyage of Tadhg* described it as "plaintive and matchless," while Saint Patrick found its match only in heaven, though he objected to the "fairy twang," an elusive unsettling discord. *Planxty* is the word coined by the great harper Turlough O'Carolan to describe such music's unforgettable beauty unfettered by conventional cadences or scales. O'Carolan owed his genius to the fairies, for he was but an ordinary minstrel until, falling asleep on a rath, he dreamed his way to the heart of music. O'Carolan's "Farewell to Music," blown by fairy breath through Irish pipes: that is how the spirit of Connemara sounds to me.

Some of my Irish friends would shrug, hearing this, and offer that it is well-known the Gentry make themselves felt in this fashion. Some would explain a bit impatiently that, as my relations are Mayo people, of course I respond to the West with such extreme emotion. Others would pour me another cup of tea, laugh gently, and change the subject. They may have these mystic encounters with the land, but they certainly don't talk about them. No matter. I know I have heard elusive inaudible music singing forth from land that is wild but nevertheless deeply known by humanity. For rituals have been performed in Connemara for thousands of years, the same rituals, in the same places, year upon year upon year, creating what wisdom teacher Christopher Bamford calls "a holy intimacy of human, natural and divine." In Connemara human consciousness has met the land's consciousness — what my ancestors called the goddess — so consistently that she reveals herself even to the outsider, even to the occasional visitor.

Old rites and folkways that rivet people to place have been preserved in Connemara with an almost unbelievable determination, for as the local proverb says, *Ná déin nós agus ná bris nós:* "Neither make nor break a custom." This conservatism extended to the use of land. There are few bogs so unspoiled in all Ireland, indeed in all Europe, as that bisected by the Old Bog Road. For years it had no name; it was just "the bog" to residents of the area, but recently it has worn the name of Roundstone Bog because of its proximity to that village. Except for Marconi's telegraph site, and that ruined halfway cottage, the bog has been empty of human occupation since it began to form some ten thousand years ago. It begins at the Roundstone turnoff and extends for twenty-five square miles. Rush and sedge and cottongrass purl into tussocks in a marsh dotted with hundreds of small surface ponds. Granite outcroppings rise from deep rich peat that Seamus Heaney calls "black butter melting and opening underfoot." Here and there, a dark slice shows where someone has cut turf for winter fires. Squads of thin-legged long-haired sheep, branded with fluorescent paint, graze lazily. Above the bog rise steep quartzite mountains called the Twelve Bens — from the Irish word for a pointed peak, sometimes anglicized as the Twelve Pins — on whose gray-blue slopes the sun plays hopscotch with the clouds.

Without a local guide to point out the hidden pathways used by generations of shepherds and turf cutters, or feet tiny enough to tread the otter trails between the shallow lakes, hiking off road is difficult. Wellingtons would be imperative for walking on the watery bogland, but footprints might leave permanent damage. There is a better way, the one I used that bright fall day. I became a bogtrotter, embracing that derogatory term for the Irish just as the word itself embraces the old Gaelic *bogach,* "soft thing." Tracing, like the clattering sheep, the maze of pink granite out-croppings brought me deep into the bog. Light kaleidoscoped the heathery mountains from southern Benlettery, "the wet-sided peak," north to Muckanaght, "naked Macha," named for the goddess whose hoodie crows flew around me like gray ghosts. It was peaceful beyond expression. I drank in the bog's rich loamy scent and the sudden sharp hits of salt from the nearby sea. Crows and merlins calling in the wind, and the soft moan of the wind itself, mixed with an occasional burst of bleating and, every quarter hour or so, the dull growl of a car on the distant road.

I had seen no red-haired girls at all.

"So," I asked Frank, "pubs and young men — where do I go to take lessons?"

"Oh," he grinned. "Oh, you!" And then he told me the story.

Once a year or so, a woman arrives in town, walking down the gentle slope from the Old Bog Road. A green scarf covers her head, a green shawl crosses tightly over her chest. She carries no satchel, so it seems she has not traveled far. It is a night when a *céilí,* or a wedding or funeral, is planned so she can mingle in a throng of strangers. She wants strangers around her, but she also wants to be noticed. It suits her purpose to be noticed.

It is evening, and the celebrants (or are they mourners?) have gathered indoors, probably in a pub. The fiddlers have finished a set, and someone begins to intone a lively *sean nós* melody, the ornate unaccompanied song of the West. The red-haired girl presses toward the center of the crowd, where she throws back her head, opens her full lips in an ecstatic breath, and begins to dance. She dances the old way, Connemara style, the way the Irish danced before anxious priests forbade the movement of anything but the feet. Her feet flash, right enough. But her shoulders also sway, her breasts heave, her arms rise lightly from her sides. Her hips swing to the quick tempo. As her green scarf slips to her neck, red hair blazes out around her milk-pale face.

Soon everyone is dancing. She has no lack of partners, the red-haired girl. She dances into the night with one and then another of the young men, finally pairing up with the most attractive. He might be a strapping black-haired fisherman, or a short tough farmer, or a gray-eyed poet. They dis-appear into the night. Bystanders hear her murmur a promise that she will take him to her house, up on the Old Bog Road.

She takes him to her house, indeed, that halfway place other travelers see as a ruin but which her young man perceives as a cozy firelit cottage. She has her way with him, and he with her, until both are sated. After that night the young man is never seen again for, like some perverse Brigadoon, the cottage of the red-haired girl disappears in morning mist, leaving only that shattered pile of rocks at the halfway curve of the Old Bog Road. Like smoke, the red-haired girl too disappears, until the next time she awakens to the call of her desire.

She has no name, the red-haired girl from the bog, but she is easy enough to identify, for old legends declare that anything red and white is fairy born. White dogs with russet ears, white cats with brindle stripes, liver-and-white cows, roan pinto horses, all such creatures bring the magic and threat of fairy to our world. Her dancing partners should have recognized their danger, for red-haired girls with milky skin — and anyone resembling them, even nonredheads wearing red petticoats — are omens of ill fortune, folklorist Lady Wilde informs us, while archaeologist Thomas Westropp records the belief that a mere glance from a red-haired girl can kill a horse or a man. But, in thrall to her otherworldly beauty and without thought of safety, lovers follow the red-haired girl, the Leanan Sidhe, the beautiful fairy mistress.

She leads her fated lovers to Tír na nÓg, a paradise island in the western ocean where no one ever ages, sickens, or dies. Dreamy days are passed in eating and drinking, dancing and making love and, when those pleasures dim, fighting fairy wars in which no one ever dies. The landscape is as beautiful as its people: castles of silver and gold rise from rounded hills covered, not with spiky gorse, but with trees that flower and bear fruit at once. "Though the plain of Ireland is fair to see, it is like a desert once you know the Great Plain," the fairy king Midir once told a mortal woman he was intent upon seducing. Yeats called it "an Eden out of time and out of space," while his contemporary, the Galway piper Steven Ruan, described it as "a place of delights where music, singing, dancing, and feasting are continually enjoyed; and its inhabitants are all about us, as numerous as the blades of grass."

Those who travel to Tír na nÓg are referred to, not as dead, but as "taken"; they are said to have gone, not to the grave, but "away." Small, common words for a vast, uncommon experience. Save for certain places and times, fairyland is invisible to and inaccessible from our world. The red-haired girl lives there with others of her kind, the *sidhe* or Tuatha Dé Danann, the "people of the goddess Danu." This race is said to have ruled Ireland until defeat at the hands of the Milesians, a myth that may encode displacement of the Tuatha Dé's worshipers — early Celts or pre-Celtic people — several thousand years ago by an invading culture. Just as their people did not go away but were absorbed into the conquering race, the Tuatha Dé remained in Ireland, omnipresent but invisible. Within Ireland's hills and beneath its lakes, these diminished gods still lead their charmed and charming lives. Shamanic peoples like the Australians, whose Dreamtime bears a striking resemblance to fairyland, readily recognize such parallel universes. As the great mythographer Joseph Campbell said, "The idea of a sacred space where the walls and laws of the temporal world dissolve to reveal wonder is apparently as old as the human race." The idea does not require any spiritual belief. A staple of science fiction and television space operas, alternative worlds can be derived from contemporary physics: the many-worlds hypothesis, in which probability curves collapse, each reality continuing on its separate course; or superstring theory, in which unimaginable worlds are hidden in the folds of a ten-dimensional universe. Fairyland is like that: intangible but quite real; out of sight, under the hill, on the wind; nearby, just not right here.

In 1869, Thomas Huxley coined the word *agnostic,* to describe his belief that divinity is utterly beyond our understanding. Although people nowadays tend to mix up *agnostic* with *atheistic,* Huxley did not necessarily disbelieve in god; he just did not think us capable of knowing much about the subject. In the way Huxley was agnostic about god, I am agnostic about fairies. I cannot agree with the old Sligo man who told Yeats firmly, "No matter what one doubts, one never doubts the fairies, for they stand to reason." Neither can I dismiss them as mere fiction, projected archetypes, or mislabeled history. For although I have never met anyone, red-haired or not, whom I suspected of being one of Them, I have had many peculiar experiences at *sidhe*-haunted places in Ireland for which the Fairy Hypothesis is as good an explanation as any I have heard.

When I was younger and more reckless, I deliberately sought the *sidhe.* Inspired by Yeats, I yearned for places "where enchanted eyes / Have seen immortal, mild, proud shadows walk," where "beings happier than men / Moved round me in the shadows." That first time over, after unpacking my volumes of Yeats and Lady Gregory at Máire's, I began inquiring in the pub after the local fairies — calling them, as I remember, by that very name. One of the patrons snorted knowingly. "Ah," he said, pausing to take a long drink of porter, "you'd be interested in the Good People then?" I leaned forward eagerly, failing to notice his correction of my nomenclature. The man waved his arm at bright-faced Gráinne behind the bar. "Bring her another Smithwick's, she'll be seeing Them soon enough, so."

The unsubtle codding stung. I had not, after all, asked for directions to the wee shoemaker's shop, the one with the red cap and the pot o' gold. I had asked a serious question about local tradition, and I did not expect such resistance and evasion. Dermot MacManus, compiling Connacht fairy lore in the 1950s, elicited the same response, saying of his would-be informants, "They are desperately shy of strangers or of any who might scoff and so they keep these things among themselves as closely as if they were not." There are limits to what one talks about with strangers, even those who live above the speaker's favorite pub. Outsiders have often derided the Irish as soft-headed mystics; how could anyone be sure I would not do the same?

But something was at work besides suspicion of strangers. With the wisdom of years, I now understand how inappropriate my question was. Ireland, like many traditional cultures, had fierce taboos against speaking too boldly of powerful beings, something I should have realized from my Alaskan upbringing. During the summer, Athabascan people never mentioned — much less told stories about — the fur people; such discussion was saved for wintertime, when bears were safely asleep and would not overhear humans gossiping about them. Similarly, the Irish did not chatter recklessly about their fairy neighbors. When it was necessary (or irresistible) to mention the *sidhe,* flattering euphemisms were employed: the Good Folk, the Gentry, or simply Them, common words hiding uncommon reality.

Chastened by my noninformant at Máire's, I went back to my books and my rambles. The West of Ireland is dotted with fairy sites, odd bits of bog and forest not visibly different from the next bit of bog or forest but possessing a certain ineffable quality that both attracts and repels. Even with a precise map, much less the fragments of oral history and folklore that were my guides, such places are hard to locate, for normal senses fail to perceive them. Joseph Campbell described fairyland as a warp in the space-time continuum: "One seems to be walking a straight line, but actually is curving past an invisible fairy hill of glass, which is right there, but hidden." But fairy leaves its traces. A road shimmers slightly, a tree pulses, a rock grows too sharply focused. There is a glassy wall upon which the scenery seems painted, beyond which everything becomes much more vivid, as though this world is a projected image of that other. Or there's a spikiness, like nettles surrounding an old ruin, a warning written in the aspect of land.

I began to understand why Celtic shaman Tom Cowan calls taboo the twin of speech. As I continued my explorations, even hints and implications began to seem the boldest chatter. Hearing the mystery nested between words, I became unwilling to speak of what I had experienced. Even writing here, I find myself hesitant. What, I ask myself, makes me so? Fear of seeming a soft-headed Irishwoman? Not at all. I have often been urged by credulous friends to speak of these matters, but even then I feel a crushing sense of unease. The taboos that surround fairy have come to seem appropriate. Each word here is mined from cavernous silence, every sentence forged from the fragments of dozens of discarded others. As Yeats said,

> *More I may not write of, for they that cleave*
> *The waters of sleep can make a chattering tongue*
> *Heavy like stone, their wisdom being half silence.*

In half-silence lives the ineffable. Anyone who has tried to write a love poem knows how far short words can fall. Fairyland is like love; tangled in words, fairy encounters seem either flat and dry or exaggerated, unreal, hallucinatory. I keep extensive journals and have a steel-trap memory, but I sometimes doubt my own experience. Did I really aim a camera at a fairy spot that broke my light meter, which repaired itself afterward? Did I really see the fairy lights on Roundstone Bog one Samhain night? Did I really step on a Stray Sod near Gort and wander for hours in a tiny clearing, unable to find my way past a sudden wall of nettles? Are there places that have whispered their names to me? Did I visit a world long past? Is there a crack in time through which I have edged? Well, yes. Yes, but . . .

I came to Ireland imagining fairyland a metaphor or a mythic well of sweet poetic imagery. What I found is that fairy — or whatever it is, that something truly Other into which I have stepped in forest and on bog, at holy wells and within stone circles — is real, and poetry the clearest way to describe its wild beauty and dangerous power. But I am not writing a poem here. To speak rather than sing of fairyland is to enter a thicket more prickly than gorse. Is truth what is impaled, or what escapes? The latter, I suspect.

❊❊❊❊❊

Despite these hesitations, I will tell you how something precious went "away." The cause of such disappearances is said to be the "fairy blast," an invisible inaudible tornado that tears things from their moorings in time and place and sets them down far away in either dimension: here one moment, gone the next. Sometimes these kidnapped items reappear, hours or days or even years after their disappearance. Sometimes they never reappear, or they come back so far from where they disappeared that no one recognizes their return. According to old lore, butter is a favorite if somewhat inexplicable target, so much so that Lady Gregory devoted an entire chapter to its protection; to keep the *sidhe* from this prize, rural Irish women placed mullein leaves or holy water in their churns. Butter itself is not the fairies' goal; they want its *foyson* — an archaic English word for "inherent vitality" or "nourishment" that remained in use in Ireland until recently — which they drain away, leaving the physical ghost of the butter behind. The Gentry steal milk too, making us spill it, then growing angry if we cry (hence the still-common proverb) as they lap its *foyson* away. Fairy food may tempt the taste buds, but it never satisfies as does our own grosser food.

Some thefts are unmotivated, flat-out fairy mischief. MacManus recorded a particularly entertaining — to reader, not to victim — incident that occurred in 1947. One summer day, the young artist Miss E. M. traveled by bicycle to Roundstone Bog, intending to paint the famously picturesque Bens. Locating a hillock that promised a good vista, she dismounted and carried her canvas up its slope, where she placed it on the ground before descending for her paints. In her brief absence, the canvas disappeared. It was a still day with no wind. Even had it been breezy, a sailing white square would have been clearly visible against the dull gray-green bog. But the canvas was nowhere to be seen. Gone, vanished, poof!

"Miss E. M. is an intelligent, sensible girl with a well-balanced mind," MacManus assures us, "and it was the outrage to all logic and common sense which irritated her as much as the waste of her time and energies."

Outrage or not, the canvas was gone. After a fruitless search, Miss E. M. gave up and ate her lunch, then casually glanced up at the hillock. There lay the canvas, exactly where she had left it, gleaming whitely in the sun. Miss E. M. later learned that her chosen work site was — are you at all surprised? — a fairy hill.

My story is something like Miss E. M.'s, with one important exception. I had not the excuse of ignorance, for I knew what I was doing: I went to a famous *sidhe*-haunted spot wearing a magnificent silver-and-turquoise necklace, one that would tempt a New York mugger, much less a fairy. The necklace itself had a peculiar history. Years earlier, a Navajo shaman had asked an Irish visitor to deliver it to Ireland, then walked away without revealing the intended recipient. The woman passed on the necklace to a stranger in a Connacht pub, offering no reason for the sudden gift. That man in turn gave it to me, another virtual stranger. Fascinated with its story and taken with its beautiful workmanship, I wore the necklace constantly, often reaching up to touch the long silver arrow that pressed into my throat.

The day in question, I decided to visit a haunted area in Connacht, one long familiar to me and mentioned in many folklore texts. On earlier expeditions, I had felt a somber watchfulness about the place. When I call it to mind, I remember an encounter with a bowhead in Prince William Sound. Twice as long as our boat, powerful enough to capsize us with a flip of its flukes, the whale surfaced nearby and lay for a quarter hour, like a huge barnacled waterbed, staring at us. Gazing steadily into its one visible eye, I wondered how this vast creature assessed us tiny humans. Like the calm alien intelligence of the bowhead: that is how the fairy place felt to me. Lawrence Durrell speaks of such assessing invisible eyes when he says that all landscapes ask the same question: "I am watching you — are you watching yourself in me?" In Ireland's fairy places, I have been watched and have watched myself being watched.

That day I put on the shaman's necklace and hiked over to the fairy place. In retrospect, I shake my head at my behavior. Whatever was I doing, wearing an object of power from another land into a place that opens onto fairy? Worse, I was not alone; for no other reason than to show off my knowledge of the countryside, I had brought along a curious companion who made me uneasy by chattering about fairy apparitions as we walked. Light and shadow dappled the ground as we neared the boundary. Nervously, I touched the silver arrow at my throat. The fairy spot, when we reached it, seemed oddly ordinary, beautiful in a conventional and earthly way, not at all conscious and alive. We chatted a bit, walked about a bit, then turned to go.

Everything seemed suddenly awry. I put my hand to my neck. "My necklace." I said. "It's gone."

The necklace was heavy; its absence was striking; it could not have fallen to the ground without catching on my clothing. Yet it was gone. Vanished, poof! I reasoned that, as we had not moved since I last touched it, the necklace must have fallen near my feet. Its silver should be shining up from the dull earth. But a methodical search turned up nothing. I choked out a feeble joke about twenty-first-century dissertations on ancient trade routes between the Navajo and the Irish. We retraced our steps slowly, scouring the ground with hands and eyes. Nothing.

Days passed. Unable to resign myself to the loss, I returned to the scene of the snatching. I am, like Miss E. M., an intelligent, sensible girl with a well-balanced mind; it was the outrage to all logic and common sense that irritated me as much as the loss of my necklace. Surely we had not searched with sufficient care. Surely a bit of leaf had covered it, or a shadow, or a slanting slate. Surely there was another explanation for the disappearance of my necklace than the lust of Irish fairies for Navajo silver.

Approaching the fairy spot, I walked slowly, studying the ground. Walking that way, you feel space become distorted. Everything seems more complex, larger somehow, than when you walk swiftly, arms swinging, eyes forward. I saw tiny golden flowers not earlier in bloom. Strange bulbous spikes of seeding ivy. Oddly geometrical arrangements of stones like undecipherable ogham. My senses began to shift, as they had not on the earlier visit. Plants, rocks, water, leaves, a feather — all seemed deeper, more complex. Things wavered, quivered, came alive. Outside the perimeter, the world as we know it. Within its boundaries, light both more slanted and more direct, glowing from the undersides of objects, coming from all directions at once.

I searched carefully, with no happier results than before. The necklace remained "away." Resigning myself to the loss, I sat on the ground and fell into what I can only describe as a silent conversation with the place, which answered in a tender breeze. What did we talk about? The past, the present, the future. Other things as well, things I cannot now recall. I do remember how the conversation ended: I asked whether there were really fairies there.

A great sudden burst of wind blasted against me, so sharply that I shut my eyes. Something hit my cheek. The wind stopped. I opened my eyes.

Something lay in my lap — a hazelnut. I looked around: there were no hazel trees in sight.

Do even Irish fairies answer questions with other questions? My pocket was full of Irish coins, for I rarely walk in fairy places without silver for an offering. I dug a hole and slipped in a few punts. I had forgotten about the necklace, so bewildered was I by the incomprehensible reply — had it been one? — to my silent question. Baffled and inexplicably grateful, enchanted by the consciousness the place once again emanated, I hiked away, in a different direction than previously.

Far from the path we took on necklace-snatching day, something glinted on the ground. And there it was: my necklace, laid out in an exact circle as though on display on a jeweler's counter. I looked down uncertainly. If it had been "away," perhaps it did not want to come back. Finally I took more coins from my pocket, thanked the Good People for returning my jewelry, offered the punts in trade, and reclaimed the Navajo necklace. It lies here on my desk as I write. No scratches or other marks betray the truth of its sojourn; if its *foyson* has been taken, I cannot detect the loss. But if it remains the same, I have changed: I feel a curious lack of attachment to the necklace, which seems to have a will and a life of its own. I wonder if it plans to travel Southwest again, bringing home a message from the Irish fairies, or if it will remain yet awhile in the Midwest. For now, it rests with me as a reminder of the mysteries. If only I could appreciate everything and everyone in my life with the same clarity of affection.

I hear the rustle of doubt from invisible readers. Surely there is some simple scientific explanation of how a shaman's necklace disappeared in a haunted spot, only to turn up somewhere else! Perhaps the clasp loosened. Okay, then. And maybe I leaned forward, so that the necklace neatly avoided catching in my clothing. That is possible, although I do not remember leaning or the release of the weight from my neck. Then, perhaps, the force of its fall drove the necklace into groundcover, hiding it from sight. Hm: not probable, as the groundcover was not deep, but again, it's possible. Then an animal or a bird carried it in mouth or paw to the place I found it and dropped the necklace, which fell into a perfect circle. Yes, well, I suppose...

Or perhaps it was just "away."

I have, to my knowledge, never been "away," despite frequent visits to fairy-haunted places. Sometimes I come back later than planned, but never with a confused sense of lost time. Most important, I have never seen those tall gracious beings who move with a dancing grace whom people profess to encounter when "away." For that matter, I have never met any of Ireland's other supernatural races, either — not wee folk like the drunken cluricaun or the shoe-making leprechaun, not hybrid beings like the devilish pooka-horse or the silkies who live like seals on coastal rocks. Belief in such creatures runs parallel to belief in fairies; Yeats wrote of a woman who assured him that heaven and hell were fictions, "but there are fairies and little leprechauns and water-horses and fallen angels." Nonfairy races live on the borders of fairy, where we can bump into them without being "taken." For leprechauns, water-horses, and fallen angels do not reside in Tír na nÓg, and they do not stage raids on our world for loot.

Butter and unpainted canvasses are not the fairies' only targets; people of certain categories are at serious risk of kidnapping. Wet nurses and midwives are frequently "taken," because the *sidhe* do not practice those professions. Those with exceptional hand-eye coordination (dart champions, beware!) are drafted for wars against the next mound over. Poets are held captive awhile, then freed to spread the fame of fairy. Musicians of genius are "taken" to play for the endless fairy dances; the fairy equivalent of a Grammy is that one day you up and disappear. When the *sidhe* have no further use for you, back you come — to find everything changed utterly, for centuries passed while you fiddled those fairy tunes. Because the released (nay, discarded) servant misses the comfort of a familiar world while laboring in fairyland, the *sidhe* provide recompense for work well done. Musicians are given memorable tunes like the famous "Derry Aire," which originated in fairy, and midwives are endowed with gifts of prophecy or healing. Poets receive an equivocal reward, a fabulous eloquence that burns through them until it snuffs their lives; the price of fairy inspiration is expiration.

Fairies also steal humans simply because they find us desirable. Babies are especially at risk, for fairies are born wizened little raisinettes, not plump pretty infants as we are. One story of how Biddy Early got her magic blue bottle involves her providing cover for a fairy kidnapping, wherein a changeling was substituted for a human babe. But any beloved person, of any age, is in danger of being "taken." Utterly amoral, fairies feel no compunction about stealing whomever — married or single, young or old, male or female — they find appealing. For this reason, it is good to be chary of tender gestures; I never heard my grandfather speak my grandmother's first name aloud, an omission meant to thwart the eavesdropping *sidhe*.

Although infatuated fairies kidnap humans of both sexes, men are disproportionately at risk. While a few randy fairy kings — like Finvarra, who "loves the mortal women best," according to Lady Wilde — prefer plain-faced humans to the beauteous *sidhe,* the fairy mistress is by far the greater danger. Finding little charm in her bloodless brethren and preferring the smoky testosterone musk of the human male, she treats men from our world like butter, to be stolen at will. The kidnapped rarely suffer, for they fall — hard, fast, completely — in love with their captors. It is not Stockholm syndrome that keeps the "taken" submissively in thrall, but rather the inventive wantonness and irresistible beauty of the fairy sweetheart.

Tall and stately, soft skinned and soft haired, high colored and sweet of feature, fairies are "so beautiful that a man's eyes grow dazzled who looks on them," says Lady Wilde. One song describes "my jewel, my fairy lover" this way: "eyes like stars, lips like berries, voice like a gentle harp." She haunts the singer:

> *I left her in the cattle-meadow,*
> *my brown-haired fairy lover,*
> *eyes like stars, cheeks like roses.*
> *When I kissed her, I tasted pears.*

A twelfth-century text describes her this way: "Her upper arms were as white as the snow of a single night, and her clear and lovely cheeks red as the foxglove of the moor. Her eyebrows black as a beetle's wing; her teeth a shower of pearls; her eyes blue as comfrey; her slender long yielding smooth side, soft as wood, white as the foam of the wave. Her thighs warm and glossy, sleek and white. The bright blush of the moon in her noble face; the lifting of pride in her smooth brows; the ray of love-making in her royal eyes." Ah, who would not follow a woman like that?

The beauty of the Leanan Sidhe — silken skin, rosy cheeks, musical voice, sweetly fragrant hair, the taste of pears — assails every one of our senses. But it's all done with fairy mirrors. The fairy mistress garbs herself in what is called in Irish a *piseog,* a fairy spell — in anglicized Scots Gaelic, a *glamour.* It is fairydom's favorite trick, to use our own senses to confuse and confound us. Just as the Stray Sod causes us to circle, elf-led, round and round the smallest space, so the Leanan Sidhe confuses us with beauty. But what is she, really? Some who penetrate her veil of illusion claim that she is no glorious queen ruling from a silver castle but a dowdy hag in a nettle-ringed shack. But such reports are few. Usually the *glamour* holds.

Mortal men cannot resist the Leanan Sidhe. Neither can Ireland's immortals, as we learn from the tale of the great warrior Cúchulainn and his fairy lover Fand. In a dream she came to him, all cloaked in red, only to beat him until he lay near death. Cúchulainn awoke to find that neither medicine nor magic could cure the injuries inflicted in the dream. For a year he lay in dire straits. Then, on Samhain eve — on Halloween, the day when the veil between our world and fairy fades away — Fand took Cúchulainn to her magical island in the West. Instantly forgetting both her bloody attack and his brilliant wife, Emer, Cúchulainn fell under Fand's glamorous spell. It took not only Emer but an entire college of Druids to draw Cúchulainn back to earthly life.

Men willingly depart fairyland only on rare occasions, and not because they weary of fairy love but because they crave, as fairies do butter, earth's simple joys. A common motif in the *imramma,* the ancient voyage tales, is the wretched homesickness of fairy captives. A particularly sorrowful *imramm* centers on the hero Bran who, lulled to sleep by mysterious music, awakened to find a wand of silver extravagantly and unexpectedly blooming with fragrant white flowers. When he touched it, a beautiful woman appeared, singing poignantly of a "distant isle / Around which sea-horses glisten: / A fair course against the white-swelling surge." She disappeared, leaving Bran rent with desire for the unseen land and its lovely singer.

He set off toward the setting sun — for, as everyone knows, the *sidhe* live off the west coast of Ireland — and was reunited with his fairy love on the Isle of Women. There they danced to the soulful fairy piper and made love endlessly in sweet grassy bowers. But despite the beauty of his

Leanan Sidhe, Bran grew so homesick that he stole a boat and escaped. With a party of other captives, he reached Ireland's welcome shores, where one eager sailor leapt ashore rather than wait for docking. The instant his feet struck earth, the man grew old, died, and disintegrated into ash. For time passes differently in fairy; this side of the gate, life dashes by; over there, it crawls along. (Applying Einstein's special theory, the *sidhe* live faster than we do, so time in their world passes more slowly.) Faced with a hopeless choice — to die in Ireland, or to live forever banished from it — Bran set back out to sea, never to be seen again. Does he still voyage there, stuck between the worlds?

Stories in which people chose an ordinary workaday life over fairy's luxury seem baffling at first glance. Fairy kidnapping should be a popular fate, offering as it does a shortcut to immortal leisure. Ireland's bogs should be crowded with men striking macho poses in hopes of attracting the red-haired girl's eye. But there is a reason to direct the Leanan Sidhe's lustful glance elsewhere, for she is notoriously fickle. When her passion wanes, she ditches kidnapped lovers back in our world: the fairy equivalent to capital punishment, for most die as Bran's companion did, the moment their feet touch earth. Those who survive reentry succumb to wasting illnesses. Nothing here compares to anything in fairyland, so the spurned suitor refuses food, drink, and love, until he goes, quite permanently, away.

Once a man has made love with the Leanan Sidhe, no other love suffices; returned to our world, he dies to return to her embrace. That was what happened to Oisín, poet of the heroic Fianna. "Taken" by the lovely Niamh of the Golden Hair, he lived happily with her until his homesickness for Ireland grew too strong to ignore. Niamh loaned him a magical horse that brought him instantly from the island paradise of Tír na nÓg to the mainland. There, stunned to discover an Ireland filled with churches but empty of heroes, Oisín fell to the ground, whereupon the fairy horse vanished. Saint Patrick himself attempted to convert Oisín, but the poet so mourned the loss of his fairy love that he died soon afterward.

The Leanan Sidhe, *la belle dame sans merci,* shortens life rather than extending it. In Ireland she rarely acts directly as executioner, though we find that motif in other Celtic lands. In Brittany, a virtual twin of the red-haired girl is Dahut, last pagan princess of the land. Assisted by sea elementals called the Korrigans, Dahut built the golden city of Ys on an island off the Breton peninsula. Dahut was said to have taken scores of young men to her bed, each for a single night of bliss. She then killed them and had their bodies tossed over a cliff into the roaring sea or buried in what they call in Ireland a "purpose-built" pit in a bog. Her hair is said to have been the color of fire.

⬚⬚⬚⬚⬚

I used to think that these ancient tales were reflections of men's fear of women's sexual desire. Mythology offers innumerable variations on the bogeyman theme, imaginary figures used to scare people into good behavior. I heard these tales as fire-red warnings to women: act on your desires, and you will destroy those you love. I saw these stories as mythic versions of the priestly rules that stiffened Irish dancing until it became only flashing feet. Women — I believed these stories warned — you must harness those dangerous desires. Fear them. Resist them. Do not act upon them.

Such messages would indeed be useful to those who feared that, unbridled, women's sexuality would contaminate lines of patrilineal inheritance — or merely require more exertion than men were willing to expend. Such rejecting messages about women's sexuality are sometimes articulated quite clearly, as when the seventeenth-century English clergyman Robert Burton, in *The Anatomy of Melancholy,* shuddered, "Of woman's unnatural, insatiable lust, what county, what village doth not complain?" But images are more powerful than words; narratives last longer in the memory than statements. Thus we find what feminist scholar Susan Bordo defines as stories that encode "fear of woman as 'too much' — that almost always revolves around her sexuality." Such a "too-much" woman is our red-haired girl, our Leanan Sidhe.

There is no question that such stories have been used to warn women against our sexuality. But that does not necessarily exhaust their meaning. Irish mythology, being polytheistic, is both/and, not either/or. Multivalent meanings are more common than not. The red-haired girl from the bog may serve as a cautionary tale for overly aroused Irishwomen, but that need not be its only — or even its primary — meaning. Myths do not long survive when they are limited to controlling the behavior of some members of a society in order to benefit others. Without a deeper meaning, the red-haired girl's legend would have faded long ago, even in conservative Connemara.

To plumb this deeper meaning, let us return to the entrance to fairy, to Roundstone Bog and the site of the necklace snatching. This side of the veil, such entryways seem nondescript, "unrecognizable, invisible to the unaware," in the words of the great Breton scholar Jean Markale. Hidden-in-plain-sight locations for fairy gateways include crossroads, little hillocks, high patches of rough ground, boulder-strewn glens, and wild clumps of trees. Size doesn't matter; one can enter fairy through a tiny door at the base of a gorse bush as readily as through the open side of a mountain. Trees are popular; a grove of ash, oak, and thorn is a sure sign of fairy presence, as is a lone thorn growing in a rocky field. Ruins — raths and lisses and dúns, dolmens and menhirs and brughs — are favored as links to the ancient past when fairies ruled. Markale points out that the *sidhe* especially delight in "intermediate zones, neither earth nor water, where all life is both made and destroyed...the alarming region of exchange between the living and the dead." Bogs — lonely and remote and swept with sadness — satisfy these requirements perfectly. For similar reasons, fairies colonize islands that look like blue clouds on the horizon, sometimes visible, sometimes cloud-hidden.

Like place, time can be fairy-haunted. Normally, temporal differential separates earth from fairy. The Wild Hunt gallops past and we hear nothing, fairies frolic in morning sun and we see nothing, although in the first instance we may feel a sudden breeze, in the second an inexplicable lifting of the heart. Occasionally, however, the door swings open. The fairies and their world become as visible and audible and tangible as anything this side of the veil. Like fairy places, such times are liminal, invisible to the unaware. The hinges and crossroads of day — dawn and dusk, when the outlines of reality are blurred — are common fairy moments. Other moments occur at unpredictable intervals, when the worlds bump into each other.

But quite predictably, on two days each year, the door swings open, the veil is shredded, the walls fall down. Old Celtic feasts mark these points where fairy and earth coincide and synchronize. On Bealtaine, the first of May, fairies wander about earth looking for humans to seduce, creating a time of risk and opportunity, of power and possibility. Quite the opposite is true of Samhain, on November 1, when fairy hills snap open, islands drift close to shore, cities rise from shallow bog lakes, and the night belongs to the destructive fairies. Even those without second sight behold the hosting of the *sidhe.* In great armies, they troop across earth, killing plants with their breath, stealing infants and midwives and lovers, waging war on neighboring fairies.

It is a night of danger, not opportunity. In olden times, people stayed indoors on Samhain, hoping to avoid the Wild Hunt; anyone walking outdoors carried a black-handled knife or a steel needle, as fairies were believed to fear metal. Should you meet the trooping *sidhe,* throw the dust from under your feet at them, or turn your coat quickly inside out in the hopes of confusing them about which direction you are headed. Few humans live to describe such encounters, for most who encounter the *sidhe* vanish forever. We maintain a hint of the dread with which our ancestors greeted Samhain when we dress up children as monsters and speak in hushed voices of razored fruit, denying and thus sustaining Samhain's fearful image.

But why should we fear to meet the *sidhe?* Because they will steal us from earth, and beautiful as fairyland is, there is a shadow upon it. However much one eats of fairy food, one is never full; however much one drinks of fairy mead, one is never drunk. Something — some *foyson,* some essential vitality — is missing in that perfect shadowless world. Our world of growth and death, death and growth, interlaced and intertwined, holds something that fairies need, something so compelling they resort to theft and kidnapping to taste it.

If fairyland is essentially unsatisfying, what of the fairy mistress? Can one ever be fully satisfied with her? Although it is never spelled out in myths and folktales, the answer must be no. Sex with the fairy lover must leave us unfulfilled, for in her lovely loving arms we can never plumb the mystery of mortality. The *sidhe,* the *Colloquy of the Ancients* puts it, "are unfading and their duration is perennial." But without an ending, we do not really understand a story; without shadow, we cannot see the shape of things. Thus the Land of Youth is ultimately terrible in its unnatural beauty. When the queen of fairyland promises that you will never die, she does not mention that you will never truly live.

Today death seems an insult, a wrong done us, something to be outwitted as long as possible. Although now we hide and deny death's presence, things were different in the not-too-distant past. By the time they reached my age, my Irish ancestors would have attended on many deaths.

They would have seen death come in the night, taking someone quietly from the side of the turf fire; they would have seen death come in the middle of the day, stealing children with fever and young people in bloody accidents. But death does not become less mysterious when one has witnessed it. Indeed, holding a cooling body from which a loving, living person has vanished reinforces rather than diminishes that mystery.

Death is the *foyson* of life, its imperfect but vital essence. Immortals never feel how much like orgasm death is in its overwhelming inevitability, in the way the body becomes both most fully physical and most utterly soul-filled at the same instant. Death is as precious and intimate as sex — perhaps even more precious, more intimate, for it can never be repeated. "Sex and death both require an entire giving-up of self," my Irish American colleague Corinne once said. "With sex it's temporary. With death, there is no longer any boundary." I understand what she means, for I held the hand of my heart's chosen as he died. Bob Shea was the kind of man any red-haired girl would love, an imperfect vital being who made everyone around him feel more alive, more passionate, more curious. I was terrified as he lay dying of cancer, for I feared that my joy in his life would be buried beneath the horror of his death. But even the years of searing pain afterward cannot dim my gratitude for the inexpressible intimacy of sharing Bob's death and for the constant, piercing awareness of the fragility of our lives that is its legacy.

It is that boundarylessness for which the Leanan Sidhe hungers, which draws her back again and again to our world. But the very chaotic imperfection for which fairies lust may be their undoing, for this changeful earth offers potential for disaster as well as creation. Our power over the *sidhe* extends beyond leaving silver necklaces at home when we go to fairy places, carrying iron on Samhain, and hoping not to be outstandingly talented in music or midwifery. Actions in our world have a direct impact upon fairy, which is vulnerable wherever it intersects with our world. Those hidden entrances may be too clever by half. What stops us from cutting down the fairy tree, from paving the bog? What stops us from closing the doorway from this side, trapping the red-haired girl and her kind to starve for *foyson* in their perfect, beautiful, sterile world?

In the past, belief in fairy punishment constrained such closure of the passages from fairy. When the *sidhe*'s invisible roadways were blocked with buildings and walls, they were said to toss stones, cause objects to fly about, even bring death and disease until the offending structure was removed and the path could once again be used. Even worse was the destruction of fairy trees, for which retaliation was quick and furious. In the 1920s, a Father O'Hara decided that his parish of Kiltimagh — right down the road from my grandparents' village — needed a new hospital. The only available land was vacant, for good reason; between the two fairy trees upon it there was insufficient space for even the smallest building. Not a soul in the village dared cut either tree, but Father O'Hara found a foolhardy farmer who, loudly mocking the fairies, did the dreaded deed. That very night, the man suffered a stroke — the term means "stricken by fairies" and is said to mark the wound of a fairy arrow — and died soon after.

Pishoguery, old superstition, long gone from modern Ireland? No. Just ask in Ulster about the American company that selected a field with a fairy thorn for their factory site. Locals strongly urged reconsideration, but the company shrugged off the warnings. Bulldozers arrived, the fairy tree was torn limb from limb, the foundation was poured, the walls went up. As the production line groaned into action, forward-thinking capitalism seemed to sing a paean of victory over backward superstition. But — and here I see Ulster folklorist Bob Curran, who first told me this tale, lean back, deepen his County Down accent, and wink just slightly — nothing ever really went well after that for the DeLorean Automobile Company, now did it?

Belief that disasters follow desecration of fairy places remains secretly common in Ireland. In 1999 in Newmarket-on-Fergus, teacher and folklorist Eddie Lenihan campaigned to save a fairy tree — not just a tree but the very Croke Park of fairy thorns, the gathering place for Munster fairies when they rode against the hosts of Connacht — slated for execution in a road improvement scheme. Eddie vociferously reminded everyone concerned of the traditional punishment for anti-fairy behavior, thereby winning an indefinite stay of execution for the tree. The road was rerouted around the tree, officials declaimed about avoidance of adverse publicity and the folkloric value of the "monument," and one could almost hear a great sigh of relief from the other side of the veil.

Such controversies have raged for centuries, ever since Saint Patrick battled the *sidhe* on a northern Connemara mountain, a bit beyond Leenane. On the peak, a fairy woman wrestled with Patrick for domination of Ireland. He won that magical battle and banished the *sidhe* forever from Ireland. Nothing against our sainted Patrick, but some seem not to have heard the news, for people still battle to preserve fairy trees. Perhaps, as Eddie Lenihan says, there is something powerful in the land itself, tangible even to strangers — something essentially and vitally Irish that is best described in the vocabulary of fairy encounters. While necklaces are still stripped off visitors at fairy sites, will not the *sidhe* endure?

They will, so long as they continue to have access to our world and its nourishing chaos. And that is far from certain. For it is not just lonely fairy thorns that are threatened: the holiest mountain in Ireland, the very place where the fairy woman battled with Saint Patrick, has come under siege. The events are surprising, for Croagh Patrick is Ireland's most beloved mountain. Tens of thousands climb it each year, their goal a little chapel near a stone circle on the peak's summit. The date of the annual climb, on the Celtic feast of Lughnasa, has led Máire MacNeill and others to argue that the "Reek Sunday" ascent replaces a Celtic feast, which in turn may have replaced an earlier one. Sixteen hundred Christian years and untold centuries before, the same ritual, year after year after year, has riveted people to the land.

I remember the first time I saw Croagh Patrick, blue against a limpid sky, a pyramid so perfect I thought it some mysterious ancient structure. I was at Carrowcastle, the farm where my grandfather was born, and my cousin Vincent was telling me how I came to be American. In 1903, he said, my grandfather — then a strapping lad of sixteen — spent a summer burying a stone. In Mayo's raw and stony land, fields were made by digging out small stones, which are useful for buildings and fences. Larger boulders were burned, encircled by blazing fire until the stone grew so red-hot that water, thrown against it, cracked it into manageable pieces. But stones too big to move or to burn had to be buried. Wheelbarrow after wheelbarrow — on poorer farms, basketful after basketful — of soil was dumped on the ground until the rock was covered deeply enough that grass could be sown.

I was standing on a fine flat field, soft with bright grass. If underneath was a massive rock, the surface showed no sign. Vincent told me that when my grandfather finished the task, he laid down his spade, announced he would not be broken by the stony land, and walked away. John Gordon walked to Dublin, took passage to London, emigrated to America — and there married a girl from Bohola, just two miles down the road from Carrowcastle.

I had been brought up singing Irish songs and writing "Irish American" under "nationality" on school forms, but until that moment I had no real image of my grandfather's life in Ireland. He had rarely spoken of it. Mayo was a poor county at the turn of the century; the joke was that the most productive crop was raising children for export. The West of Ireland is gloriously scenic, but scenery is not butter. Cold, hungry people lack the leisure to appreciate nature's aesthetic values. As playwright Martin McDonaugh says of Connemara, "All you have to do is look out from your window to see Ireland. And it's soon bored you'd be. 'There goes a calf.' "

It is easy to idealize the old ways, to imagine that ancient life was easy as well as simple. That life was far from perfect. Howard Rock, my Eskimo grandfather, used to grow angry at strangers who came to him hoping to learn the secrets of Eskimo shamanism. He would lean forward in the dull darkness of Tommy's and speak just loud enough to force the petitioner to bend forward. "Make you a deal," Howard would say, "I'll tell our secrets. You just have to lose all your teeth and die of tuberculosis at forty." We shared many a laugh at the startled disbelief that spread across the listener's face just before he excused himself and darted from the bar.

To my grandfather, America was Tír na nÓg, a fairyland in the West. He did not expect to go "digging for gold in the streets," as the Percy French song goes. He only wanted to find — and he did find — a livelihood that let him raise himself and his children out of poverty. His grandchildren have done even better. Grandpa never traveled, except for that one trip home when he was eighty, yet I come and go from Ireland at will. He never even went to high school, yet I have had the benefits of higher education as both student and teacher.

Who would I be, had he not emigrated? Some of my Mayo cousins still work the land, strong farmers on rocky soil that over many years has been brought to fruitfulness. Had some not left, life would have been harder for all. There was not enough to go around — not enough land, not enough jobs, not enough money. Even in the 1970s and '80s, my younger cousins followed in Pop's footsteps because they could find no work at home. Now, as Ireland experiences the economic benefits of European

Union membership, thousands of exiles are returning home. They want to raise their children in Ireland, as my grandfather could not. And they don't want to live in poverty while they do it.

And so moneyed interests threaten holy land. In 1993, Andaman Resources and Glencar Explorations purchased mineral rights to the slopes of Croagh Patrick. Their intention was to mine gold. Ever since prehistory, gold has been extracted from the hills and valleys of Ireland. The Irish National Museum is filled with splendid Celtic gold objects, treasures of the nation. But ancient ways of mineral extraction — the antler-bone pick and woven basket — did little damage to the land. Industrial-strength gold extraction, by contrast, tears the land's skin, plundering right down to bedrock, then uses cyanide to leach the rubble. Three million tons of rock are churned up for every ton of gold extracted.

Gold holds no romance for me, for I grew up surrounded by the residue of its extraction: great blond tailing piles a half-century old, rocky hills that still support little vegetation. I have clambered around old dredges and seen the ghostly iron buckets still lined up, poised to be filled when the vein gave out and the effort was abandoned, museum and mausoleum for dreams of wealth and leisure. A gold mine on Croagh Patrick? The thought steals my breath away. Many others feel the same; opposition from pilgrims and farmers, pagans and tourists has brought the project to a standstill. But not to a halt, for the companies are still fighting to reopen the mining scheme.

Saint Patrick was not able to evict the fairies from Ireland, but we may yet manage what millennia have not. In spite of his victory in saving the Newmarket-on-Fergus fairy tree, Eddie Lenihan is despondent about the future of the fairies. "The old culture is almost gone," he wrote me not long after the victory, his backward-slanting writing growing twisted as a thorn tree as he grew more heated about Ireland's losses, "and soon will be, no matter how we may wish it otherwise — and there are very few people who wish it otherwise. All that matters now in this wonderful new Ireland is money, status, show and — nothing, really. Because there's nothing behind the veneer."

Having come to believe in our own *glamours,* we are creating a world in which fairies are unwelcome. Even if we leave open the doors between our worlds, what good is butter from which the *foyson* has already been drained? My friend Tom Hannon mourns, "Patricia, I hate to say it, Patricia, but we were better when we were poor. Truly, Patricia, truly. Much as I hate to say it." And I, who have flown in a fossil fuel–powered aircraft to drink tea with him, am silent. Would my grandfather, who left Ireland so as not to be broken on the wheel of poverty, object from the grave? Why do I keep thinking the fairies hold the clue, that there is some third way in this apparently inevitable war between a decent life and magical land?

⊠⊠⊠⊠⊠

Out on the Old Bog Road, I walk upon the granite bones of the earth. "The wet center is bottomless," said Heaney, but it is not so. Ireland used to be one-fifth bog, but in the last half century, 90 percent of that bogland has been destroyed. Roundstone is a blanket bog, one of the last undeveloped examples in Europe. It could be gone within my lifetime. Mined out, all its peat removed. Eroded away by those picturesque grazing sheep, whose numbers have tripled in a decade with the help of EU subsidies. Destroyed by encroaching conifer forests, planted by commercial pulp manufacturers. Paved to create an airport to service yet-unbuilt resorts. Or turned into a dump. Boglands across Ireland are being used — legally and illegally — for burials. Where women once buried butter to preserve it, a newly wasteful society now buries plastic butter containers.

Perhaps, from the perspective of geological time, the loss of an Irish bog would not be especially significant. Nor would be the elimination of human life, for that matter. Other ecological niches, other species, have been destroyed by geological processes, climate shifts, meteors, glaciation. Roundstone Bog shows the scars of such ancient change. In the very heart of the bog is a patch of volcanic rock: Boolagare, named from the tradition of women spending the summer together there, milking and making butter. In that tiny area, Roundstone geographer Tim Robinson says, the most ancient Ireland shows through "like floorboards under a worn carpet." For the now-green island was, geologic ages ago, a chain of seabed volcanoes into which a tectonic plate smashed during some unremembered catastrophe. The earth moves and changes, gradually or cataclysmically. Does it really matter what we do?

How can it not matter?

In one of his early poems, Yeats describes the way fairies steal us: by promising us a beautiful deathless world. Is it not all we desire?

Where the wandering water gushes
From the hills above Glen-Car,
In pools among the rushes
That scarce could bathe a star,
We seek for slumbering trout...

But to join the fairies, to leave this "world more full of weeping than you can understand," the child must abandon all homely earthy pleasures, "the calves on the warm hillside . . . the kettle on the hob." In the end he goes away, "solemn-eyed . . . to the waters and the wild," forever preserved from death but never having known life. And we, Yeats's readers, know that he has lost more than he has gained, that the brown mice bobbing around the oatmeal chest are far, far more vital than the mingled hands and mingled glances of a fairy dance.

To remember deeply is to be wise. The world of the *sidhe* is called the "land of youth" not only because fairies do not age physically, but also because they need never bear responsibility for their deeds or their consequences. But ours is not the world of the *sidhe.* When we pretend that it is — when we push away awareness of death and decay, when we bury the refuse of our overly complicated lives like strange sacrifices in bogs — we lose more than we gain. Only by embracing our mortality, by honoring the cycle of life and death, can we live our lives fully. Only by honoring the earth's rhythms can we survive as a species. There is no bog huge enough to bury a discarded earth. Those who seek to avoid death, to live forever in a fairy shadowland, are doomed to get exactly what they fear. Even fairies know that, just as they know that there is no real ecstasy without pain.

I call myself an agnostic about fairies because what happens in Ireland's fairy places defies my understanding. Something plays with me, steals from me, gives back to me, answers questions I have not yet even learned to ask. Whether we call this power the *sidhe* or elemental powers or god or the universe, it exists to remind us that there is more to this world than our mechanistic philosophy allows. The red-haired girl from the bog is a story of the passion that other world has for us and of our own desperate passion for it.

Dusk came on over Roundstone Bog, that day. Hours passed, but I could not make myself leave the silent land. Feelings rushed through me like the sighing wind: remembered losses, stinging anger at feeling those losses again, confused guilt, panic at not knowing how to balance contradictions, piercing sorrow at the fragility of beauty. But even as those feelings surged through me, I felt something else as well, a kind of joy that is not separate from pain and that cannot exist in isolation from it, a great tearing hunger to live in this world as fully as I could, until I heard the wailing of the fairy woman at my death.

The hoodie crows called. The articulate wind sang in my ears. I stood on the granite bones of the bog. Above the Atlantic, the sun set in a blaze of red and gold, clouds streaming out like flame-colored hair against the encroaching night.

Chapter Four

Intoxication

I t happens whenever I start talking about Ireland. "Tell Hare Hunting on the Burren," Paula demands.

Paula has been my friend long enough to have heard all my stories, and she knows what she likes. "Come on, tell Hare Hunting."

Invariably, I demur. And with good reason. Hare Hunting is a story that can be misunderstood, could give offense. Besides, it shows me in less than the best of lights. I like ones in which I appear mystical and fey, sensuous and profound. Hare Hunting — well, it betrays my wilder self. "Nah," I say, shrugging, casting eyes upward. "How about..."

Paula, anticipating my refusal, holds me hostage to her plot. Turning to the others, she urges, "Get her to tell Hare Hunting. It's the best." And to a chorus of *"come on's,"* I finally give in and give it out.

"Give it out." Tell us a story, it means. Or recite a poem, sing a song, relate a joke. Add to the merriment. Don't hold back. "Give it out, now, girl." I like the generosity of that Irish phrase, the implication that stories and poems and songs are kinds of currency. As of course they are, especially in Ireland, where eloquence has been prized since prehistory; an early poem claims no one can have dignity without fine speech. "You wouldn't be tired of listening to him" was high praise in Lady Gregory's time, when storytellers — *seanachies* — brightened the desolation of rural life, telling tales in dim smoky cottages from Samhain to Bealtaine. Today, despite a few decades of bellowing about television as the ruination of conversation, the Irish can still talk circles around most anyone else. A cup of porter to lubricate the vocal cords, and soon the *craic* begins.

Not that everyone in Ireland is a great storyteller, but pit the worst in Connacht against the best in Chicago, and I'll lay odds on the Irish one. I count myself lucky in knowing some of the finest talespinners in a storytelling nation, like Bob Curran and Dan O'Donohue, with whom I spent the first Samhain of the new millennium. In antiquity that was the night of stories, and today's Samhain festivals — from Cape Clear over to Dublin, from Lough Gur up to Kiltimagh — continue the tradition. Ours was no festival, just a few of us in a dim smoky pub listening to some of Ireland's best. Dan, a magician as well as a *seanachie,* pulled a deck of cards from his pocket and executed a story-trick before kicking the ball over to Bob, who in my honor related Irish-inspired vampire tales from America. Yes, television blasted from the next room, but at our table stories flowed as freely as beer.

"Tell the Car Factory," I urged Bob. So what if I have heard it before. It's a grand story, worth hearing again. And so he told about the Ulster fairy tree, and the warning against murthering it, and the Americans ignoring the warning, and the bulldozer advancing on the tree and . . .

Once again, I appreciated the way Bob piles detail upon detail, puts on accents and characters, draws out the suspense until its laughing release at the end, when the DeLorean company suffers the inevitable fate of those who offend the Other Crowd. Bob's speech is as carefully crafted as his prose. For spontaneous utterance is but a rough draft; stories are made not in the telling but in the retelling. In repetition after repetition, the perfect phrase is found, the most effective pause, the most colorful verb. And the best stories are never finished; they always remain partially fluid, ready to be poured out again into a different vessel.

I grew up among storytellers; there's nothing like a long arctic night to stoke the narrative fires. Bush pilots stack up especially well against Irish *seanachies*. Irish Alaskan bush pilots? Now there is a category to conjure with. They can hold people spellbound with wild tales of arctic adventure. But setting and action do not alone comprise a good story; style is more vital than substance. I remember Jack Smith, a pilot who could talk the tail off an Irish bull, telling me that any decent storyteller could hold you rapt by describing a door opening. The worst thing, he contended, is when you're well into it and someone interrupts: "Hey, that's not true, I was there, let me tell you what really happened." Unless, of course, the contradictor uses the same material to forge a better tale than your own.

So when I first came to Ireland, I already knew how to spend the currency of stories. After figuring out the bus route to my grandparents' hometown — no thanks to that man in the Galway station — I went north from Gort into Bellavary, the nearest stop to Bohola. There I asked directions to my cousins' farm and was told it was "just a mile up the road." So I started walking. Just as the Irish blessing promised, the road rose up to meet my feet. And kept on rising. After an hour, I realized I must be lost and stopped to ask directions from a friendly woman at the door of a trim cottage. Smiles and nods were offered. No, she told me, I was certainly not lost, indeed, I was almost there, it was right up the road, just about a mile.

This process repeated itself at intervals as I grew more and more exhausted and confused. Each time I stopped to inquire, I was assured the family farm was "just a mile up the road." Thus I encountered the "Irish mile," an infinitely expansive measure that reaches from wherever you are standing to wherever you are going. Not that anyone intends to deceive. The Irish do not actually lie, but neither do they disappoint you with the truth.

And so I walked, asked directions, heard "just a mile up the road," started off again. Six or seven miles later, sagging beside my cousin Nora's turf fire, I related the saga of my journey. The children began to trickle in, and the other cousins. With each entry I was urged to describe how I had walked from Bellavary, stopping for directions and trudging off after hearing it was "just a mile up the road." Inevitably, with each telling, the tale lengthened, grew richer with detail. Polishing my words, honing my timing, I emphasized my tourist innocence against the helpful fraud of the locals. My audience assisted. If I forgot a clever bit, someone gently reminded me; if I missed a local name, someone murmured it. By dinner I had told Just a Mile Up the Road twenty times, and some of my cousins had heard every one.

But I digress. Hare Hunting on the Burren had been requested, right?

It was my first summer in Gort. I was single and young, living above a pub. A wildish thing — the term poet Eithne Strong coined for head-strong young Irishwomen. My landlady, Máire, was determined to get me properly settled, and so she introduced me to every bachelor farmer she knew, none less than twice my age, all with good field drainage and mothers already dead. But fine Burren pasturage was not bride price enough for me. I would find my own friends, thank you, and wildish ones at that.

One night the crowd went up the Burren for some home brew. Not poteen, that illegal whiskey I had first tasted when Emily Saint John Collins stole into the pub and served us out of a little flask right under Máire's nose. Poteen was raw stuff, fiery, that hurt going down. The Burren home brew — sloe wine, soda sweet — went down easy. We drank and sang. We drank and recited. We drank and talked, growing wittier with every bottle. It was all grand *craic* until someone tried to relieve herself and fell backward into a fury of nettles. Then we realized how strong the sweet stuff was. Lurching and stumbling, beyond thinking of the danger of driving in such condition, we headed for the Volkswagen bug we had driven over from Gort.

I remember little of the drive home except stark granite streaked with moonlight. The boreens were clear of traffic, so we made it safely to Ardrahan. The next morning, I awakened in a faintly familiar house. Stumbling out to the kitchen, I faced a ghastly sight. Silhouetted against the window was the long body of a hare, dangling from a ceiling hook, its throat cut over a bowl where blood formed a dark mirror.

I do not remember shrieking, but I must have done, because the others came running, only to exclaim in shock and alarm. Wherever had the hare come from? Our host was certain it had not been there the night before.

Dodgy memories surfaced. Out of the collective fog, someone remembered that we had gone hare hunting on the Burren. Now, hares in Clare are rarely on the thoroughfare, but on the back roads one can see them hopping about clearly enough. The trouble was, we had no weapon. Or did we? Was there not one close to hand?

The VW bug.

No one remembered whose idea it had been. No one remembered how many hares we had aimed at and missed. No one remembered hitting the victim or putting it in the boot of the car. No one — no one at all — remembered butchering our prey in the pale dawn.

We were that drunk.

At this point in my tale, all are laughing, no doubt remembering their own wildish youths. So I have to pause a bit and let the silence gather before I give out the punch line:

Worst of all, no one remembered who was driving.

No matter how many times I tell this story in her presence, Paula always leads the laughter when I finish. I then urge her into her own party piece, Why Can't the Irish Do Anything Right? I enjoy it as much as she enjoys Hare Hunting, and not just because I was there when it happened. But I will leave Paula's story to Paula, except to say that it's a good one, especially the part about being held hostage for seven hours, unfed and unwatered, by a maniacal monologist who . . .

Ah, now then, that's Paula's story. I will only say that it begins on a stormy winter night in the shadow of the great Ox Mountains. It was Paula's first visit to Sligo, but I had been there before, right after that encounter with the Irish mile in Bohola. On the trail of Yeats, that first time over, I dreamed of seeing Innisfree and Dooney Rock, the hazel grove and the hills above Glen-Car, the Rosses where the fairies foot it half the night — places of the poet's Sligo childhood. And, of course, his grave, where I would solemnly ponder the epitaph Yeats composed for himself: "Cast a cold eye on life, on death. Horseman, pass by."

In that little city perched on the banks of the Garravogue, rimmed about with great bluffs and sweeping hills, I felt lonely and remote. I passed by everything but Yeats's grave and another up the road in Ballyshannon, that of William Allingham who wrote that poem I had recited in childhood, the one with the refrain about "wee folks, good folks, trooping all together." Somehow I found myself drawn to cemeteries, where unsettling incantations shivered through my mind. Afterward I sought out pubs where I sat for hours feeling raw and prophetic, writing blood-drenched poems shot through with words like *pitiless* and *sorrowful* and *death,* even one in which that butchered Burren hare appeared as an omen of destruction. Soon shocking news arrived: running to help a threatened neighbor, a dear friend in Alaska had been shot, his death bleeding into my poems even at that distance. It was, in Dylan Thomas's memorable phrase, my first death, the one after which there is no other, the one that made me consciously mortal.

Afterward, Sligo seemed a sorrowful place, full of bells tolling funereally. I attempted without success to determine whether my death-clouded poems preceded, followed, or were simultaneous with my friend's murder. Something similar happened years after, when I woke from red dreams of carnage to write strange twisted poems about human sacrifice until, at dawn, I heard radio reports of mass suicide in Jonestown. What telepathic trapdoor, I wondered each time, had poetry opened beneath me?

My Celtic ancestors — whose very word for poet meant "seer" — could have explained. To them, poets were magicians and prophets, what Jerome Rothenberg called "technicians of the sacred." Poets had access to occult knowledge called *fíos* or *imbas,* a sudden simultaneity of inner and outer worlds that folklorist Dáithí Ó hÓgáin describes as "fire within water."

Think of poetry as a tree, rooted in the past, extending through the present, into the airy future. Celtic tradition married speech and spirit; poets used chanted revision to forge poems from their visions. Becoming a poet back then took longer than becoming a doctor does now. Years were devoted to memorizing almost four hundred tales in sixteen categories, including cattle raids, voyages, and elopements. Only after mastering that repertoire did one learn composition, practiced in silence and darkness, the better to open to *imbas.* Those years of rote learning strengthened memory to the point where writing was unnecessary, for poems were "composed in the mind and not on paper, retained in the memory and not in books, recited to audiences, heard and not read," in the words of Rhys Carpenter, a scholar of oral literature. Completion of a dozen years of study entitled the poet to wear a costume symbolizing her ability to move between worlds: the *tuigen,* a multicolored cloak of feathers from swans and mallards, birds equally agile in several elements; and the tinkling belled branch — gold, silver, or bronze, depending on the level of skill — that represented the tree of life and of poetry.

Had I lived then, had I been a poet then, I would have been familiar with many altered states of composition: *imbas forasnai*, or "light of fore-sight," in which after chewing raw meat — bull, pig, even cat — I would recite incantations into my hands; *teinm laeghda,* or "illumination of rhymes," in which I would use metaphors to prognosticate; *dechetal do chennaib,* "composing on one's finger ends," a kind of psychometry that brought instantaneous knowledge that was just as instantaneously spoken. Like other *banfhili* (woman poets), I would have been also *bandrui* (a druid), a member of what religious theorist Marie-Louise Sjoestedt called Ireland's "scholar-magician class." Prophecy and poetry gave poet-druids great power. Literary critic Walter Ong tells us that in oral cultures, names grant power over the objects named. Because the basic poetic technique — metaphor — names one thing, then changes it to another, a poet could transform the world. Had I lived then, had I been a poet then, my transfor-mative power would have been both feared and revered.

But I knew none of this as I sat scribbling in the Sligo pubs, not far from Lissadell, ancient stronghold of the Ó Daillaighs, whose poetic blood courses in my veins. Had I somehow tapped into my heritage? Or was there something about the land itself that ratcheted open the trapdoor through which I fell? Near Sligo are places of great visionary power: the plain of Mag Tuired, where winged Mórrígan chanted her people to vic-tory over their enemies; Cruachain, where a *bandrui* prophesied bloodshed to great queen Medb: everlasting Asseroe, where beautiful mystic voices ("singing a song of ancient days, in sorrow, not in pride," Allingham said) lured Medb's granddaughter, Ruad, to her death in its cascade. In that vor-tex of mythic power, as my friend's life poured from his distant wounds, I visited cemeteries and wrote sorrowing poems. Sligo was not a place I could easily forget.

Memories of that haunting Connacht city finally drew me back, accompa-nied by Paula on her first trip over. Barely able to see the road in a wild rainstorm, we located our lodgings — whoops, that's Paula's story again — on the slopes of Knocknarea, the mountain that looms above Sligo town. Next day in a dim dawn I rose to a warm welcome breakfast. Paula had warned me not to expect her until late, so I had time to ascend the sum-mit before she downed her second cuppa. Instead I poured more tea and read an outdated newspaper. An hour dragged by; I ran out of tea. Should I order more? I stared into my empty cup.

Why such dragging restlessness? I forced myself out of the breakfast room, got my coat, pushed open the massive front door onto a cold raw day. The path up Knocknarea began just steps away. But again I dawdled, leaning over the stone fence to judge how far — not very — down the steep slope I could see. Then, my back against the fence, I stared up at the fog-shrouded mound called Miosgán Meadhbha, Medb's nipple. Such cairns, common in Ireland, transform mountains into breasts, the earth into a woman's body. Over a thousand feet high, Knocknarea's cairn is proportionately huge. Within it, wild queen Medb was said to be buried in a never-excavated tomb.

From the muddy field behind me, a pony whinnied. I turned to scratch its ears, its skin warming my hands. I had forgotten my gloves. My hat, too. Perhaps I should go back? Perhaps climbing Knocknarea was not a good idea on such a morning? Again, that resistance. Again I fought it back. No one was about. I picked up a pebble from the roadside, following local tradition that adding to Medb's cairn brings your heart's desire. I set my feet on the path. Wind tore at me. What could I see from the top? The clouds that grayed the sky would soon utterly block the view. But I pushed on.

Then, almost to the cairn, I stopped. This was silly. I could barely see the road below through the blur of fog, much less the reportedly spectacular sea view. Might not tomorrow be clearer? I threw away my stone. It clattered down the path.

My descent did not take long. At the bottom, I stopped again to pet the pony. "Stupid, huh?" I asked. "You think I'm stupid? Come all this way only to miss Medb's lump?" The pony nuzzled for a lump of sugar. "So what if I didn't go up. So what if I'm not going to get my heart's desire." My mind twitched like the pony's ears, still irritated by my irritation with...

Ah. That was it. Ah, yes. I knew why I turned back shy of the summit. I did not much like Medb.

Most of Ireland's heroines and goddesses — Brigit, Macha, Danu, the hooded Cailleach — offer images of womanly power I gladly embrace. But Medb? I knew her from the "Iliad of Ireland," the *Táin bó Cuailgne,* the epic *Cattle Raid of Cuailgne* I had read years earlier in Thomas

Kinsella's famous translation. Even in English Medb dominates the *Táin* just as Knocknarea dominates the Sligo horizon. But not with her charm; she is aggressive, greedy, demanding. Oh, yes, and haughty, self-willed, and irresponsible. Although the *Táin* may be Ireland's *Iliad,* there is a difference: "While the great epic wars of Greece and Ireland were both initiated because of a woman, Medb, unlike Helen of Troy, drew up the battle plans," critic Maureen Waters points out. "An unscrupulous and masterful virago," archaeologist Proinsias MacCana calls Medb. "Devious and bloodthirsty," says historian Peter Berresford Ellis. Sounds about right to me.

Lots of women disagree. Miriam Dexter, the brilliant Indo-Europeanist who has devoted years of study to Medb, finds her a fascinating vision of feminine agency. Elizabeth Cunningham writes marvelous witty novels in which a red-haired, willful, passionate Medb appears as a Celtic Magdalene. Irish poet Nuala Ní Dhomhnaill assumes Medb as a feminist persona, declaring "merciless war," *Fógraim cath gan truamhéal,* on any man who insults her dignity. I appreciated their visions of Medb. I wanted to share them. It was just — well, I just didn't.

I returned from my failed raid on Medb's mound to find Paula pushing blood pudding around a mess of hard fried eggs. Had my diviner's eyes been open, I would have noticed gathering clouds of culture shock and predicted the stormy outcome of Paula's mounting belief that the Irish Can't Do Anything Right. But I saw nothing. And I certainly did not foresee the saga about to unfold, the epic series of misadventures that Paula — once her usual sunniness had returned — would craft into her party-piece recitation.

Despite the worsening interior weather, the sky was clearing slightly. We set out toward the round nipple-cairned breasts of Carns Hill. Beside the shores of sweet Lough Gill we drove about confusedly, looking for the tiny sign indicating Ireland's most beautiful holy well. Then, rounding a curve, we found it: Tobernault, nestled in its dense hazel grove in the protective shadow of a hill. The irritations of travel, the morning's difficulties, and our navigational confusion all dropped like heavy cloaks from our shoulders as we entered the holy precinct. The only sound was water surging from a rocky cleft and bubbling between gray flagstones. Even before we saw signs demanding silence, our voices dropped to murmurs.

Meditatively, we followed the stations, small piles of stone topped with crosses. My senses sharpened in the silence. Had I never visited a holy place, I would still have recognized Tobernault, so saturated is it with what Walter and Mary Brenneman call "loric power," a centripetal force that pulls us to places deeply linked to story. An Irish holy place, they say, is "like the nest of an animal, full of intimate odors, sounds, and artifacts." Those who come from such a place know it like family. Mention its name, and they picture its seasons and weather; mention its name, and all its stories are implied. Irish holy places and their stories are literally incomparable, for rather than belief in abstraction palely reflected in a physical object, loric space is intensely specific. There is no "real well," no perfect pattern; there is only this well, the one right here, this Tobernault.

Tobernault's lore is deeply Catholic, or so it seems: heaped stone stations, great Mass Rock, paired Lourdes grotto and Crucifixion. Even on a wet winter day, candles flutter beneath the Virgin's statue. Within the clear well itself, a plaque proclaims: "O Mary conceived without sin, pray for us who have recourse to Thee." But although today's dedicatee may be Our Lady, legend suggests an earlier lady of the place. Tiny indentations mark the well's stones, reportedly left by Saint Patrick when he "sained," or depaganized, the water by penetrating it with his staff. Local tradition alludes to the well's former owner. Called the "well of intoxication," Tobernault's waters are said to invest hurling players with great speed and skill. Even more telling is the well's "pattern," its sequence of required prayerful movements. Those stone stations mark a sunwise circuit, a miniature royal progress, pointing to the well's ancient role as an inauguration site. They point too to Tobernault's original owner: the goddess of sovereignty who married the local king, a lady now forced to find her favorites among sporting heroes.

That goddess was the fertile earth, the hilltop cairns visual reminders of her presence. In loric sensibility, "earth" means not an abstract planetary whole but innumerable separate places, each simultaneously the goddess. Therefore, ancient Ireland had hundreds of kings, each ruling a tiny territory, a few people. Not a hereditary office, kingship was earned through strength, intelligence, and vigor, as divined by druid-poets and authorized by the goddess. A king's reign lasted as long as he satisfied the goddess. An ancient poem describes her gifts to a worthy ruler: sunny skies, dew on the grass till midday, no wind stirring the cows' tails till noon, wolves stealing no more than one bull calf from each byre. "Truth in a ruler brings milk and corn," we are told, but an unworthy king brings "famine, dryness of cows, ruination of fruit, dearth of crops." A land mirrored its king as a well reflects the sky.

Marriage of goddess and king united her invisible realm with the visible world he ruled. Wells like Tobernault, whose waters bring underground refreshment and fertility to the surface, symbolized their connection, and Tobernault's hazel trees — magical to the Celts — reinforce the symbolism. Roots in earth, leafy crowns in air, trees connect invisible and visible. The king himself was a "world tree," folklorist Dáithí Ó hÓgáin argues, pointing out that *bile,* Irish for a sacred tree, metaphorically means "protector." The king-as-tree "stood between heaven and earth and thus kept both in equilibrium for the welfare of his subjects."

If Tobernault was a well of inauguration, it is clear who Patrick evicted with his well-penetrating staff: the goddess of earth and earthly abundance, the king's judge and lover, a goddess whose names and stories are as uncountable as her holy places. Sometimes she is Flaith, which means simply sovereignty, the power and responsibility of rulership; sometimes she is Étaín, sometimes Ériu, after whom Ireland is named, sometimes winged Mórrígan. But most often Lady Sovereignty was the very goddess whom I had avoided on Knocknarea. The well of intoxication belonged to the one whose name means "drunkenness": Medb, lover of the *ard rí,* Ireland's high king.

In the *Táin,* Medb is never called a goddess. Was she not simply a human queen wearing a goddess's name? It seems easy enough to find the answer: just look in the book. But the *Táin* was composed long before writing came to Ireland. Its origins are lost in prehistory's mists; we do not even know if one poet or many created the tale. For the last half century, since Milman Parry established the orality of Homer's works, scholars have debated the genesis of ancient masterpieces. Mircea Eliade believed that epics echo visionary journeys, while Georges Dumezil contended they describe and support social structures. However such tales originated, they were sustained through oral repetition; our words *epic* and *voice* are cousins. But repetition is not reproduction. Themes and motifs remained constant, but new ideas were folded into epic tales, new characters added, links established to other tales.

For untold generations, poets sang of Medb's cattle raid. Then along came the written word. Literacy was viewed with suspicion by the Irish, whom Lady Gregory said believed that "there is no man able to read books who can tell a story out of the mouth." Writing's disadvantages flowed together with its advantages. Some tales were preserved, true, but most of those in the bardic curriculum were lost. Those that survived were altered in their very essence. As Walter Ong points out, literate folks picture words as having tangible reality, perhaps resting on pages in books like this. But in an oral society, words disappear even as they are spoken.

In our visual culture, we speak of insight and self-image and good prospects; we get some perspective or an overview; we understand someone's point of view in order to see things their way. But a world based on ear rather than eye unfolds like a story rather than appearing like a picture, in total, all at once. Media critic Paul Rodaway has remarked that sight is before us but sound surrounds and penetrates us; we can detach from the seen world simply by closing our eyes, but we cannot shut out the sounding world. Hearing is our deepest sense, first to develop in the womb, last to go as we die. Spoken stories flow freely as water or beer; written down, their form is forever frozen. On the birthday of a written text, a spoken one dies.

No one knows what scribe entombed Homer's words, but we know who transcribed Ireland's epics. "In Ireland writing was a child of Christianity," says Proinsias MacCana. Today's *Táin* is a monkish version of a story whose original we can never hear. Fair play to those who preserved the tales of their ancestors. But are monks necessarily reliable recorders of pagan material? MacCana contends that they deliberately chose to "suppress or to soften traditions of native myth and ritual that clashed too blatantly with the central doctrines of Christianity." And no figure clashed more blatantly than Medb, whose residual divinity Miriam Dexter contends is "underlined by the vehemence with which she is derided."

That vehement derision explains my trouble with Medb, whom I saw through the eyes of her enemies. But even monks were occasionally intoxicated by Medb — as, for instance, in the *Táin*'s opening scene. Abed with her husband, Ailill, Medb enumerates her reasons for choosing him. "A miser would be all wrong, because I am so generous," Medb explains. "Gossip starts when a woman opens her hand more freely than her husband. The same is true of courage, for I fight and win my own battles, so a timid man would not be right for me. And jealousy — impossible, for I always have one man in the shadow of another." What a speech! Were this all I knew of Medb I would have climbed Knocknarea no matter the weather. But the rest of the *Táin* — Medb's recklessness with men's lives, her deceit, her willingness to prostitute her daughter — well, that stuff put me off her.

But back to the pillow talk: Ailill claims he owns more than Medb does; Medb dismisses his claim; to settle things, they have their possessions dragged before them. Cattle and servants parade through the bedchamber to be counted. And yes, Ailill has a sensational bull. Born in Medb's herd, White Horn was "unwilling to live under the rule of a woman" (feel a heavy, misogynist hand? perhaps a monkish scribe?) and moved over to Ailill's. Medb's fierce resolve to have the bull's equal leads to a four-hundred-mile round-trip raid on Ulster and to death — lots and lots of death.

As the epic of cattle theft and bloody mayhem proceeds, I find my sympathies dissolving. I want to say: get back down on the pillow, girlfriend. Take it easy. Lie down, Medb, enjoy your man. It's just a bull.

But to understand a story is to understand those for whom it was told. The *Táin,* recited to crowds of inebriated warriors, provides endless brawls, lists of glorious deeds, paeans to heroes. We see Ferdia, fighting his own foster brother, Cúchulainn. The hosting of Connacht against Ulster. The wild cries of the final battle. All stuff to warm a man's heart. But women were listening as well, women who knew marriages as unions between families, sealed with a bride price paid for twenty-one years. Women who knew ten different kinds of marriage, of which only one — the union of equals — allowed a woman to be co-lord with her husband. Women who understood what Medb had at stake: her right to make contracts, to buy and sell herds, to cultivate her lands — in short, her sovereignty. I imagine these women cheering Medb as she took lovers and discarded them, stopped the battle while she relieved herself, stole what she needed to assure her equality. I imagine, too, that when the Brown Bull of Cuailgne killed White Horn, only to die of his battle wounds, they understood that Medb, equal again, could finally lie back and enjoy her colord, just as they would enjoy their own after the banquet ended.

Those warriors and ladies, children of pagan Ireland, would have recognized the goddess behind the queen. Despite monkish sniping about "following the rump of a misguiding woman" and about how "it is the usual thing for a herd led by a mare to be strayed and destroyed," I too could find, shadowing the written *Táin,* the goddess who sang in the clear spring of the spoken epic. Tobernault pointed me toward this hidden Medb,

stirring my desire to understand "the fair-haired wolf-queen, proud of posture" described in the *dindshenchas.* Where to find her? Easy to say: on a
hill so deeply linked to sovereignty that even those who have never seen it
call it "royal." On Tara, seat of the high kings of Ireland.

※※※※※※

In Ireland's loric landscape, where the goddess inhabited all places simultaneously, Tara's king was more a spiritual than a political leader of the
innumerable kings who married the innumerable regional goddesses. His
prestige derived from Tara's symbolic meaning in Irish spiritual geography. Ireland's provinces corresponded to the four directions: Connacht to
the west, Ulster to the north, Leinster to the east, Munster to the south. But
there was also an invisible central pivot around which the directions
turned. In the visible world, Tara was that point; Medb was its goddess;
and her husband was Ireland's high king.

From the first, Tara's prosperity was linked to its queen. In the *Book of
Invasions,* the poet Tuan describes Tara's history, which he witnessed not
only in human form but as an eagle, a salmon, a stag. In early times, Tuan
tells us, a king named Eochaid ("horse") married queen Tailtiu, after which
"there was no wetting save only dew, and no year without harvest; false-
hoods were expelled from Ireland in his time." But Eochaid's reign ended
in his defeat by the Mórrígan's hosts at Mag Tuired. In the fray the victor,
Nuada, lost an arm. Disfigurement barred him from rulership, so a substitute named Bres ascended Tara's throne instead. But if whole in body, Bres
was disfigured in spirit. He even refused beer to a poet!

Kings were required to be generous, to dispense the goddess's bounty
to all her children. To such openhanded kings, poets sang praise songs that
magically increased the land's abundance. But a stingy king? What's a
poet to do? Simple: compose a satire. Like this one: "You crooked withered shaggy dog, you starved pot of trouble, you odious clown carrying
your bag in cold hands." As diviner of the goddess's satisfaction, the poet
both judged and administered judgment; thus the glossarist Cormac fanci-
fully derives the word for poet, *file,* from "poison (*fi*) in satire, and splen-
dor (*li*) in praise," while a medieval manuscript warns us that poets'
tongues have two compartments, one for honey, one for venom. *Aer,* the
oldest Irish word for satire, also meant magical incantation. Aimed at an

errant king, satire raised fiery boils or other disfigurement that ended his reign. Such was the case with Bres, who offered a poet only three little crackers for a meal. The poet paid him back with Ireland's first satire:

Without food upon his dish,
without cow's milk upon which a calf grows,
without a man's abode under the gloom of night,
without enough to reward poets, may that be the fate of Bres!

Bres's lack of generosity cost him the throne; Nuada, fitted with a silver prosthesis, replaced him. His first act was to bring four treasures to Tara: a cauldron that could not be emptied; a spear that never missed its mark; a sword that always found its victim; and the stone of destiny, Lia Fáil. The first three of these Otherworld treasures are now back in the cave from which they came, but Lia Fáil still stands at Tara.

Lia Fáil was the first ancient monument I saw in Ireland, Tara the first ancient site. Over the years I have returned many times, seeing Tara under siege by tourist armies in green summer, empty and windswept in gray winter. My favorite Tara memory is of one autumn day when mud reached my ankles, wind stole my hat, rain saturated my sweater, and I had the place all to myself. It was Samhain, when Tara's doorways are supposed to open, when the Other Crowd motions us to come on over and lift a glass with them. If ever there were a time and place that door should swing open, shouldn't it be Samhain on Tara? The wind a bullroarer in my ears, I wandered the raths, made circuits of the holy wells, placed my hand on Lia Fáil. But nothing happened to me, that day or any other, on Tara hill.

No matter: Tara is what its chronicler Michael Slavin calls "one of the best windows we have on Ireland's pagan past," and a window is as good as a door. But to see through Tara, the eyes of imagination have long been needed. "Tara, though she be desolate today, once was the habitation of heroes," says a tenth-century poem. Tara is just as desolate now; I have overheard more than one tourist question all the fuss and bother over ruts and bumps on a small green hill. But as shape-shifting Tuan asserted, that hill shadows virtually all of Ireland's history, its fifty monuments — most in ruins — extending from the star-graven Mound of the Hostages, built five thousand years ago, to a church dedicated to Saint Patrick, only two hundred years old.

That windy Samhain, alone on Tara, I envisioned the place as it would have been millennia ago. Warriors and ladies from all Ireland's provinces would have passed between the green ridges of the ceremonial way, gathering for the Samhain Assembly, the *feis Temro* — a celebration "without theft, without wounding a man; without feats of arms, without deceit, without exercising horses." So what did everyone do with all their time? "Constant drinking throughout the week," the old poem answers, for which reason the assembly was sometimes called "Tara's Drinking Feast."

The biggest drinking feast of them all was the king's inauguration. Slogging through the slick mud, I reached the place where it would have begun: the Forradh, or seat of judgment, from which protrudes Lia Fáil. Beneath its limestone phallus, tests were conducted to determine whether the goddess accepted the royal hopeful. A mantle had to fit him exactly, a chariot bear his weight, and its horses accept him at the reins. Two stones had to rear back to let him by, and Lia Fáil had to scream at his touch. If the king passed these tests, a poet would be wrapped in a bull's skin for the *tarbfleis,* or bull divination, in which a poet ate raw beef until he sank into a stupor, whereupon a "spell of truth" was chanted. Whoever appeared in the poet's dreams was deemed the rightful king.

But these were just the preliminaries. If confirmed by the oxblood-drenched poet, the king advanced to the *banais rí,* the main act in the inaugural drama. Exactly what this phrase describes is unclear. Giraldus Cambrensis claimed the king-elect ate raw mare meat while bathing in horse broth, but some doubt the ancient historian's report. More likely, a less barbarous rite concluded the feast: the king drank from the cup of the goddess.

I wanted to climb Rath Medb that wet Samhain, to stand where the ancient inauguration had climaxed, but an impassible moat left me staring up from the road. I imagined Tara before that road was built, and myself a lady from Connacht watching the queen act as the goddess, holding out a chalice to the man who would be king. "Smooth shall be thy draught from the royal cup, 'twill be mead, 'twill be strong ale," I could almost hear her say. In my vision, queen and goddess, goddess and cup, cup and contents, all blurred into each other. And so they should, for all are Medb. "A man cannot be king over Ireland if the ale of Cuala does not come to him," says one tale. Cuala was Medb's father, Medb herself the ale. In drinking from her cup, a man drew into himself Medb's intoxicating power.

Interpreters often say that Tara's ritual symbolized and was followed by sexual union. My sister Eileen can explain the connection between drinking and sex: one always leads to the other. But hold on a minute: drinking symbolizing sex? Saint Patrick knew patriarchal sexual symbolism when he saw it; he stuck his staff into the goddess's well. (Saining, indeed.) But drinking from Medb's cup recalls a child nursing at the breast rather than a man penetrating his lover's body. Or perhaps the cup's intoxicating contents represent even more intimate fluids? Holy wells from which ale was brewed, like Tobernault, flow beneath rather than from the nipple-cairned breasts of the earth goddess. If the king's action symbolized sex, it seems more a receptive than an active sort, more yin than yang.

But is not kingship the peak of masculinity? Not really: a king is no more a man than ale is a grain of barley. Inauguration means utter transformation. Like honey turned to mead, man through inauguration becomes suddenly and irrevocably king, child of the goddess and her tender lover. In ancient Ireland, such transformation was otherwise limited to poets — who became "the wind of the sea, the stag of seven battles, a hawk on the cliff, the greenest of plants, a salmon in the river," as the great Song of Amairgin has it — and to divinities. Such shape-shifters moved in a shadowy Otherworld where boundaries blurred between inside and outside, above and below, masculine and feminine. Rath Medb opened onto liminal space. There a man lifted the cup of the goddess. And a king put it down.

Tara's inauguration ritual is unlike any found elsewhere, and no one knows how deep in history its roots are. The rite may preserve pre-Celtic motifs, for according to shape-shifting Tuan, Ireland's primordial settlers invented brewing to preserve summer's bounty of grain. But unlike the Greeks, who stored wine for year-round use, the Irish used beer as a seasonal indulgence. Cauldrons for brewing have been found by archaeologists, but no ancient version of the six-pack — no litter of beer-storage vessels — has been unearthed. Beer had to be consumed before it soured, which led to periodic drunkenness that was absorbed into the ritual year. Beer was ripe in its cauldrons at Samhain, just in time for an eruption of cosmic disorder that was reflected and reinforced by earthly drinking bouts.

No approbation was attached to drinking beer rather than milk or water. Samhain drunkenness was an expression of potent virility — hard drinking, stiff ones — as we see in *Mesca Ulad,* "The Intoxication of the Ulstermen," a comic poem about drunk warriors carousing about the countryside. Now that beer is available in all seasons, the Irish are imagined to drink without ceasing. But Irish drinking is more complicated than stereotypes allow; the Irish are as abstinent as they are alcoholic. For centuries per-capita alcohol consumption in England has equaled that of Ireland, but we see no cartoons of boozy Beefeaters. Ireland is distinguished not for drinking but for binge drinking, as the Donegal T. D. Mary Coughlan recently argued when she deplored the "ruined lives, premature deaths" brought on by such behavior, which may have its roots in ancient Celtic Samhain boozing.

As for me, despite my wildish hare-hunting youth, I exemplify Bachman's theory that most drinking, Irish or otherwise, decreases with adult responsibility — settling down, my landlady in Gort called it. Yet not everyone settles down. Coming from a family of several self-confessed alcoholics and a few unconfessed ones, I know firsthand the turbulence and disorder caused by those swimming in denial and drowning in drink. Tara's drinking rituals unsettled me almost as much as monkish visions of that misguiding mare of a Medb. Yet if I could penetrate the *Táin*'s derisive surface to embrace the intoxicating goddess, could I not also appreciate Medb's primary sacrament, her communion? Could I not see Medb as the higher power — perhaps, in her case, the "deeper power" — of which Alcoholics Anonymous speaks?

To do so requires a deeper look at Irish kingship. Today drinking slackens social obligations, but Tara's inaugural draught tightened them. I have known more than one overserved man who fancied himself quite the prince. But such men could never pay the tab for Medb's red ale, which held the king hostage to *geasa,* magical commands and prohibitions. Generosity was primary, but each kingship had additional rules; Medb forbade Tara's king to remain in bed after dawn, while other goddesses had other rules. The king of Munster could not camp for nine nights consecutively on the Suir River; the king of Connacht could not travel to Clare in a speckled cloak. Carousing about the countryside with the lads? Falling off the *geasa* wagon? Not likely. That could cost the throne — and more.

The dire penalty for negligence is depicted in the poem "Da Dearga's Hostel." When Conaire, grandson of the goddess Étaín, first reigned at Tara, its abundance — "acorns up to the knee every autumn" — reflected his righteousness. Then, one after another, he broke his *geasa*. When a king failed, so did the land; starvation loomed like a dark cloud on the horizon. A poet's satire could raise boils on Conaire, but that was insufficient retribution for such consistent sacrilege. So a divine ambush was set up in the hostel of Da Dearga, nephew of the Red Goddess of sovereignty. After Conaire was lured inside, a terrifying hag appeared and assumed an incantatory posture. When Conaire asked her name, the hag rattled off a score of strange words before smiting him with unquenchable thirst and setting the house ablaze. "All the liquid in the house was spent extinguishing the fire," the epic says. So Tara's gilt cup was taken to all the rivers of Ireland, but their waters receded at its approach, and Tara's king died in agony.

⊠⊠⊠⊠

Who is this hag who pulls back the cup of refreshment from the lips of the king? All but two of the names she offers are elsewhere unknown. Those familiar ones are titles of the Mórrígan, a triple goddess whose name means "death queen" and who is an ancient form of Lady Sovereignty. Her mate was the king of gods, the Dagda; together they comprise an Otherworldy reflection of Medb and her king in the surface world. As queen of poets, the Mórrígan composed Mag Tuired's victory incantations. As queen of prophets, she stood astride rivers predicting mayhem. As battle queen, she protected her land and its people. She is Medb's mirror image, for while Medb offers the cup of sovereignty, the Mórrígan snatches it away.

The two comprise the feminine heart of the *Táin*. If monkish copyists buried Medb's divinity beneath heaps of derision, they were unable to contain the Mórrígan. She flies around as a carrion crow, swims in rivers as an eel, races across the land as a wolf. She is a fearsome ancient hag, then a gloriously vibrant maiden. When she screams, warriors drop dead. When she does her laundry, more men keel over. She is wildly contradictory. Does she hate Cúchulainn or lust after him? Does she wish to further Medb's plot or hinder it? Just when you think you've got a fix on the Mórrígan, she changes shape or direction. I imagine priestly editors throwing up their hands every time the Mórrígan stuck a wing into the story.

But she remains in the epic background, for what poet Nuala Ní

Dhomhnail calls her *banulachta,* her "womanness" or female power, clashed even more blatantly with Christian doctrine than did Medb's. Medb resisted being controlled by her husband; the Mórrígan, a force of life and death, was utterly beyond control. That she shadows so many narratives suggests her ancient primacy, but we have no story in which she plays the central role. Who knows what epics have been lost and what they said about the Mórrígan?

But if none of her major myths survived the transition to literacy, there is a more primary text to consult: the Irish land itself. So I pulled out that compilation of place lore, the *dindshenchas,* and there she was, right enough, "the mighty Mórrígan, shape-shifting goddess, envious queen, fierce of mood, cunning raven-caller." Now, where did it say she lived?

"In the cave of Cruachain, her fit abode."

Cruachain? Medb's home, where she had her pillow talk with Ailill?

⁂

I had never been to Cruachain. Most visitors to Ireland, even those who seek out mythic places, never get there. Tourists besiege Tara; Knocknarea gets its share of the action; but Cruachain? One of ancient Ireland's five seats of power, it is hard even to locate today. No tiny red italics, signifiers of historic sites, mark it on the standard tourist map. Books on Irish antiquities passingly mention Rathcrogan in Roscommon — a wee village near Tulsk, don't you know, up the road a bit from Castleplunket and Strokestown, and not a metropolis among them — a fact I filed away in case I was ever in the vicinity. But the one time I was, en route to Sligo, I missed the turnoff at Longford and found no compelling reason to turn back.

The Mórrígan provided that compelling reason. Though the monks put me off Medb, the wild winged Mórrígan — shape-shifter, poet, prophet — pulled me in. As my normal haunts are nowhere near Cruachain, I planned an expedition for a Samhain morning. Why then? Because every tale set at Cruachain begins on Samhain: Medb's cattle raid departs then, the drunken Ulstermen turn up at Medb's doorstep then, the Mórrígan flies forth from her cave on that day. Cruachain, like Tara, is an Otherworldly doorway, and it is on Samhain that such doorways swing open.

That gray morning I hit the road early, with my Connemara friend Barbara and Maggie, over from Florida. We retraced in reverse the route

Paula and I had taken on that memorable trip, passing right by the pub where Barbara had convinced Paula that the Irish Can Do Something Right. After misadventuring down from Sligo, Paula and I must have looked like women in need of a stiff drink, because Barbara had gotten us quickly into a pub where a musical session was in progress. Silver-haired silver-voiced Barbara Callan composed delightful comic ballads. That night, in her broadest Connemara accent, she sang my favorite:

O woeful conshternation, what will we women do?
For all men from here to Maam and down to Timbuktoo
will be roaring like Niag-a-ra on this potent drug Viag-a-ra,
caushing conshtant agg-ara-vashun to the likes of me and you.

As we put Connemara behind us and shot toward Cruachain, I reminded Barbara how her song had worked magic on Paula's attitude. To clue Maggie in on the events in question — without, of course, telling Paula's story — I described how I had tried to clear the atmosphere by offering Paula Irish language lessons.

"But," Maggie demurred, "you don't actually know..."

"Hey!" I shot back. "I know *tubber* and *lios* and *bally.* Once you've got 'holy well' and 'fort' and 'town,' you just make the rest up." *Ballinaspittle?* Town of the big spitters. *Tubbercurry?* Holy well of the Indian food. *Lissivigeen?* Fort of the vegetarians.

Maggie and Barbara groaned and grinned.

Critic Vivien Mercier claims wordplay is the basic form of Irish humor. If so, I am resoundingly Irish. It runs in the family: my father once described my "two bedroom/one path" cabin in Fairbanks as "uncanny," while my own personal best was asking a friend who had just thrown a bit of stale French bread at me to "stop causing me *pain.*" Wordplay is to me pure magic, and punsters bards of barbs, or what feminist theorist Claudine Hermann calls "thieves of language," redistributing meaning like cattle. The Irish are prodigious at such thievery; look at the famous Irish bull, "a metaphorical statement stressing apparent connections which are not real," as Maureen Waters has it. The best bull is so subtle that the listener is unsure whether it is blastingly brilliant or utterly stupid. Thus we have "half the lies told about me aren't true" and "I can't see in the dark, barrin' I was a cat." Or the famous bull of Sir Boyle Roche, member for Kerry in the Irish House of Commons in the latter part of the eighteenth century: "All along the untrodden paths of the future, I can see the footprints of an unseen hand." Bulls are poetry astray. As Anglo-Irish novelist Maria Edgeworth said, "the Irish are an ingenious generous people" and the "bulls and blunders of which they are accused, are often produced by their habits of using figurative and witty speech."

Americans are jokers; the Irish are wits. Of course there are Irish jokes of the Bridget-brace-yourself sort and labored puns like that ancient crack about the difference between the Mayo women's track team and leprechaun bunko artists (those cunning runts). But the best Irish humor is organic, rooted in story like a tree in rich soil; it shares with Ireland's holy places a loric quality, each witticism reflecting its context. For instance, take "it's an illusion." Hardly a witty line, eh? Now hear the whole story: as a young man, Dan O'Donohue worked in Foley's, a pub pictured on a famous postcard that shows a bright yellow propane tank sitting beside a red doorway, taken one gas-delivery day. For years, tourists would arrive bearing the postcard, stare at the space beside the door, shake their heads, and depart to find the "real" pub. So Foley painted a propane tank on the wall, then printed "it's an illusion" above it, just below "Guinness is good for you." The photographer returned for another shot that became another postcard. And because of photography's flattening effect, the illusory propane tank looks just as real as the doorway next to it.

What makes this story especially enchanting is that the publican was a retired magician, an illusionist like Dan himself. Sleight-of-hand tricks might seem an odd sideline for a storyteller, but Dan's schtick is quite in line with the Irish belief that magic and storytelling and poetry are all related arts of transformation. Poets were masters of illusion who could call forth the *ceo druidechta,* or "fog of druidry," to pass unnoticed through crowds. But did fog shroud the poet, or did the poet turn into fog? Tuan tells of being fish and bird; Amairgin of being a wave of the sea, a salmon in the well, a tear of the sun — both shape-shifting through practice of *feth fiadha,* the art of semblance. But did the poets actually change their shapes or, as Joseph Campbell contends, through magic or eloquence alter their audiences' perceptions?

We still know the Gaelic word for a spell, a *glamour* that makes us see whatever the poet or illusionist desires. Today, women are called glamorous with no sense of the secret deceit implied. In the word's original sense, Ireland's most glamorous goddess is the Mórrígan, whom we find in the epics shape-shifting away. When she wished to seduce Cúchulainn, she was a ripe maiden; to curse him, she turned into a right hag. To fight Cúchulainn in the water, she became an eel; on land, a wolf. In her own cattle raid on Ulster, the Mórrígan was a woman red in skin and hair, nails and teeth. But the moment Cúchulainn challenged her, she turned into a blackbird.

Not very glamorous in the contemporary sense. But glamorous people are sexy — are they not? — and shape-shifting, says mythographer Christine Rudvere, is invariably a signal of sexual prowess. And the Mórrígan's sexual appetite was as huge as her body. On Samhain eve, she straddled Connacht's river Unius to wash her nine long braids. Along came the Dagda, that curious king with his beer belly and his matty hair, wheeling an enormous mallet (really? a *mallet?*). Overcome with lust, he made love to the Mórrígan then and there, his performance so vigorous that she rewarded him with a couple of new magical incantations.

This tale, so full of weird unsettling power, verges upon the obscene. Medb's sexuality is similarly queen sized, and her lover — named "Semen, Son of the Big Stallion" — of appropriate endowments. Whoever said size doesn't matter never met the man after whom Lia Fáil was called *Bod Fearghuis,* Fergus's Rod. How big was Fergus? Seven fists fit inside his penis; his scrotum filled a bushel bag; seven women were needed to satisfy him. Medb's own appetite was even more impressive; it took thirty-two men to satisfy her. Medb's other bodily functions were also what Miriam Dexter calls "prodigious"; when she urinated, she carved out three deep canyons. Think about it: with a bladder that big, what ought we to think about Medb's other internal spaces?

Medb was *flaithuilach,* a lovely Irish word that includes the word for sovereignty, *flaith,* and that means both nobly generous and sluttish — both giving out and putting out. The enormity of her sexual appetite makes Medb, by Vivien Mercier's definition, a comic character. Comedy is intimately tied to sex, Regina Barreca claims; cracking a joke is like making a pass, and "laughing together is as close as you can get to a hug without touching." I would go further: laughter is a kind of intercourse, a spontaneous and uncontrollable shared bodily experience. (Some say laugher is like sneezing, but I personally have never had anyone bring me to sneeze, then sneeze along with me.) Anthropologist Matadev Apte has discovered a universal belief that women who tell jokes are wildish things, their laughing mouths reflecting lower openings. Humor's assertive sexuality may explain why women are just supposed to smile brightly as men tell jokes — the bunny in the headlights look — but never tell them ourselves.

⊠⊠⊠⊠

But I must have been sick the day we covered this at school. I've been a joke teller — I even know some clean ones — all my life. I'm a wild witty woman who as often as possible indulges in just what Plato warns against: abandoning myself to violent laughter. And I chose my friends accordingly. So it was a merry trio crossing the hills of Connemara and the wet plains of east Mayo. Through Castlebar and Swinford and Ballaghadereen we went, telling stories, singing songs, making jokes, slowly ascending toward the highest point on Roscommon's limestone plain, ascending high enough that I had to swallow sharply to take the pressure from my ears, ascending so slowly that I might have driven right past Cruachain had Barbara not suddenly cried out, "Look!"

Look? At what? All I saw was a little car park and a small sign.

I pulled in, and we scrambled out. It took a moment to bring the setting into focus. A sign announced the hillfort, or rath, after which Rath Cruachain, anglicized as Rathcrogan, is named. But what stood before us was low and unassuming. I looked around. Was there another site nearby, a larger one, more appropriate to Cruachain's mythic stature? No. The wee hill was it, the famous capital of Connacht where Medb's fine palace stood, where she launched the raid on Ulster, where the great bulls met in fierce and final combat. I had expected something like Tara, with sign-posted ancient monuments mobbed by sightseers. But Cruachain was just a field bumpy with mounds, and on that wet November day not another soul was about.

Unspectacular as it seems to the untrained eye, the Cruachain complex is, according to archaeologist Michael Herity, "unequalled on any other site in Ireland and out-rivaling the best in the whole Celtic world." In the center of seventy ancient monuments — ceremonial passageways, burial mounds, souterrains, holy wells, standing stones, and raths — rises Medb's small rath. Originally a natural hillock, it was shaped in ancient times into a rounded breast whose aureole of ditches circled a nipple-cairn. A century ago or so, a few thousand years after it was raised, the cairn was razed by local farmers greedy for building stone. But the rath's breast shape is still clear.

We started up Rath Cruachain, skirting puddles, dodging livestock. I did not expect to see much from the low summit. But five minutes later I gasped in surprise. A wide vista opened around us. I could see for miles in all directions over what Yeats, who knew the site from when he lived in nearby Sligo, called "Cruachain's windy plain": blue Connemara in the west, a grand sweep of farmland out to the east, dark forests around Lough Ree to the south, the low Shannon hills to the north. Most startling was the enormity of the sky. I felt lifted into a watercolor of cloud and light, great washes of gray on pale blue with startling bursts of the brightest white. The low sun seemed close, and the great black cloud looming in the southwest, and the dark diagonal of rain to the north.

We wandered rapt in an airy sense of space and a ghostly sense of history. It was like walking through a multiple exposure. A low green hill. Women circling its summit. The shadow of a palace and an ancient cairn. Shades of warriors, faint echoes, a clangor of swords. A poet's melodic harp. A strapping red-haired queen choosing her favorite. All Cruachain's stories unfolding around us — but fogged, blurred. Irish places often seem this way to me, storied significance flickering upon current emptiness like movies on a dull screen. In memory, I see Cruachain as both a lonely hill and an epic seat of power. Without knowing its stories, would I have seen just the first?

The day was dying, and we far from home. We had not yet found the Mórrígan, so we turned our backs to the sun and walked to the edge of the hill fort. Our shadows fell, long and eerie, down the side of Medb's rath, across the field, across cattle and hedgerows and ponds and boreens. Perhaps a hundred feet long, our figures joined together at the base, forming a vast black three-headed monster.

"Smile like the Mórrígan," I said, snapping a shot.

Then we were off in search of her. Signs lead to Medb's rath, but the Mórrígan's cave is a different story entirely. It appears on no map; no signs point the way; guidebooks offer little more than its name and general location at Cruachain. Nevertheless we started off confidently enough, for Barbara had been to the cave before. Within minutes our confidence sagged as everything jumbled together into rural sameness, every boreen looking just like the last, and the next. Once, twice, three times we drove past Rath na dTarbh, the fort of the bulls. We stopped for directions, being told — what else? — that the cave was but a mile away. Each time we set off confidently in the direction pointed out, only to find ourselves back again at the bulls' fort.

Sunset was nigh when we finally found a tiny gate beside a narrow road. From the boot of the car, Barbara produced wellies, waterproof trousers, and jacket. On her earlier trip, she had watched while others descended, but this time she would go down while we waited above. Suited up, Barbara led us into a field knee-deep in mud. Struggling to keep our footing on the single narrow strip of firm ground, we crept single file along the barbed-wire fence. Twenty feet later, we stood next to a thorn tree atop a large stone.

"Here we are," Barbara said.

I looked around. The Mórrígan's cave is called "the hell-mouth gate of Ireland," which sounds yawningly huge. In Tulsk's little museum we had seen its photograph: a vulva-shaped cavern perhaps two stories high. But Barbara stood before a chest-high flagstone above an opening the size of a fireplace.

"This is it?" I said disbelievingly.

"This is it," said Barbara.

The cave's mouth was slick with gray mud. Barbara ducked under the entrance stone and slid down the souterrain. She duck-waddled a few feet, her head hitting the ceiling. Then she was out of sight. We called after her. No response.

Marooned on a small solid island in a mud sea, Maggie and I passed the time sharing what we knew about Oweynagat — Uaimh na gCat, the cave of cats. No one knows whence the name derives; cats appear rarely in Irish myth. Robert Graves mentions an oracular cat cult devoted to "a slender black cat reclining upon a chair of old silver" in a cave. There was a cat who mangled Ireland's chief poet Senchán Torpéist for his satire calling felines "hanging-down cowtails."

Senchán was rescued from the feline assault, only to die later because of Medb, Tom Hannon told me once. "Some of the verses of the *Táin* had been lost, you see, Patricia," Tom said, "and Senchán knew that the only way to retrieve them was to go to the Otherworld. And so he did, Patricia, he called up the spirit of Fergus himself, and from him learned the lost verses. Then, Patricia, at a royal banquet, the poet came forth, all wan and pale, and recited the verses, and fell over dead." A single recitation was enough, for other poets in the hall memorized the missing verses even as the dying Senchán spoke them.

Despite Oweynagat's name, its lore centers on cattle, not cats. The Mórrígan, who corralled her Otherworld cattle there, punished a woman for letting a bull into the cave. And a calf was said to have disappeared down Oweynagat, emerging twenty miles to the north with a woman holding onto its tail. No such underground route exists today, an alteration explained as the work of the devil. Because Irish myth has no devil, no hell, we know these Christian words point to rather than hide the cave's original identity. "Hell" is the Otherworld, and "the devil" is the goddess who rules there.

⌗⌗⌗⌗⌗

In addition to the Mórrígan, two other goddesses are said to live in Oweynagat: triple-headed Ellen, a fearful creature from a ninth-century text whose name means "incantation," and Cróchan Crogderg, the mysterious red woman after whom Cruachain is named. Cróchan came from Tara as handmaiden to the goddess Étaín, lover of the god Midir. Infuriated by her husband's affair, Midir's wife had slapped Étaín with a branch of magi-cal rowan wood, transforming her into a pool of water, a worm, and a fly, each for seven years. As her fly life ended, Étaín drowned in a cup of beer. A princess drank the beer down, swallowing Étaín. Now in mythology, drinking is like having sex — haven't we heard that before? — and so, nine months later, the princess rebirthed Étaín, as lovely a woman as she had been a goddess.

Years later a man named Eochaid desired to become king of Tara, even going so far as to schedule his inauguration. But "they could not convene the Festival of Tara for a king who had no queen," says the *Tochmarc Étaíne*. Eochaid searched the land for a wife, settling on the fair Étaín, who offered him the cup of kingship on Rath Medb.

Étaín had forgotten her earlier life, but Midir's love was undiminished. He came to Tara, murmuring in Étaín's ear, "Though you may think the ale of Ireland delightful, the ale of my land is even more so; warm sweet streams flow through the land, the choice of mead and wine." His words stirred no remembrance; Étaín remained faithful to her human husband.

Midir then challenged Eochaid to a card game, with Étaín as prize. He won; one kiss, and Étaín's memory flooded back. Transforming themselves into swans linked by a golden chain, Étaín and Midir flew away through an open window.

Because the queen's departure ended Eochaid's right to Tara's kingship, the erstwhile king pursued the escaping couple to Midir's palace. By a marvelous sleight-of-hand, a substitute queen was provided so that Étaín could remain with her beloved. The doting couple moved to Connacht where, at Oweynagat, Étaín's pregnant handmaiden — a woman red from her skin to the hair on her head, so red she was called Crogderg, "blood-red" — gave birth to a daughter. That daughter was Medb.

Is Cróchan Crogderg another name for the Mórrígan, who also appears as a red-skinned woman? Is Étaín another name for Medb? The linked myths, with figures shape-shifting into each other, are difficult to disentangle; perhaps they were meant to be. The Mórrígan was the mate of the Dagda, whose cauldron went to Oweynagat after its removal from Tara. Cróchan's name means "cup" or "cauldron," which in turn, Tom Cowan points out, means an entrance to the Otherworld, "a miniature well." Cróchan's daughter is the cup of intoxicating red ale. Cup, cauldron, woman, goddess, cave, holy well, ale — Cróchan and Mórrígan and Medb — all blur together. And all focus on a tiny opening under a rock by the side of a small field off an unmarked road somewhere in Connacht.

⊠⊠⊠⊠

Dusk was gathering around us in that muddy little field, blurring the edges of the world. The sun sat at the horizon. It was the point in mythic time when the Mórrígan drove her cattle back into Oweynagat. Every night at sunset they entered the Otherworld through the cave's souterrain entrance. But that Samhain, only the sun's beams angled like a crowd of weary cattle into the tiny opening of Oweynagat.

Suddenly, myth ripped through the veil. From our left came a loud bellow. A red cow lunged toward us. Around her, cattle gathered and began to lumber in our direction. Cattle appeared in the field before us. Then, from the right, more cattle. The fields around us filled with cattle, moving toward Oweynagat, making a strange urgent noise. Soon a crescent of cattle — a score or more — surrounded us, roaring.

We looked at each other. "Hey," Maggie said, "don't ask *me* what they're up to. I raise horses."

"We're a great team," I answered. "I only know about moose."

We made little wan jokes. Did we look like the Mórrígan? Was it feeding time? Were Irish cows carnivorous? Was that big one a bull?

I was not so much frightened as uneasy. The bovine behavior seemed rawly meaningful. The cattle stared at us, alternately raising and lowering their heads, singing antiphonally to sky and earth. One bellowed, then another, their huge voices rumbling through our bodies, their breath steaming with each roar.

Barbara was nowhere to be seen. No sound came forth from Oweynagat. Had she fallen, been injured? Did she need help?

The cattle roared. Maggie and I stood in the reddening sunset.

Then Barbara's head appeared at the cave's mouth. We ran to her. She could not get out of the cave. The slippery mud gave her feet no purchase. As one, Maggie and I each grabbed an elbow and dragged Barbara from Oweynagat. Filthy, cold, and spent, she grinned broadly. At the car, she stripped off her muddy outer garments, and we piled in for a long drive west.

Barbara was ebullient. Where she had left our sight, Oweynagat opened up into an underground cathedral. It was easy to stand up, she told us, easy to gain a footing, easy to move about. She had shone her torch on the rock ceiling high overhead, the rock floor beneath, the striped rock walls. At what seemed to be the cave's center, she had prayed and sung, feeling a strong maternal presence. "Magical," Barbara said, "it was utterly magical."

Happy as I was for Barbara, I was also envious. Why had I not prepared to descend into Oweynagat? Why had I not borrowed waterproof clothing, bought a torch? Or sacrificed a sweater to the Irish winter and gone down as I was? Had my nerve failed when I saw that tiny opening? Would it fail again if I returned to the Mórrígan's cave? Seeing the womblike cavern seemed the whole point of our journey. And I had missed the point.

But the meaning of experience often reveals itself not in the moment but later, through story, just as the meaning of visions often appears in revision. When I told the tale of Cruachain, the bellowing cows seemed a mere curiosity, remarkable only because of their mythic connection to the Mórrígan. But every time I retold the story of our expedition, every time I wrote of it in journals and letters and poems, those cattle gained significance.

It took a storyteller to tell me why. When my friend Falcon River was visiting Chicago, I took her to Greektown for their famous flaming cheese. Falcon is the sort of person that Irish Alaskan bush pilot Jack Smith had described, someone who can enchant you by describing a door opening. And like all good talespinners, she loves listening to stories as much as telling them. So there we were spinning yarns. I reached the part where Maggie and I were midwifing Barbara out of the cave when Falcon stopped me.

"The cows." Huh? "The cows. What about the cows?"

I replayed the scene in my mind: the bellowing cows, the sun's slant light, Barbara's head appearing at the cave's mouth...

"Why, they stopped bellowing when she came out."

Falcon studied me. "What did you say she was doing down there?"

"Wandering around, praying, singing."

"Ah. There you go."

I stared at her.

Falcon knows how to milk a moment. She speared a piece of cheese, spread it on bread, ate it slowly. Finally she resumed. "Now, that was strange cow behavior. They rarely bellow like that. Usually when a cow is calling to a calf. Certainly not in herds. And cows are prey animals. Like hares. Those big ears? They need them to hear predators creeping up on them."

Whatever did big ears have to do with the price of beer in Ireland? Falcon milked another moment dry. "Think what Barbara sounded like to those cows. Her voice, resonating against the walls of the cave, ringing in those big floppy ears. Like nothing those cows ever heard before. I think — " and she paused for emphasis, "I think they were singing back."

Singing back?

In that instant, everything shifted. My vision went double, as it does when I see both past and present at Ireland's haunted holy places. I saw a different world from what Plato imagined in that cave where he said we watch reality's shadow dimly cast on rocky walls. I saw another cave, one where Otherworldly power replenishes and sustains our surface world — neither more real than the other, neither an illusion, neither a reflection of ultimate reality. In that Otherworld cave I saw a cauldron that can never be emptied, a cauldron that shape-shifted into a dark winged queen who shadowed and sustained a wild willful daughter, who gave power to a generous king.

I saw the breast-shaped hill of Cruachain that echoes the cup of its cave. I saw a woman singing in that cave, its shape repeated in the soft ears of cattle singing back to her. I saw two women standing as the poet stands, between the worlds, midwifing meaning from experience through story, story that rings in the cave of our ears, its sounds dying even as they are born. Story that enters us, penetrates us, borne into our dark interiors to resonate in our blood, our bones. I saw myself standing at the entrance to the Otherworld while my friend descended to its depths. And in that intoxicating moment I knew that we all stand there always, that the Cave of Cruachain is everywhere, that the great white bull and the brown ceaselessly dance the marriage of dark and light, Otherworld and here, spirit and body, that the story of Medb and the Mórrígan has no beginning or any ending...

"Oh yes," I said to Falcon. "Oh yes. They were singing back."

Chapter Five

Becoming Native
to This Island

With relentless beaks, a squad of crows attacked a winter field. It was a fine fair field, sweeping upward in the pale sunlight toward a dark bulwark of rhododendrons surrounding a single gnarled oak, beneath which three ruddy cattle grazed. Welcoming this peaceable scene as an excuse to slow my journey, I parked on the verge and walked to the field's iron gate.

Shrieks rent the air as another crow spiraled down to invade the feast, some carrion invisible from the roadside. Black birds of battle, I thought, Macha's winged servants. How appropriate to encounter them as I traveled to her ancient stronghold near Armagh.

Something caught my eye, something fluttering in the chill wind. A flag. How odd, I thought, a flagpole in the middle of a field. And what was that atop it? Red, white, blue. I vaguely recognized the pattern. The Stars and Bars? Whoever would be flying the Confederate flag over here?

But no. There were too many crosses, and the colors were in the wrong places. What was it?

The Union Jack.

Without realizing it, I had crossed the border. I suddenly felt light-headed. My breath escaped in a painful sigh. I had not known that I was holding it in.

It was mid-afternoon, and the conference in Belfast to which I was traveling started that evening. Eight hours earlier I had left Dublin, intent on beating the morning traffic up the N1. Suburban sprawl stalled me, then Drogheda's usual congestion. Even so, I should have been at the border well before noon. But I had been killing time, finding one then another reason to postpone crossing, for the first time, into the North.

North. It is a touchstone word for me, one that in most contexts connotes home, familiarity, a known place. A northerner most of my life — one of those rare people who can unsettle Canadians by describing their country as "down here" — I hear in the word *north* moose and aurora, pastel shadows on snow, blueberry bogs and white birch. Whenever I am dislodged from my moorings, I dream of flying like a raven over intricate braided rivers, among mountains up whose rocky faces scramble sharp-footed sheep. Always, in the dream, I am heading north.

This is, I realize, an eccentric reaction to the word. Most temperate-zone folks hear *north* as winter and darkness. Rather than arabesques of asparagus grass and lingonberries on the floor of a boreal forest, they envision white treeless wastes. North is fright, loneliness, even desperation — Perry bent against an impossibly frigid wind, ghost ships held captive by eerie unbreakable ice. North is the farthest remove from home, a place where Frankenstein's monster wanders mournfully, distant from all the known safe world. There is one exception: American cities. Our prevailing winds blow south, carrying odors toward society's less fortunate. In our cities, north signifies purity and cleanliness, in contrast to the down-and-dirty South Side.

North is also directionally "up." Because our maps are oriented with north at the top, we unconsciously picture things tending southward as though pulled by gravity. Moving north, we imagine, entails significant, even Herculean, effort. Students look at me oddly when I describe the Laurentian Divide, above which rivers flow north. "But isn't that uphill?" their quizzical expressions imply.

North is an oddly fractal word, etymologically related only to words about itself, like "northerly" and "northward," or to the people who come from that direction, Norse and Nordic and Norwegian. Yet behind its unyielding glacial face, north is secretly solar, conceptually linked to the sun's motion. North is classically defined as the cardinal point opposite the sun's position at noon. That definition presumes a northern hemispheric vantage, for when you observe dawn from the earth's alleged topside, you see the sun roll southward toward midday. As the year progresses, the sun rises daily further south, as though retreating in dread. Watching sunrise up here, north stands to our left, so words for "left" are tainted by the direction. Our English word derives from European originals that meant worthless, old, weak. Thus "left behind" is a reasonable locution, for why not discard the useless? And how about *sinister:* Latin makes the word for "left-handed" even more threatening than in English, while the French *gauche* means clumsy, awkward.

In Irish, the solar symbolism of directions is even closer to the surface. North is *tuaisceart,* a word implying left-handedness; cousin words are *tuais,* arrogance; *tuaithe,* curse; *tuairech,* foreboding; and *tuaichthe,* anguished heart. By contrast *deisceart* means south, right-handed, turning sunwise. A relative, *deiseal,* means to move as the sun does — by extension, to follow nature's order; whatever moves left, anti-sunwise, implicitly goes against nature. What the world calls Northern Ireland is to the Irish *An Tuaisceart,* "the North," six counties separated from the other twenty-six by the British Parliament in 1921. Politics aside, to speak its name evokes an ancient hidden dread.

Americans call the region Ulster, but that incorrect usage is rarely heard in Ireland. An Tuaisceart is only part of the ancient province, for three Ulster counties — Cavan and Donegal, and Monaghan, whose name I bear but to which I have no ancestral connection — were left in the Republic at partition. The names of the other six counties of the North have been familiar to me since childhood. There is Antrim, whose green glens call us home. Armagh, where bold Phelim Brady lived. Danny Boy's Derry, Nell Flaherty's Tyrone. Star of the Country Down, Fermanagh

Highland Reel — names that roll off my tongue as easily as Mayo and Galway. I never saw these counties, though not for lack of opportunity: residing at Annaghmakerrig, I was just miles shy of the border; vacationing in Carlingford, I looked at the blue-gray Mountains of Mourne sweeping down to the sea. But I never crossed into the North.

Not that I feared violence; tourists are rarely targeted by Irish sectarians, and besides, I could as easily get killed in Chicago as in Belfast. Not that I lacked interest; a list of mythic sites — topped by Emain Macha, hill-fort of the goddess — invited exploration. But something kept me south of the border. As much as the word *north* comforts me, the phrase "the North" threatens, for generations of my mother's family have played their parts in the patriot game. I have been to Kilmainham to find the cell where great-uncle Pa was interned and to Portlaoise to visit a cousin imprisoned for conveying explosives in his car — headed, of course, north.

My grandfather was fiercely anti-British. Although John Gordon never to my knowledge lobbed a bomb or ferried explosives, he planted incendiary devices deep in our hearts. Pop regularly trumpeted the strains of British rule: evictions, poorhouses, famine. He taught me about the Battle of the Boyne and Cromwell's massacre at Drogheda, about quislings and Black-and-Tans. Pop described how he escaped Mayo poverty, just a few years before the Easter Rising, by stowing away on a boat to England, where he planned to earn passage to America. British attitudes toward the Irish infuriated him. "They made us sleep in latrines," Pop would say, still furious after half a century. As a perplexed girl I pictured people in sleeping bags on the floors of large public rest rooms, before learning that Pop meant the bothies, shacks with no separate toilet where immigrant Irish laborers stayed. Pop would not forgive anyone of English heritage, no matter how many generations removed. Once I brought a new boyfriend to meet him. All he had to hear was his name. "British," he said, and turned away.

As soon as I left home, I became a Quaker and stopped singing rebel songs, but good intentions alone do not extinguish the rage of generations. Once, hanging by a strap on the London tube, I glimpsed the hot depth of my conditioning when I found myself calculating how many faces around me were colonial — Pakistani, South African, Irish. Just then a blond, thin-nosed woman bumped against me. Hate-filled words at the ready, I turned as though invaded. That woman may not have been English, but she —

well, she *looked* it. In a flash, I categorized her as the oppressor I had been reared to hate and fear. Swallowing my words, I realized that although I may not boil like my grandfather, something still simmers. I never went to the North, not to avoid British territory, but to steer clear of a stormy internal terrain.

And so, that winter day, I found reasons to forestall my arrival at the border. There was tea to drink, and the paper to read right down to the adverts, and then — oh yes! — I needed to find some tubes of that lovely effervescent vitamin C. Finally exhausting my excuses, I started north again. Major Road Works (I always envision a portly military man) halted me near Julianstown; I listened to Irish-language radio, in no hurry at all, at all. Then, at the Drogheda traffic circle, I spied a familiar brown Heritage Site sign. Of course! I could drive over and take a tour. Perhaps Clare would be free for tea. Then I could take a good long browse at the bookstall. I could kill another few hours, by which time I would surely need lunch.

Postponing the border crossing was my excuse that day, but in truth I rarely resist an opportunity to follow the Boyne as it meanders through Meath's low hills to Newgrange, the place that is my spiritual touchstone. I discovered it by accident, that first time over, when my CIE tour bus to Tara stopped at three other significant places: something called the Brugh na Bóinne; the field where the Battle of the Boyne was lost (or won, depending on your perspective); and Drogheda Cathedral, where we could pay respects to Blessed Oliver Plunkett's petrified head. Packing a book, I planned to debark only at Tara. I have never yet trodden the soil where, in 1690, Billy of Orange trounced the papish James and, although Oliver has ascended to full sainthood, I have still not made his head's acquaintance. But Newgrange drew me then, as it draws me still, into its mysterious spiral recesses.

The CIE did not invent Newgrange tourism. During the Celtic Iron Age, pilgrims left offerings — Roman coins, a sweet little copper ring, an extravagant spiral-scribed brooch — at the then three-thousand-year-old mound, even though they could not reach the site's spiritual core through the collapsed entranceway. Pilgrimage dwindled after the fourth century when Saint Patrick gave his famous shamrock sermonette on nearby Slane hill. But Newgrange's significance was never forgotten; six centuries later, poet Cinead Ua Hartacáin sang of the Brugh na Bóinne, the divine palace on the Boyne. As elsewhere in Ireland, fairy rumors kept the place hallowed in the folk imagination, though not sufficiently to preserve stones from its outer ring from being crushed for a road extension.

Then, less than a decade after King Billy's victory down at the river bend, quarry workers uncovered a lavishly ornamented boulder at the entry of a three-chambered cairn, soon identified as the legendary Brugh. Antiquaries thronged to the site, each proposing a different history. Governor Thomas Pownall of Massachusetts pronounced it a naval monument of Phoenician provenance. Colonel Charles Vallancey of the Royal Irish Academy believed it to be a shrine to a Persian god. Both were wrong, as were those who envisioned a Celtic druid's temple. For like its relative Stonehenge, Newgrange was ancient before the Celts migrated to — or invaded, depending on your point of view — Ireland.

If Newgrange was not built by the Celts, then by whom? Not by Ulster's first visitors, who twelve thousand years ago chased game into land that had itself, millions of years earlier, drifted over from Scotland to collide with another continental fragment drifting north. Settlement began around 7000 B.C.E. Though a rising sea had swamped an early land bridge, Ireland's northeast tip remained visible from across the waters. Foragers boated the few miles over to colonize the mouths of Ulster rivers, where they found oyster, crab, lobster, and other shellfish in abundance. Later came farmers who advanced southward to the Boyne valley, where rich glacial soil supported dense oak forests. By 3300 B.C.E., Ireland's forest had yielded to field and pasture. We do not know if these first strong farmers, or later immigrants, erected the stone monuments that stretch across Ireland like a necklace on a fair woman's neck, for their builders left no records save enigmatic, strangely moving petroglyphs.

Myth agrees with archaeology on the wavelike pattern of Irish settlement — or invasion, as the texts prefer it. According to the *Book of Invasions,* Ireland's first settler was Noah's daughter Cesair, who arrived with a boatload of maidens and a handful of men. Cesair was followed by Fomorian giants, who were evicted by beer-brewing Partholonians, who were killed off by plague, whereupon the hero Nemed brought over his people. The Fomorians grabbed back the land, but Nemed mustered the Fir Bolg to oust the Fomorians for good and all. Their reign was ended by the Tuatha Dé Danann, who lost Ireland to the Milesians.

Got all that? No? Ah. Then just picture a series of invasions: people riding cold gray waves from Scotland or Spain (or Alaska, if we believe the Internet ranter who contends that Ireland was settled by Eskimos) and disembarking in Ireland, usually in Ulster. Some were migrants, forced by war or climatic change to seek a new home; some were invaders looking for gold, cattle, or women to steal; some were a bit of both. As the myth shows, each arrival had to find acceptance within a preexisting society or, more likely, fight his way in. One group of immigrants — or invaders — put down roots, then put up stone monuments that later arrivals admired and held sacred.

Whoever they were, Newgrange's builders were remarkable engineers, both social and technical. That first time, I stood with the other tourists near a stout menhir, marveling as our guide pointed out the location of the timber city that housed the builders of the complex's forty mounds. At Newgrange, hundreds of workers had hauled a quarter-million tons of rock, including cobbles from the Mourne Mountains, up a high ridge overlooking the Boyne. There they arranged almost a hundred kerbstones around a three-hundred-foot-diameter mound over an inner chamber oriented toward winter solstice dawn.

These ancient people were artists of genius. My first taste of megalithic art was Newgrange's entrance stone — a bit like discovering European art at the Sistine Chapel, for the recumbent glacial giant, deeply incised with spirals, is a masterpiece. I fell behind my tour group, entranced by bas-relief still sharp five thousand years after stone tools had cut into gray granite. Three straight lines bisected the composition; related designs unscrolled to each side. I felt a compulsion to reach out and trace those lines, especially the unusual triple spiral on the left. But at a sharp command from our guide, I rejoined the group, ducking through a doorway beneath a narrow transom and squeezing through a stone corridor into a tiny inner sanctum. The central room and three antechambers — the whole forming a kind of tubby shamrock — were exuberantly carved with stars, bars, lozenges, meanders. And suns: a dozen blazed forth from stone. In the farthest chamber reappeared the triple spiral from the entrance stone. The mysterious symbols seemed to hold some spiritual significance, to meet "a ceremonial or spiritual or symbolic purpose," as archaeologist Claire O'Kelly put it.

Our guide described how a shaft of light enters through the lintel — called the roofbox — to penetrate the mound's dark recesses on winter solstice and winter solstice only. This solar orientation, long rumored, was also long dismissed as too sophisticated for Stone Age primitives. Archaeologist Séan O'Riordain derided the "jumble of nonsense and wishful thinking indulged in by those who prefer the pleasures of the irrational and the joys of unreason to the hard thinking that archaeology demands." So Newgrange's restorer, Professor Brian M. J. O'Kelly, did the kind of hard research archaeology demands — occupying Newgrange on solstice to witness "a pencil of direct sunlight travel through the roofbox and right along the passage." Skeptics then argued that changes in the obliquity of the ecliptic, the earth's wobble, meant that solstice now dawns slightly farther south than when Newgrange was built; surely those ancient pagans did not know what we moderns have just discovered. Finally someone did the math. In 1974, just two years before my first visit, surveyor John Patrick ascertained that the roofbox allows for changes in the sun's position from the time of Newgrange's construction into the indefinite future. The solar drama was no accident.

Hearing all this, that first time at Newgrange, I felt a shudder of longing. A sunbeam illuminating an ancient cairn on the year's darkest day — how the archetypal image stirred me. My mind began to churn. If I started saving right away... if I found a sitter for the cat... if I put in for time off work.... Such longing is common, so common that the waiting list for Newgrange solstice was a decade long before admission was converted to a yearly lottery. But my resolve did not diminish as the years passed. I applied and reapplied, was refused over and over. Finally my dedication — and, okay, some phone calls to the Department of Antiquities from my uncompromising Aunt Della — paid off. With just time enough to book a flight, I was approved to enter the monument on December 21, 1986.

After all those years of waiting, I flew into the stormiest Irish winter in a decade. I drove to Slane in lashing rain. All night, wind howled like a berserker around the Coynington Arms. I slept poorly, plagued by vague dreams — jet-lag fantasies? — of grim sacrificial rituals. I rose hours before dawn, restless and unrested, and plunged into wet darkness. My hopes as low as the sky, I wound along the watery boreens to the shrouded mound.

At Newgrange, I joined a waterlogged group under umbrellas useless in the slanting rain. At 9 A.M., with nary a hope of a sunbeam, we were led inside. The lanolin odor of Irish wool filled our nostrils in the surprising warmth, for Newgrange's roof design includes runnels that make it the

only place in Ireland that has been dry for five thousand years. Site man-
ager Clare Tuffy eloquently described what we would see, could we see
anything. A photographer staged a mock sunrise with strobe flash, then we
all trooped out. Next day's Dublin paper pictured me on the front page as
the solstice visitor who had traveled furthest to be rained on.

But if the winter sky had no pity, Clare Tuffy did. Newgrange's
builders apparently understood meteorology as well as astronomy, design-
ing the mound so that sunlight enters during the five days when the sun's
southward movement stalls — hence "sol-stice," sun-standing-still — and
thus multiplying the chances, even in Ireland, of a clear dawn. When Clare
offered me a chance to return on December 23, I eagerly accepted. But that
day was as dismal as the solstice itself had been. Leaving Gort at 4 A.M. in
a desperate storm, I prayed the eastern sky would be clearer. But through
Athlone and Kinnegad and Trim and Slane, the storm raged on.

I arrived to join a sorry soggy cluster of hopefuls staring toward a dark
horizon. Noncommittally, Clare oriented us. There, over there, she pointed
to the southeast, that's where the sun would rise. I noticed the conditional,
hope bleeding away. But was that a bit more light, a bit less cloud? Ah,
well, maybe not. Was the rain slowing a trifle? Maybe so? Clare's voice
was low and careful. "I think we might see something!" We scampered up
the slope, over the entrance stone, through the stone corridor, into the
chamber.

Clare extinguished the lights. Darkness covered us. Not a photon
penetrated Newgrange's stone heart. My own heart began to pound. With
excitement? No: unreasoning dread. What would happen if the sun did not
enter the cairn? Nothing, I told myself, no big deal, always next year, plan
to return. But something primal seemed at stake. My hands shook, my
stomach knotted, I grew faint. I prayed silently, desperately — to whom,
to what, I do not know...

A sunbeam bolted across the darkness.

Audible gasps, then the sound of sobs. Someone fell to her knees.

I had imagined the sun creeping in like a cat, illuminating the room
gradually with soft dim light. But it slashed in like a sword. For a quarter
hour, I stared at the light's improbable bronze against the floor's sandy
blackness. Then, slowly, so very slowly, the light withdrew. Like a delicate
girl, the sun stepped down the corridor, leaving us again in darkness — but
a darkness kissed by light.

We filed forth into a storm. The sunbeam had been so brilliant that I expected a clear sky, but only a tiny opening in black clouds marked where the sun had risen. Yet even that weak sun was intoxicating. Sunlight drenched me. Light was everywhere, behind me, above me, everywhere. I felt reborn, baptized with light, saved from darkness, lost then found again. Before that morning, I had thought Newgrange mysterious and beautiful. That gray winter morning it became more, became my spiritual touchstone. Because as I stood staring at the point of dawn, I knew — not believed, not theorized, but *knew* — that the earth provides for us, that we have air enough to breathe and light to see by, water enough to quench our thirst and food to sustain us. Whenever I am lost or despairing, I remember that solstice morning and know comfort once again.

No doubt my intoxication resulted from staring fixedly at a fingerwide light beam after a period of impenetrable darkness. Was Newgrange designed to create this intense physiological effect? Perhaps, perhaps not. Individualistic European humanism assumes we are the measure of all, and therefore that such a building should have been built for human experience, but the ancients might not concur. They may have felt it sacrilege to invade the sun's domain or believed the sunbeam's power could be dissipated by human presence. We can only speculate about whether Newgrange's builders celebrated rituals inside or beside the stone chamber on solstice mornings, and what those rituals might have been.

But such speculation is rife, usually beginning with the assumption of a male solar deity to whom rituals were offered. In the 1700s, Vallancey translated the name Newgrange into *Grian-uagh,* the *uagh,* or cave, of *grian,* the sun (actually, if unaccountably, it means "new farm building"). Although *grian* in Irish is feminine, Vallancey anointed Mithras, a Persian barely known in Ireland, as the mound's designated deity. Three hundred years later, Martin Brennan called the Brugh "a great feat of non-verbal communication" whose "message transcends the barriers of language." What was that message? The same Vallancey heard: that the mound houses a sun god.

But we have no proof the ancient Irish thought the sun male. To the contrary, evidence points to a goddess of the solar mound. Leaving aside the often-argued theory that spirals are a pan-European goddess symbol, there is Newgrange's ancient name, Brugh mná Elcmair, "palace of the woman of Elcmar" — referring to Bóand, goddess of the Boyne. A more common name, Brugh na Bóinne, is usually translated "the palace on the river Boyne." But *na* means "of," not "on"; "the *brugh* on the river" would be Brugh ar Bóinne. Brugh na Bóinne means "the *brugh* of Bóand," the palace of the goddess. The possibility of the site's deity being feminine rather than masculine is now acknowledged at Newgrange, where guides carefully refer to "the god or goddess of the mound."

The change struck me on the tour I took after detouring off the Belfast road. I remarked upon it to Clare — after all these years, she is still there, now as director — when she joined me for tea. "That's policy," she nodded. "We don't force one interpretation over another." We sat companionably in the new café, reminiscing about taking tea in the old days in her office, a little square shed now used as an admissions gate. Clare remembers each of the dozens of solstices she has witnessed at Newgrange — "ah, yes, you were the rained-out one, where the sun came two days late." She also recalls the various stages in Newgrange's reputation, from a time when tourism was minimal to today, when the mound's triple spiral seems ubiquitous in Ireland. "I just saw it on a yogurt advert," she said. "It's everywhere, not just on jewelry and scarves — everywhere. It's become a sort of national symbol." Why is that? I asked. She put chin on hand and pursed her lips. "Maybe because nobody owns it. Other Irish emblems — the wolfhound, the castle, even the harp — they all belong to one group or another."

Surely not the shamrock? I asked.

Clare shook her head. "Christianization."

Forget shamrocks, I offered; Newgrange has real rocks. Clare grimaced and laughed. Then, hearing I was bound for the North, she exclaimed, "Oh, you'll be nearly to Emain Macha. You must stop. Oh, you definitely must." Emain Macha. The name tugged at me like an insistent relative. I pulled out my map. There it was, perhaps forty minutes away. I had hours before the conference, time enough to visit Macha's fort. Another time, I might have recalled an errand, gone back to Dublin rather than cross the border. But I was already headed to Belfast. Emain Macha it would be.

⊠⊠⊠⊠⊠

Instead of going back to the N1, I meandered north from Slane on little back roads, farmland boreens. By my calculations, the border lay ahead twenty miles or so. I envisioned something like the Alaska-Canadian crossing: a gate with uniformed guard asking what my business was, how much money was I carrying, how long would I be staying. I rehearsed answers. Could entry be denied? Would there be enquiries about my family history? I began to wish for iron nerves. I pictured accordion wire inside the walls at Portlaoise, the young soldier who wrote down every word I spoke, my unsteadiness after my shoe soles had been removed to search for contraband.

Then, without warning, I was across. No guards, no tollbooths, no checkpoints. Not even a welcome sign. I had thought I was lingering in the Republic yet again, but suddenly I was in the North, leaning against an iron gate watching the Union Jack flap in the breeze.

Across the field, the crows screamed.

Had I gone to the North a dozen years earlier, during the Troubles, I would have encountered soldiers and checkpoints in Europe's most heavily militarized rural area. Had I come during the marching season, had I gone to the tense encampment at Garvaghy Road in Portadown, I would surely have seen armed cars and armed men. Had I stuck to the N1, I would have noticed money changers at the border. My old road map, from twenty years ago, lists approved border crossings and warns, "A motorist crossing the frontier by roads other than approved roads is liable for very severe penalties, including confiscation of the car." My new map has no such warning.

I had encountered nothing. On one side of the border, crows and hay; on the other, crows and hay. Rivers, oceans, mountain ranges are boundaries, hindering the passage of birds and plants and humans. But lines on a map are less real than those that spiral across Newgrange's stones. Unless something marks a border — a gate, a sign, an armed guard — a traveler can cross unaware.

Still screaming, the crows flew off to the south.

I studied my map. To my right a great blue-gray mass dominated the horizon: Slieve Gullion, apparently, indicating that I was southwest of Newry, a town I had avoided while staying in nearby Carlingford. Back on the road, I tried to detect *northness* in the land. Until I saw that Union Jack, I had felt no difference. But afterward, the fields seemed a bit larger, the houses a trifle more substantial, the roads wider. I remembered how, when I first came over, I had been warned by my aunt against speaking to

Travelers — well, no, she said "tinkers," the far less polite term. At the time, I could not tell a tinker from a tailor — everyone looked Irish to me — but within a few months, I found myself noticing a subtle height of brow, a slightly different set to the jaw. Like Mark Twain discerning the Mississippi's wave patterns, I found it impossible to unlearn what I had been taught. The best I could do was to make a point of always speaking courteously to Travelers.

I suddenly realized that here I, like the tinkers of whom Della had been so suspicious, was part of a persecuted minority. My car had Irish plates; I had fleeting visions of being stopped by *gardai* — or whatever they called them up here. I drove carefully, afire with fantasies of detention by armed men. I forced away these unsettling thoughts. Emain Macha lay near — among the North's mythic places, the one I most longed to see, a great ritual center named for a goddess.

But which goddess? Irish myth offers three distinct goddesses named Macha. To further complicate matters, she is said to have been part of a stormy trinity with Babh, crow-goddess of battle, and the great underworld queen Mórrígan. Because of that association, Macha is called a war goddess, though the meaning of her name ("earth" or "field") more readily suggests a divinity of fertility and abundance. Besides, only one of the three Machas — Macha Rua, red-haired Macha — would be uncomfortable at a Quaker rally.

But although called a goddess, Macha Rua may have been historical, if we believe the *Annals of Ulster,* which say that in 377 B.C.E. she became queen of all Ireland, reigning for seven years. Macha Rua's father was one of a trio of Ulster kings whose rule was contingent on satisfying three conditions: abundance of the edible acorns called mast; unfailing efficacy of fabric dye; and safety for women in childbirth. When Macha's father died, drowning in the legendary cascade at Ballyshannon, the other kings denied her the throne. So Macha made war upon them and won. The enemy princes, banished to the Burren, were the five oafs we met in chapter two, those who set upon Macha in disguise as the Cailleach. Ulster's warriors threatened the thwarted rapists with death, but Macha assigned them to dig a rath, a hillfort, whose outline she drew with her bronze neckpiece. That rath is Emain Macha.

The building of Emain Macha positions the story in a period when Ireland might have seen woman warriors like the contemporaneous Celtic queens Boudica and Cartimandua, who fought the Romans in England. The Roman Ammianus Marcellinus claimed that every Celtic woman, not just the queens, was warlike: "especially when, swelling her neck, gnashing her teeth, and brandishing her sallow arms of enormous size, she begins to strike blows mingled with kicks, as if they were so many missiles set forth from the string of a catapult." Perhaps such words were mere propaganda. After the Celts nearly conquered Rome, its citizens had cause to demonize their powerful enemies. And to the anxious male Roman, nothing seemed more demonic than a strong, armed woman.

The real extent of Celtic women's participation in battle is unclear. Celtic warfare pitted one champion against another, and we have no records of women in single combat, although the law written by Columcille in 590 C.E. excluding women from military service suggested that there were, indeed, warrior women, as does the *Lex Innocentum* of Adomnán, which, a hundred years later, reiterated the ban. Historical queens may have been not warriors themselves, but strategists who sent champions out to fight. Miranda Green suggests that while men cast spears at opposing armies, women cast spells. Support for this view is found in the writings of the Roman geographer Tacitus, who describes black-robed priestesses screaming like crows, creating a commotion beside the battlefield. Perhaps they personified Babh, who in her crow form devoured those killed in battle. By late Celtic times, Macha and Babh were conflated in the image of war's carrion bird, according to ninth-century Cormac, who glosses Macha as "Crow...one of the three Morrigna." He also defines Mesrad Machae, "the masts of Macha" — originally the acorn test of Ulster leadership — as "the heads of men after their slaughter," referring to the Celtic warrior fashion of wearing heads of conquered enemies on the belt. (Cormac would have found Oliver's slowly shrinking head a capital homage to Macha.)

But Macha Rua's readiness to take up arms was not shared by the other Machas. Macha wife of Nemed — the invader who cleared Ireland of forest and Formorian and whose name seems to mean "sacred grove" — foresaw the disastrous cattle raid Medb would inflict on Ulster and died of mourning, hardly the behavior of a war goddess. Similarly antiwar is the most famous Macha, a member of the Tuatha Dé Danann called Grian Banchure, or "the sun of womanhood," described in the *dindshenchas* with the lovely title of "Macha who diffused all excellences." In the story called

Noinden Ulad, or "The Debility of the Men of Ulster," we learn that this Macha married, to his great fortune, a human widower named Crunnchu mac Agnomain. He did not court her; she arrived out of nowhere one day, walking *deiseal* around the house before wordlessly entering the kitchen as though it was hers by right. All went well until he decided to attend the Assembly of Ulster, to be held at the House of the Red Tree. Knowing her husband's boastfulness, Macha disapproved, but Crunnchu promised to speak no word of her. With her grudging permission, Crunnchu set off for the hill fort that would soon bear his fairy wife's name.

Macha's fears were well founded. As the king's horses pranced forth, Crunnchu bragged that his wife could best them in a race. The comment reached the king, who commanded Crunnchu to prove his statement. The king's servants hauled Macha, heavy with child, before the assembly, and announced that her husband would die unless she ran against the king's team. Macha begged the king to delay the race until she delivered. But the king, hoping Macha's pregnancy would slow her down to his advantage, refused.

"The fleet silent woman stripped off her clothes and loosened her hair," the *dindshenchas* relates, and the race began. Macha crossed the finish line before the king's steeds were halfway around. But the exertion brought on labor. The goddess brought forth two babes, a boy and a girl, and then died. "When a time of oppression comes," Macha cursed as she died, "the men of this province will be overcome with the weakness of a woman in childbirth for five days; to the ninth generation it shall be so." Whenever Ulster was threatened, Macha's curse struck, with only the great champion Cúchulainn exempt from its effects.

This strategic weakness underpins the plot of the *Táin.* When Medb's warriors marched toward the Cuailgne Mountains near Carlingford, where the great brown bull lived, Ulster's defenders fell to the ground in predictable distress, leaving Cúchulainn to battle Medb's champions alone. So fiercely did he fight that, by the time the Ulstermen recovered, few Connacht warriors were left standing. Ulster won against outmatched Connacht, but Medb had stolen Donn Cuailgne away using the back roads, achieving equality with her husband at great cost of life.

Ironically, given Macha's warrior-thwarting curse, Emain Macha — the name means "Macha's Twins" — is now called Navan Fort. But it is no military fortress. Its earthworks, which mark Ulster's sacred center as

Cruachain does Connacht's, stand just outside the city where, until he lost his head, Oliver Plunkett served as primate (I always envision a chimp in vestments). Armagh — Ard Macha, "Macha's height" — remains an ecclesiastical center, a host of churches and cathedrals suggesting its ancient sanctity. There I stopped to see the only known image of Macha. For centuries part of the Protestant cathedral's decoration, the granite bas-relief shows the goddess with arms raised threateningly, breasts bare, legs bent. Her posture recalls the Sheela-na-gig, but her face is hard, angry, not laughing like a Sheela.

Emain Macha lies just beyond the town's borders, atop a large glacial drumlin carved into embankments. The site saw use from the Neolithic onward, which may account for the successive Machas, each associated with a different mythic race. Its mound, originally thought a Neolithic tumulus like Newgrange, was revealed by excavation to be an Iron Age temple. Nothing quite like it has been found elsewhere. Five rings of oak posts — nearly three hundred of them around a massive central tree pillar, proposed by Anne Ross as the Red Tree from which Ulster's legendary Red Branch warriors were named — formed a west-facing building. After construction, the building was filled with limestone boulders to create a mound. A fire burned the protruding timbers, then the mound was covered with turf. Archaeologists believe that the entire process — timber building, stone filling, fire, turf covering — was executed as a single ritual, while Dáithí Ó hOgáin proposes the destruction of the temple by invaders.

⋈⋈⋈⋈

That winter day, except for a young father and his son, I had Emain Macha to myself. It rained steadily as I spiraled upward. The mound itself is unremarkable, but the view from its summit is breathtaking. I rested against a huge bare beech, taking in the peaceful winter landscape — the same landscape Ulster's warriors would have seen when they faced Medb's troops, who had marched from Cruachain on the Monday after Samhain. It was a surprise attack, and an unorthodox one. Winter was traditionally the off-season for Iron Age Irishmen for whom cattle raiding was sport, a kind of ancient All-Ireland match. Men were maimed and killed in the raids, and glory gained, but real war was fought against invaders trying to take land, not against cousins stealing cattle.

From Emain Macha's summit, I saw clusters of leafless trees, dark bastions against the green and bronze of winter fields. What would have been the view from the hill in ancient times? More trees, certainly, although nothing like the impenetrable forests that began to fall with the first farmer's arrival. Farmers need fields for planting and grazing, wood for burning and building. Myth tells us that Nemed personally cleared Ireland's first plains — eleven unnamed fields, then one named for Macha. Nemed's myth truncates history, which according to the *landnam* ("settlement" in Old Norse) theory followed this pattern: first small areas were cleared for gardens; as soil wore out, gardens were moved to freshly cleared land while earlier clearings became pasture for increasingly important herds; slowly the abandoned clearings became the great plains of ancient myth.

We do not know how the earliest settlers viewed the forests, but the Celts deeply reverenced trees; indeed, the word *druid* is related to that for *oak*. According to brehon law, trees came in classes just as people did — the list went from *airig fedo*, or "nobles of the woods" like oak and yew, through *aithig fedo,* "commoners of the woods," including alder and willow, right down to *losa fedo*, or "bushes of the woods," that included gorse — and there were appropriate penalties for inappropriate cutting. This sense of arboreal sanctity continued into Christian times, when the mystic Columcille proclaimed from his sacred grove in Derry the sinfulness of cutting down oaks.

But in 1169, Norman law invaded Ireland with its alien concept of privately held land. Land became property, a resource for extraction and sale. Much of Ireland's forest literally sailed away as the tall masts for England's imperial navy. But sufficient forests — called "fastnesses" in Ireland — remained, and rebels used them as citadels, so Elizabeth the First ordered all Irish woodlands destroyed. Of two million cleared acres in Ireland in 1700, nearly one and a half million had been deforested in the previous century. In many cases land was sold to English entrepreneurs for less than its timber's value, making "the feathers pay for the goose," as the saying went. Soon treeless Ireland was importing wood for building, and only a fraction of Irish land remained in Irish hands. One of the great poems in the Irish language mourns the destruction of the woodlands of Kilcash: *Cad a dhéanfhaimíd feasta gan adhmad, Tá deire na gcoillte ar lár:* "What shall we do without timber, the last of the woods is fallen."

An Ulster song with a piercing plaintive melody remembers ancient attitudes in the face of the new extractive economy:

Oh bonnie Portmore, I am saddened to see
Such a woeful destruction of your ornament tree,
For it stood on your banks for many's the long day
Till the long boats from Antrim came to float it away.

Oh the birds in the forest, they bitterly weep,
Saying where shall we shelter, where shall we sleep,
For the oaks and the ash are all cutted down,
And the walls of bonnie Portmore are all tumbled the ground.

Today native Irish woodlands are, according to ecologist Eoin Neeson, all but extinct. As the great forests disappeared, invading plants appeared. With early farmers came seeds, some imported intentionally but others carried over unwittingly in animal fodder and packing. Exotic edibles, ornamentals, and weeds released into deforested regions spread further and faster than the same plant on undisturbed land. In Ireland, such plants arrived like Normans: first invited over, they laid claim to more and more land. Where once oak and ash had shadowed the ground, now were fields of marrow and potato, gardens of roses and rosemary. Language remembers the successive invasions. Oak (*dara*) and ash (*fuinseog*) have true Irish names, but marrow and potato, rose and rosemary came more recently, their names *mearog* and *prata, rós* and *rós Mhuire* immigrating along with them.

The invasions continue; Ireland today has fewer native plants than any other European land. Irish has no word yet for rhododendron, none for fuchsia, though they are two of the island's most common species today. I remember the first time I saw fuchsia blooming in Ireland. It was at the Liscannor holy well. The plant looked familiar, but its size — it towered over me — was bewildering. I pulled a branch closer and examined the blossoms. Fuchsia? Wasn't that a small potted plant on my mother's porch? But fuchsia this was, big as you please, escaped from Irish gardens to the roadsides to intertwine with native brambles in tangled hedgerows. Rhododendrons seem, at first glance, to be similar escapees. They are, however, native to Ireland — or were, in the Gortian stage some 425,000 years ago. Changing climate killed off the rhododendron, which were re-introduced a century ago. Finding Ireland's acid soil ideal and facing no natural enemies, rhododendron is now strangling the remaining Irish oak forests.

The difference between an immigrant — a plant that drifted down a river or arrived in the scat of crows — and an invader is simple: us. But our imports are not necessarily sinister. I once asked Athabascan healer Audrey Sunnyboy what she thought about nonindigenous plants. It was the year that dandelions were spotted on the borders of Denali Park's fragile alpine ecosystem. Alaskans, themselves tenacious pioneers, turned out in squads to uproot the yellow invaders. But these same Alaskans build noto-riously expensive structures to nurture tropical nightshades; I once calcu-lated that my first crop of greenhouse tomatoes cost me $100 a pound. Audrey's answer surprised me. "If plants come here, it must be because we must need their medicine," she said.

On Emain Macha, I felt overwhelmed by the sense of invasion of which even the trees seemed to speak. I looked out to the north where, twenty centuries after the *Táin,* conflict continues. Perhaps we should not be surprised. In Ulster — as in Palestine and the Balkans — cultures col-lide like tectonic plates. Myth and archaeology agree that for nine thou-sand years, wave after wave of settlers arrived on these shores. Except for the first foragers, each arriving group encountered the resistance of earlier settlers. Three hundred years ago, another group boated over from Scotland — this time, not foragers or farmers, but poor Protestants forcibly removed from their land. The ensuing conflict over their presence repeats the pattern of Ulster history.

But those who objected to the new arrivals were former immigrants gone native. The ancient peoples of Ireland — whether we call them Fir Bolg and Fomorian and Milesian as the myths do, or Neolithic and Celtic as do archaeologists — each by turns became Irish. The same transforma-tion can be traced in historic times. The Normans became "more Irish than the Irish," as the saying goes. And who is more Irish than Yeats, that Anglo-Protestant? From Ireland's beginnings, each arriving people has gone through the process that Wes Jackson calls "becoming native to this place." Ulster's Protestants are the latest to embark upon this adventure.

The sun was lowering itself in the western sky. Time to get moving again. As I descended Emain Macha, I found myself humming

"Carrickfergus," a haunting air I have known since childhood. Checking my map to locate my route from Armagh, I was startled to realize that Carrickfergus was just above Belfast on the sea. My eyes drifted across Ulster, my mind moving like a radio dial as I heard snatches of inner melody. Beautiful Kitty with her pitcher of milk from the fair in Coleraine. Bangor and Donaghadee, with six miles between them. Lovely Martha, flower of sweet Strabane. My Lagan love. Familiar songs in this unfamiliar land.

But from the black letters that spelled B-E-L-F-A-S-T, no melodies came, only a list of names in a news announcer's piercing voice: Shankill Road, Stormont, Ormeau Road, names connected with the Troubles. John Hewitt intones such a litany of struggle and fury and violence:

> with compulsive resonance they toll;
> Banbridge, Ballykelly, Darkley, Crossmaglen,
> summoning pity, anger and despair,
> by grief of kin, by hate of murderous men,
> till the whole tarnished map is stained and torn,
> not to be read as pastoral again.

Like Banja Luka, like Jerusalem, the name Belfast calls forth images of war: burning overturned cars, the silhouette of an angry boy lobbing something at a soldier, slogans defacing the walls of poor tiny homes. I know there are in Belfast tidy gardens of roses, bookstalls with shelves of poetry, cats soaking up sun in shop windows. Yet those are not the images that rise unbidden at the name.

⊠⊠⊠⊠

As I drove into the city, I saw no evidence of conflict as the peace process wound forward once again. It was a gray winter day, rainy and cold, like any rainy cold winter day anywhere in Ireland. Realizing how long I had been driving, I stopped for gas, filled my tank, went inside to pay. When I handed my cash to the clerk, I received only a stare in return. Looking down, I realized I had neglected to change punts for pounds. I dug out a credit card and stood, wordless, as my sale was rung up. I returned to my car in a furious blur. That store clerk was Protestant, I raged to myself —

of course he was, aren't all merchants, aren't half the Catholics in Belfast unemployed. He had recognized me as Catholic and tried to humiliate me, acting as though my Irish punts were worthless, rejecting my people by rejecting my money. Opposing this voice was another that pleaded calm down, calm down, anyone can see you're American, there was nothing ill intended, thirty years of Quakerism must count for something, calm down.

I had no proof the clerk was Protestant, just as I had no proof the woman on the London tube was English. But he *looked* it, I thought, although I cannot say what it means to look Protestant. Do I look Protestant now? How many years does it take? Head down over the wheel, mind and heart racing, I wondered, how do people live here? How do they stifle their fear and rage? How do they handle the unrelenting sense of historical oppression? Then I thought, this is how black people feel in America. This is how my dear friend Howard Rock felt, an Eskimo in an invaded land. And suddenly I recognized my own invader's heart. Recognized what it is to love a land to which you have no right, only a yearning to make a home. Recognized that I was only singing half the song.

"It is a hard responsibility to be a stranger," Ulster poet John Hewitt says. I am a descendent of such strangers, people who left their native place to find a new one. My first known Monaghan ancestor, great-great-grandfather Michael, came from Meath to join the Union Army during the Civil War — not to free slaves but to gain citizenship. He married Mary Farrell of Longford, whose obituary makes no mention of her Irish birth, nor do their granite headstones in West Point Cemetery; they erased their Irishness to become American. Michael and Mary emigrated to make better lives for themselves, just as John Gordon and Margaret Dunleavy did fifty years later, just as Scottish settlers did who became part of the Ulster Plantation.

People move around; that is history's most unarguable fact. I live on land stolen from its original inhabitants, who probably stole it from even earlier ones. Once in place, people naturalize themselves. Michael Monaghan, Mary Farrell, and Margaret Dunleavy never saw Ireland again. Except for that one trip back when he was eighty, my grandfather stayed in America. Perhaps it is for the best. I am one of fifty million Irish-heritage people around the globe. If we all returned to our ancestral homeland, there would be no more cheery cottages surrounded by green fields;

we'd be cheek-by-jowl across the midlands and out to sea. We are all of us invading rhododendrons; we cannot just be potted and sent back where we started. We must learn to become natives where we land.

Shaken by my outrage at the petrol station, I drove to my lodgings on the Antrim Road. My hostess was a woman dressed in exquisite taste, friendly but politely distant. Most of my Ulster friends can tell Protestant from Catholic on sight, but I cannot. I do not usually worry over this deficiency, but that night I found myself examining pictures on the high papered walls until a photo of Lourdes sent waves of relief flooding through me. "Safe! Safe! She's Catholic!" This atavistic tribalism unsettled me. I have not entered a Catholic church for years; I call myself Quaker and pagan; yet, in the North, I felt my face betrayed me. Suddenly, I felt Catholic again.

That night I sat up by the fire with my hostess, drinking tea and eating sweet cakes. She was from Omagh, where a year earlier an IRA bomb had killed twenty-eight people, wounding two hundred more. Two of her relatives were hurt, one maimed for life. Although my hostess spoke calmly, she stirred her tea relentlessly, back rigid, eyes unseeing. I recognized the behavior of the traumatized. She had not been back to that part of Omagh. She had not gone back, she repeated. She wanted to remember it as it had been. Before. Before. I sat mostly silent, wrenched by a kind of familial guilt. It could have been my uncle who convoyed bombs into that tiny Northern town. It could have been my aunt, hearing from the police that her husband had been jailed. It could have been my cousin, learning the names of girls her age, dead at her father's hand.

I once asked a jailed cousin how he had decided political change was worth the lives of children. "Don't you always ask the hard questions," his next letter said. He never directly answered me, reciting instead the litany of oppression my grandfather taught me. These men the world calls terrorists offer historically documented reasons to kill. I am certain that if I spoke to my cousin's Protestant counterparts, I would hear equivalent reasons, for evil has indeed been done, and on both sides. And so both sides hold tight a map of history dominated by what Protestant peace leader John Dunlop calls "a mountain of memories" that shadows daily interactions like Slieve Gullion does South Armagh. Like the *dindshenchas* that tell the mythic story of each hill, each stream, Ireland's place-names tell of cultural collision: the Siege of Derry, the Battle of the Boyne, Long Kesh, Enniskillen. I have seen grown men cry when they speak these names. I have seen fists clench when they hear these names. And I have looked into the unseeing eyes of those who cannot locate, on this map, the road out of the past.

Garvaghy Road. Omagh. The Bogside. The *dindshenchas* of conflict.

It continues because, as Ulster poet Louis MacNeice says, "each one in his will / binds his heirs to continuance of hatred." I have myself been so bound. As my grandfather recited Irish history, he taught me what Church of Scotland minister Alan Falconer describes as the "coercion mentality" of the Catholic Irish. Through centuries of occupation, we have forged a set of images that define us as victims, our lands stolen, our religion suppressed. Protestants, by comparison, have a "siege mentality" that positions them in the midst of dangerous antagonists who would eradicate both lives and culture. My reaction to the clerk was typical; my heart speaks so fluently the language of fury, resentment, and resistance that I interpreted his silence as yet another victimization. The clerk, if he had been indeed Protestant, may have read my offering of Irish punts as yet another proof of Catholic desire to rule — to overrule — his country. In tectonic collision zones like Belfast, such tiny interactions form a mountain of misunderstanding soon engraved with what Croatian theologian Miroslav Volf calls "the spiral of vengeance."

But immigration — invasion — is inevitable. My grandparents left Ireland for America, my parents left the Lower (then) Forty-Eight for Alaska, I left Alaska for the Midwest, all of us pursuing a better life. The cost? The sensuous familiarity of place, a cost that I have paid. Although I am not native to Alaska — that word is reserved for its indigenous people — I know its plants and seasons and animals, the taste of lingonberries and of upriver salmon, the acrid smell of fall high-bush cranberry, the pink ripple of aurora. Decades of travel in Ireland have made it a second homeland, where my senses recognize the bright red of winter haws and the sharp green of monkey puzzle, the light tang of gorse and the languid wetness of winter dawn. In the Midwest, I am what the Irish call a "blow-in," a fine botanical word that captures my feeling of having just arrived on winds of change. Moving there, I experienced the sense of mournful dislocation Hewitt describes:

. . .*Often you will regret the voyage,*
wakening in the dark night to recall that other place

or glimpsing the moon rising and recollecting
that it is also rising over named hills,
shining on known waters.

In midlife, I find myself in a land where, for the first time, I do not recognize the plants: what is edible, what blooms when, what sets seed when. Scents are new; seasons change differently. After several years of feeling unsettled, I found a park whose great woodlands remind me of both the demesne of Coole and the boreal arboretum near Fairbanks. There I study the fractal shapes of Midwestern trees. Some, like light-needled tamarack, I recognize from Alaska; others, like thick-limbed beech, from Ireland; some, like alder and willow, from both. But there are so many to learn: honey locust and sycamore, gingko and magnolia. The first time I recognized the lacy winter dance of catalpa, I felt a cascade of relief, as though I were finally putting down roots, as though I might yet become what Hewitt calls "as native in my thought as any here."

When I moved, I suffered dislocation but no danger. How different for those ancients who aimed small boats at a blue cloud on the horizon. Although they must have missed familiar berry patches and hunting grounds, they had no time to mourn. Before stores of food from home were exhausted, it was imperative that they learn what was edible, what poisonous, what rare, what common. As Virgil said, "it is well to be informed about the winds, about the variations in the sky, the native traits and habits of the place, what each locale permits, and what denies." But without pocket botanical guides and time to experiment, how did they survive? I believe the American legend of the first Thanksgiving — when the Wampanoag showed the English how to make succotash from beans and corn, how to hunt wild turkey, what berries were ripe and ready — encodes the normal progression of settlement, earlier peoples helping newcomers become natives. That more bitter truth of American settlement, exemplified by the murder of the Roanoke chief Pemisapan when he refused to support indigent English settlers, does not erase the fact that friendly exchanges also occurred on this continent, just as they must have in Ireland.

In such friendly exchanges, I believe women played an important part, for their gathered foods accounted for as much as 80 percent of the nourishment of prehistoric people. I envision a female invader learning from a friendly native which plants could cut a child's fever, which were tasty and nourishing in spring soup, which made a good insect repellant. This picture comes readily to mind because that is how I learned, from older wise women. I have a memory — among many memories — of being led to a secret patch of chanterelles, a woodsy nutty mushroom that preserves well, in a stand of primal spruce. Liz Berry had brought along foraging bags, but we found so many mushrooms that we stripped off our shirts and made additional sacks out of them. We returned home half naked, giddy with abundance, forever bonded in our secret harvest. Surely that day repeats a common pattern in gathering economies.

Such friendly intercourse was not the only way immigrants became native. I know that from looking in the mirror. I am Irish on both sides — left and right, as my grandfather used to say. But I have fair hair and pale eyes, probably the heritage of Viking invaders. Historically, the Vikings did not build settlements in the Irish west or midlands, lands from which I trace my ancestry. They raided, they raped, they were gone. "The sea spewed forth floods of foreigners over Erin," says the *Annals of Ulster* for 820, "so that no haven, no landing place, no stronghold, no fort, no castle might be found, but it was submerged by waves of Vikings and pirates." My blue eyes are the genetic imprint of one of those pirates.

And who was she, my long-ago ancestor, first of her dark-eyed family to bear a blue-eyed child? Some young woman, nubile and strong, kidnapped from her village and subdued by force? Was she gang-raped, so that she did not even know which of the yellow-haired invaders left her with child? Or was she an older woman who endured the invasion of her body to save her children? And the child. Was the child accepted by siblings and cousins? Did he grow up angry at rejection? Was she hurt by village gossip about her absent father?

But in spinning this fantasy I have perhaps been trapped by that coercion mentality Falconer describes. It is possible that these eyes, this fair hair, are products not of rape but of love. Let me conjure another vision. Let me see my foremother as a lusty woman so enchanted with the piercing blue eyes and bright hair of the muscular Vikings that she offered herself for a night, or many nights, of passion with one or more. Let me imagine that ancient pirate whose eyes I inherited came back, year after year, when he went a-viking from his northern home. Let me picture him dying, my ancestress by his side, happy after years of love.

I am both immigrant and invader, descendent of immigrants and invaders. I am Irish; it cannot be otherwise. I may even have Protestant blood, despite generations of Roman Catholicism. My grandfather used to deny fiercely that Gordon was a Scottish name. "In Mayo," he instructed us, "Gordon is an Irish name." When I learned there was a Gordon tartan, I was baffled but continued, as instructed, to deny we were Scottish. Yet after Pop died, we learned that the first Gordon had arrived in Mayo less than two hundred years ago. East Mayo, where the "Irish Gordons" live, is near enough to Ulster that my maternal ancestor was probably a Scots blow-in, more likely Presbyterian than Roman Catholic.

Who knows the secrets of his genes, the truths of her body? The Polish woman with Hun eyes. The black man with Cherokee hair. Our genes travel like migrating seeds until we are all mixed and mingled. No one is just "Irish" or "American," "Catholic" or "Protestant." Theologian Miroslav Volf speaks of "the power of the remembered past." But what of the unremembered? "What is forgotten cannot be healed," says futurist Lionel Chircop, "and that which cannot be healed easily becomes the source of greater evil." To make peace among ourselves, we must make peace within, embrace our varied heritages: the hated and the loved, the rejected and the cherished. We become native by learning our land's seasonal variations; we become human by accepting that we are a mixture of native and immigrant and invader.

⊠⊠⊠⊠⊠

I wish I could say that my first trip to the North enabled me to overcome the coercion mentality of my upbringing. In truth, I remained on edge, coiled like a spring under pressure. I did not, as far as I know, carve any deeper that spiral of vengeance or add sand to the mountain of cultural antagonism. But I continued to think of the weekend as "my trip to the North." My unconscious alienation from the region led me to check maps and lists of mythic sites so that I would not miss anything as I retreated southward. I decided to conclude my visit to An Tuaisceart by climbing the goddess's mountain, Slieve Gullion.

The sky was low and black when I reached Newry. Although it sounds like an English name, Newry derives from the Irish for "the yew tree on the beach"; said to have been planted by Saint Patrick, the eponymous tree lived for almost a millennium. Newry sits at the head of Carlingford Lough, no ford at all but a fjord named for an otherwise-unknown Viking named Cairlinn — or perhaps for a hag of that name, for some scholars consider *cairlinn* a Norse equivalent to the Scots Gaelic word for cailleach, *carleen.* For centuries, the long ships from the north seas used Carlingford Lough as an invasion route to Meath, where my Monaghan ancestor was born. Was it through that long gray fjord that my blue eyes reached Ireland?

North of the lough loom the great volcanic mountains of which I sang so often as a child, an immigrant song about being forced from a beloved land for economic reasons, about how even gold-in-the-streets London does not compare to misty peaks rising above narrow waters. "For all that I found here, I might as well be where the Mountains of Mourne sweep down to the sea." But I suspect, like most immigrants, the singer did not return for lovely Mary, the wild rose who waited for him. In the past most immigrants, most invaders, traveled a one-way road. But between long-distance telephone and e-mail, I rarely pass a day without knowing the weather and the gossip from both Alaska and Ireland. Like other modern immigrants, I return regularly to the lands I know and love. For the first time, perhaps we can become native to a new place without abandoning the old. Doing so may allow us to welcome newcomers to our lands instead of meeting them with iron weapons as they step off the boat.

The rain intensified as I turned southwest to Slieve Gullion, part of a strange geological ring-dyke, the result of a brutal tectonic collision. The mountain looked ominous, unwelcoming, its bulky profile capped by black clouds. At its foot, a small cluster of oaks reached great empty arms into the wet winter sky. I pulled to the roadside, welcoming a chance to walk in what the druids would have called a *fednemed,* a sacred grove, anglicized as nemeton. Most Irish hardwood forests, like Coole's Seven Woods, were planted by English landlords, but this vestigial nemeton seemed part of no demesne. Even more unusual, it was free of rhododendron. I walked easily through the open forest, kicking acorns beneath damp leaves: the masts of Macha, ancient Ulster's test of proper rulership.

The great leafless trees caught the rain, so only mist reached me. I leaned against a massive oak, its trunk a dozen times larger than my own. The ancient Irish were astonishingly efficient at land clearing; it would have taken only a half hour to fell that tree with a stone ax. Hard work though it was, forest clearing offered tangible results: forage for cattle, crops for farmers. But the purpose of stone mountaintop cairns is baffling. Why drag tons of rock up steep hills to build such structures? Why spend hundreds of hours chipping at hard granite with stone tools to make spirals and meanders, stars and bars? Was it a way of becoming native to this island, of rooting oneself in a new place?

Winds hit me as I left the forest. I could no longer see Slieve Gullion, now wrapped in storm clouds. Somewhere high on the peak was my goal, a cairn facing southwest that forms a twin to Newgrange. As the crow flies, the sites are only a few dozen miles apart, and at winter solstice, they echo each other. After peering into Newgrange at dawn, the sun looks into Slieve Gullion's stone cairn at dusk. Irish winter days are short, the nights long. It takes the sun but seven hours to cross the solstice sky. But in those hours, the border between light and darkness is traversed, the spiral of the seasons turns, the world twirls again toward spring.

The storm struck in full force as I started up the mountain. Ireland's climate is mild, but winter storms can be fierce. Wind tore at my jacket and my hair as cold rain poured from the sky. I struggled to stay upright, unable to get a foothold on the slippery slope. After a few steps, I retreated to the dry warmth of my car. Perhaps I could drive to the sum-mit. I started up the steep road, but it was like driving into a waterfall. Water cascaded down the blacktop. Even if I managed to ascend, descent would be impossible.

So I turned my car south, heading back to Dublin town. Ah, well, there were many places I would never visit, I thought, still clinging to the unexamined assumption that I would never return. But near the oak neme-ton, I was struck by a sudden surge of longing for the Northern places whose names I had known for so many years: Coleraine, Strabane, Carrickfergus, names that sing sweetly in the mind. And yes, Omagh and Portadown and Shankill Road, names that frighten me but which I must acknowledge. Mountains of history, an endless litany of wrongs, the spiral of vengeance, all had kept me from passing over an imaginary line into a land peopled by strangers who look like me, strangers who like me are part of the vast human diaspora. But once I had crossed that line, what kept me from returning?

Had storm clouds kept the sun from entering Newgrange, that year I stood within it, I would have come back time after time until I saw that bronze sunbeam pierce the cairn's black heart. A storm in Ulster had kept me from Newgrange's twin, but it had pierced open my heart, reminding me that An Tuaisceart is Ireland, full of song and myth, poetry and beauty. Driving through Ulster in that winter storm, I began to plan my return. I would linger in pubs where Ulster Irish is spoken. Find the dolmen in the Silent Valley of the Mournes, the ogham stone at Kilnasaggart, the portal tomb at Ballykeel and Knockmany. See the Poet's Glen and the Quaker village at Bessbrook, stand on the shores of Lough Erne and climb Slieve Beagh. And, I promised myself, I would see Slieve Gullion again, some winter solstice, when Ireland's ritual landscape unites north and south in the light of transformation.

Chapter Six

THE WELL OF HER MEMORY

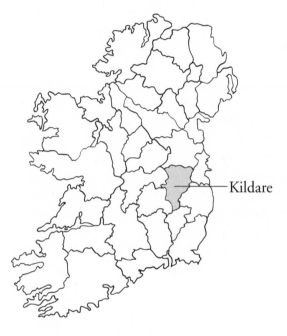

Kildare

I t was just past dawn on a soft day in January. Three pilgrims moved through the mist that swaddled the Curragh like a cold white blanket. The muddy path led straight for a time, then made a sudden arbitrary curve to the left, then right, before straightening out again. Arbitrary, for the land was gridiron flat; whatever the road bent around would have been invisible even on a clear day.

The low clouds erased the Curragh's distant edges, so the pastureland seemed endless. Endless and primeval. No fence, wood or stone, divided its vast acreage. Except for the power lines buzzing above us, we could have been in Celtic times, when the midlands were checkerboarded with such enormous pastures whereon grazed the cattle and horses of the *tuath* — the people and their land, so deeply connected that a single word sufficed for both. Now there is only this shred, this parcel, this never-plowed fragment of the old way of communal landholding. The Curragh, unfenced and untitled, is Ireland's last such link to Celtic times and ways.

It was winter. Winter in Ireland means dark and rain and mud and chill that aches in your bones. It means short wet days and long wet nights. Cold that runs damply down the sides of stone walls. Ashen fields, rubbly with last year's hay. Winter, which began as the sun lost its vigor at Samhain, still held sway as we neared Imbolc, or so the cold and the damp proclaimed.

But spring was near, near as the sheep who materialized out of the fog near a spiky outcropping of granite. Seven ewes — legs splayed, heavy bellies resting on the wet greening grass — glared up at us. Lambs kicked within them, hidden as spring on a foggy January morning. The bitter chill and the ashen fields gave no clue to the nearness of a new season but, like the lambs, spring was "in the belly" of winter, for that is the meaning of the word Imbolc, the name of the festival we had come to Ireland to celebrate. Soon spring, in all its robust fragility and wild insouciant joy, would arrive as suddenly as birth, which, like death, is always sudden no matter how fervently anticipated or feared.

A sharp sound from the left. Heavy pounding. We stopped, frozen in place. Three thoroughbreds emerged from the mist and raced past on a barely visible track. The center horse, a sleek black mare, tossed her head wildly, demanding more freedom from a rider who kept her tightly reined. Two accompanying roans galloped steadily, matching strides, their riders upright in the stirrups. Then they were gone, their hoofbeats dulling as white mist swallowed their dark forms.

We resumed our walk up the muddy path to the top of the Curragh. Before we left town, Sister Phil had warned us, "Be careful. Horses have the right of way on the Curragh." So we had been prepared for the explosion of animal energy we had just witnessed, prepared to find riders even so early on the Curragh plain. We were also, we hoped, prepared with directions to our destination. Sister Phil had assisted the other pilgrims onto a bus, but we had our own car. "You can't drive onto the Curragh," Phil told us, "so park on the road and walk in. Meet up with us at the top — you can't miss it."

"You can't miss it." How often have I heard those words in Ireland? And how often have they led to an hour of wandering down high-hedged boreens looking for "the big ash tree: you can't miss it," or "the house highest on the hill: you can't miss it," only to find groves of enormous trees and rows of homes each exactly as high on the hill as the next. The top of the Curragh? Could such flatness have a top? Surely a glacier had ironed down the land in prehistory, for we could have been in Illinois — except for the mystic mist, except for the ewes pregnant in January, except for the racing thoroughbreds — rather than in county Kildare.

Kildare is anglicized Irish, from Cill-Dara, "the church of the oak." The compound joins the two greatest influences on Irish spirituality, Christianity and paganism, symbolized by their quite different places of worship. Whereas Christians worshiped indoors, their sacred places contrasting with the unsanctified world outside the walls, the Celts found holiness in places of natural power, especially those marked by great oak trees. The Roman Pliny tells us that "they seek the oak tree for their sacred grove, and no ceremony is complete without its branches." In Kildare there was once an immense oak honored by the druids; under it was built, according to Christian legend, first a nun's cell, then a church and an abbey. Although the religion practiced there changed, the oak continued to be regarded as holy. Even five hundred years into the Christian era, its wood was deemed magical, if broken from the tree rather than cut. That sacred oak, gone for untold centuries, lives on in Kildare's name.

Just as neither church nor oak can be abstracted from Kildare's name, so can neither be removed from Irish spirituality without leaving it truncated, distorted. Paganism and Catholicism in Ireland are joined twins that cannot be separated. They are not opposites, as archaeologist Proinsias MacCana has pointed out, for in Ireland pagan ways and Christian beliefs formed an "extraordinary symbiosis." Not — notice this — a synthesis. Not two things melded into one, not one submerged into another, but two entities that combine for the benefit of both, interdependent though still detectably separate. Like lichen, from which neither fungus nor alga can be extracted without killing the whole, paganism and Christianity in Ireland need each other to live. And nowhere is this more clear than in the figure of Brigit, goddess and saint, whose sanctuary under the vast spreading oak on the edge of the Curragh was a temple in Celtic times, a convent in Christian times — and is today a gathering place for those committed to bridging the chasm between Ireland's Catholics and Protestants, between pagans and Christians, between men and women.

Bridging the chasm is an appropriate image for this endeavor, for *bridge* is itself a Brigit word. The Celtic word Brigit — actually a title rather than a name, meaning "high one" or perhaps "bright one" and used of the goddess as we use *lord* of god — was anglicized into Bridget; in turn, across Ireland and England, towns near ancient shrines to the goddess were called by names including "bridge," as in Bridgeport and Bridgetown. In Irish, the word is pronounced "breed" or "bride," leading to yet other compounds. Brideswell and Tubberbride are towns built near Brigit wells; McBride and Gilbride, from the Irish Mac Giolla Bhríde, are surnames of those devoted to Brigit. The word Brigit also survives as a name for Irish women, usually in the form of Bridget and in the nicknames Biddy, Bridgeen, and Bridey.

Bridey Duffy. That would be her name if she lived today: Brigit, daughter of Dubthach. That is, if we credit the early writings claiming that a child named Brigit, who would grow up to become Ireland's most important female spiritual leader, was born at Faughart in 450 C.E., less than two decades after Saint Patrick's legendary arrival. She was born at dawn, exactly on the threshold of her mother's home. Born of a pagan father and a Christian mother, one a noble and the other a slave. Born to straddle the two eras of Ireland's religious history and to be a bridge between them.

Some contend that she never lived, that there never was a woman who grew up to refuse an arranged marriage, to establish the most renowned convent of the early Christian era, to guide the spiritual journeys of both men and women. Brigit is simply the Celtic goddess in a nun's habit, say scholars like Miranda Green, who suspects a "false historicity" in the saint's legends. There may have been historical women named Brigit who attained positions of significant influence in the early Celtic Church, but all those miracles — Brigit hanging her cloak on a sunbeam, healing the sick with her bathwater, curing blindness with a touch of her hand — are fabrications of a Church that wished to bring an immensely powerful and beloved goddess under its influence. Such is the argument of those who find no historical evidence for the saint's existence.

But perhaps it is not necessary to deny the saint to affirm the goddess. As Irish feminist scholar Mary Condren has pointed out, stories are often as important as facts, for people act upon what they believe whether it is factually true or not. And stories have been told for 1,500 years about a sainted woman of Kildare named Brigit. There may, indeed, have been such a woman, pagan by birth but Christianized with the rest of Ireland. The Celts named their daughters for goddesses, just as Indian girls might today be named Sita or Devi after Hindu deities. Before Christianization, we know of pagan women named after the goddess, like Brigit Brethra, the renowned lawyer to king Conchobar mac Nessa. After Christianization, the custom survived. Even so, there seems to have been early concern about a saint with such a patently pagan name. One curious tale explained away the difficulty. A trinity of ghostly Christian clerics paid a visit to the unborn saint's pagan uncle to demand that she be named Brigit: "So the druid was apparently divinely inspired by a Christian apparition to give the baby the name of a prestigious Celtic goddess," says Miranda Green bemusedly.

Even had she not been given the name at birth, a canny administrator — as Kildare's sainted abbess must surely have been — could readily have assumed the name, and thus the prestige, of the local goddess when she established her convent in the druidical sacred place in Leinster, province of the rising sun. Or, as the great Celticist R. A. S. MacAlister has argued, the head of the priestess college in the rich midlands may have tradition-ally assumed the name of the goddess; one such dean, after converting to Christianity, could have taken the whole sisterhood with her and become the basis for the saint's legend. There may not have been miracles, but surely there was some abbess in early Christian times whose influence is felt down to the present.

⊠⊠⊠⊠⊠

A gorse bush shattered open the white Kildare morning, its shredded yel-low blooms like tiny explosions in the mist. We saw nothing to indicate where we would find the other pilgrims, the hundred or so who had gone by bus ahead of us. Most were Irish people who defined their morning's activity as Christian devotion. Among them were a few who refused to acknowledge Brigit's Celtic past, but most were easy with the knowledge that "ah, wasn't she a goddess before ever she was a saint," as one put it. For them, the fact that the saint's identity blurs into that of the goddess presents no problem; it is, indeed, part of Brigit's appeal, the way she

permits the embrace of the pagan past for those who wish nonetheless to
remain within the community of Christian believers.

One Irish acquaintance calls them "light-green pagans," people who
want to enrich their Catholicism with the feminine energy of the goddess.
That pale leafy tone has been standard for Celtic Christianity from the
start. In fact, a light-green tinge extends across Europe as well, and not
only because of the influence of Irish monks. Except for the tragic era of
the Inquisition, the Roman Church was historically tolerant of indigenous
beliefs. In this it followed the lead of Caesar's imperial legions, who
applied the *interpretatio Romano* to religions in conquered areas so that,
for instance, the Celtic healing goddess Sul gained the surname of Minerva
and the woodland lord Cernunnos was called a form of Mercury. In the
same way, the Church kept vestiges of ancient ways alive to the present.
Mariolatry — the excessive, nearly heretical honoring of the mother of
Jesus that served as a hideout for suppressed goddess worship — has been
a thorn in the Church's side almost since Mary died. Suspicious "saints"
with names like Priapus (Roman god of erections, without even a name
change) have only recently been expunged from the rolls. Ireland's glorious Saint Patrick, whose historical reality is far from conclusively attested,
might have joined Priapus in the dustbin of sainthood, save that it is impossible to revoke a canonization that never occurred and, like Brigit's,
Patrick's sainthood is older than the formal sainting procedure.

The Protestant Reformation was, in large part, a rejection of this *interpretatio Christiano*. No more disguised pagan rites! was the cry of the
reformers. No more goddesses tricked out as saintly nuns, no more gods in
episcopal attire! The early European settlers in my part of the Americas
were steeped in this tradition, which meant that conversion differed from
that in those other Americas where Catholicism embraced aspects of indigenous religion. Where the Spaniards colonized the Southwest, we find the
flagellation sect of the Penitentes, built upon an earlier self-sacrificing rite.
In Canada, where French Jesuits landed, we find the Micmac who, not seeing a priest for several hundred years after their group baptism, created their
own version of Catholicism melded with their ancestral religion. In the
Caribbean, African slaves and indigenous people employed Catholic
imagery in the creation of religions like Santeria and Voudoun. In Mexico,
Guadaloupe — the Mary of the Americas — took over the sites, symbols,
and duties of an Aztec mother goddess, Tonan. But in the United States,

pagan-rejecting Protestantism was the rule. As a result, we do not have five hundred strains of Christianity, one for each ancient nation; only the Handsome Lake religion of the Mohawk joined ancestral Indian ritual to Protestant belief. For the rest, sacred sites were (and are still being) destroyed, old festivals were not sustained, and the symbolism of land-based spirituality with its explicit connection to each region has been lost.

My friend Ray, brought up a Mormon, likes to say that in America even the Catholics are Protestant. Catholic immigrants may have been pre-dominantly peasants, steeped in old pagany ways, but their priests were more rejecting of aboriginal as well as imported ancestral beliefs. As a result, American Catholics tend to be more embarrassed than their Irish cousins by our non-Christian past, dismissing old rituals and beliefs as "superstition." Ireland is less rigidly dualistic. The old Celtic holidays are still built into the Irish calendar as the first days of the central months of each season: February, May, August, and November. Imbolc is Brigit's day, just as it was in Celtic times; in summer, people climb Croagh Patrick and other harvest hills, calling the holiday Garland Sunday rather than Lughnasa as the Celts did; Samhain remains as important as in Celtic times, but instead of the dead slipping back under the lifted veil of time, the living visit the resting places of the dead on All Saints' Day. Only the randy feast of Bealtaine had its pagan undertones bleached away; crowning Mary as Queen of the May substitutes for other, juicier ways of worshiping the feminine power.

American pagans are as puzzled by Ireland's symbiotic religion as are their Christian cousins. I have an American friend who went to Ireland with the intention of celebrating the ancient holidays there: the solstices and equinoxes, and the Celtic feasts directly between those solar points, eight seasonal rituals in all. She imagined herself dancing at Lughnasa on a sacred mountain, flirting by a Bealtaine fire with a strapping red-haired lad, invoking and releasing the ghosts of the dead at Samhain, all in communities where the traditions had remained unbroken since prehistory — in short, she dreamed of finding a land that echoed her own paganism. My friend had no doubts about whether she would recognize other pagans. Didn't they share the same beliefs, the same basic calendar of rituals? Wouldn't there be ecstatic drumming, rhythmic dancing, invocations of the goddess? She expected some culture shock, some adjustment to Irish ways, but she did not question that she would find her spiritual kin.

She was wildly disappointed. The Irish, she told me later with frustration from the reassuring comfort of California, are entirely Catholic, are pagan no longer, have utterly abandoned the old ways. But I know farmers who use the word *pagan* as casually as *tea* or *pint*. I know people who light Bealtaine blazes with their friends, and not just to burn off gorse. I know artists who use ancient motifs in their work and singers who write traditional music with words redolent of the goddess. I know shamans and herbalists and even a nun who considers herself a reincarnated druid. Any of these would seem pretty pagan to — well, to my mother, for instance.

Perhaps my friend, who went around Ireland asking people — directly, to their faces — whether or not they were pagans, didn't realize that the Irish language has no words for either "yes" or "no." Even when speaking English, the Irish cling to this linguistic habit. If you asked those friends I mentioned whether they are pagan, their answers would be something like these: "Who isn't a pagan, when you come down to it?" or "Isn't everyone born a pagan, so?" Or a question will be directed back at the questioner: "Are you interested in learning about the old ways, then?" or "Now, isn't that a bold question to be putting to me when we've just now met?" or the inevitable phrase to forestall further nosiness, "Won't you have more tea?"

These are equivocal answers to be sure, but perhaps there can be no simple "yes" or "no" to the question. My friends go to Mass on Sunday and do other devotions, novenas and rosaries and the like. This is more than formal observation; they find great meaning and sustenance in their faith. One tells me he feels a thrill "like a new spring" when the host is raised at Mass after the consecration. Another never fails to bless himself before every meal. To most American onlookers, this looks Catholic indeed — devoutly so. But that first man celebrates ritual on the old Celtic holidays and believes fiercely in the powers of the land; the second takes the goddess as a matter of course: "Sure don't I live in her backyard?"

The American definition of paganism is especially suspect among the Irish, too, when it seems to imply adherence to some British cult. The fact that most of the self-proclaimed "witches" in Ireland are English does not escape comment, and notice is also given to the number of American tourists who traipse through on pilgrimages to these minor celebrities and make no inquiries about local beliefs. Having confronted one too many orthodox Gardenerians — followers of the mid-century English style of witchcraft invented by Gerald Gardener — a friend on the Burren changed his way of talking to Americans. "I used to say I was pagan, because I honor the spirits of the land," he told me. "Now I just say I'm a farmer."

Whether or not they call themselves pagan, the Irish retain vestiges of their old polytheism. As the great scholar of religious psychology David Miller explains it, monotheism inclines toward either/or thinking: either something is divine, or it is not. The sacred and the mundane are thereby separated by a vast unbridgeable chasm. This leads directly to a dualistic worldview that in turn, he argues, leads to exclusivity, even totalitarianism. By contrast, polytheism encourages a both/and approach. A flowing brook is both a body of water and a goddess. That goddess, in turn, is both internal and external, immanent and transcendent. Instead of duality, we find multiplicity: Ireland's goddess is Danu in one breath, Brigit in another, Mary in the third. With such a polytheistic worldview, it is possible to be fully Catholic and fully pagan at the same time.

Pagan? Christian?

Won't you have more tea?

We three pilgrims, trudging at dawn across the great wet expanse of the Curragh, were Irish by heritage but American by birth and uprearing. None of us Catholic, we each honored the goddess in our own way, whether through scholarship or creative work or ritual. What had brought us together, what had lured us to Kildare — Paula and I from the Midwest, Diane from California — was the Brigit revival, references to which were cropping up with increasing frequency on websites and in magazines and in conversations with friends on both sides of the water. Other than knowing on which weekend the festival would be held, we were unsure of what would occur on Imbolc in Kildare. But we had come to Leinster convinced that any rituals held in Brigit's sacred place on Brigit's feast day would satisfy our seeking souls. We would not be disappointed.

We had met up the previous evening at the very spot where, several days later, the celebration of the goddess-turned-saint would conclude. Our meeting place was in the cemetery behind the Protestant cathedral of Saint Bridget, a few blocks away from the Catholic church of Saint Brigit. Dense night fog wrapped the cathedral that night like cotton swaddling. We had difficulty locating our goal — not only because of the darkness but because of the sodium vapor lights beaming yellowly on the walls of the medieval building. Picking our way across uneven graves and among slanting headstones in the chiaroscuro of deep shadow and harsh glare, we had sought out a tiny rock-walled place that I had first seen some months earlier, when I had traveled from Connemara to Kildare following reports that Brigit's sacred flame had been relit.

It had been a gray blustery fall day when I made my first visit to the site. I had walked through the town square past a somber stone statue of Brigit, sporting not only a T-shirt in support of Kildare's historic try at the All-Ireland football championship but a fetching Lily-White headband as well. (When Kildare lost to Galway, a local woman told me with brisk assurance, "Ah, well, don't you know Brigit's attention was wandering that day.") Just off the square I found the cathedral, a cross-shaped fourteenth-century building bejeweled with stained glass. I did not even put my head inside but instead stepped off the gravel path and walked around to the rear, to an old grassy graveyard below a tall pencil-shaped monastic tower.

I had been told that, behind the cathedral next to the tower, I would find the most famous Brigit site in Ireland. In retrospect I am not certain what I expected to see, probably something grand, monumental, arresting. What I found was — not much, really, just a square of granite bricks around a pit into which several slate steps descended. Those stone walls surrounded nothing but rainy air and a few flagstones where, tradition has it, Kildare's central shrine once stood. A small iron plaque on the far wall proclaimed: "Saint Bridget's Fire Temple, restored, 1988."

The fire temple. At that very spot, for uncounted generations, nineteen women had tended a perpetual fire in Brigit's honor. Each took her turn alone, feeding the flames — perhaps with Irish turf, perhaps with wood from the sacred oak — and fanning them with branches, for to blow upon the sacred fire was prohibited. Each night, under the holy women's ministrations, Brigit's fire burnt pure and clean, never leaving a trace of ash in all those centuries. Every twentieth day, the women gathered to pray, "Brigit, this is your fire, and it is your turn to tend it," before abandoning it to the goddess. Miraculously, the fire was always found, still blazing brightly, every twenty-first morning.

In addition to its twelve centuries of sanctity as a Christian shrine, the site may have an even more ancient history. Many believe the site's dedication to Brigit predates the arrival of Christianity, that it was originally a goddess temple whose rites were taken over by nuns who replaced the ancient priestesses. Thus it may have been in use for as long as two thousand years first under Celtic, later under Christian, guardianship.

The ruined fire temple, like many other sacred sites I have visited around the world, revealed more to the inner than the outer eye. As I stood there, I could sense the shadows of those priestesses, those nuns, hovering like ghosts over the small stone plaza. I could hear, in my mind, women praying to their goddess, their saint: "Brigit, excellent woman, sudden flame, may the bright fiery sun take us to the lasting kingdom." In my mind, I could hear them singing rich songs in praise of her:

Brigit, gold-red woman,
Brigit, flame and honeycomb,
Brigit, sun of womanhood,
Brigit, lead me home.

You are a branch in blossom.
You are a sheltering dome.
You are my bright precious freedom.
Brigit, lead me home.

Uncountable generations of honor and respect for feminine spirituality had flourished at the very spot where I stood. Incalculable years when no man had entered a sacred space reserved for the goddess and for the women who served her. I stood there motionless, that fall day at the empty fire temple, emotion sweeping through me like the Irish wind, warm tears mingling with the cold rain on my cheeks.

There is no absolute historical proof that Christians adopted or adapted a pagan ritual at the fire temple where I stood, but circumstantial evidence is strong. Similar temples have been found at other Celtic sites, most notably in Bath in southwest England, where the healing goddess Sul, called Minerva by the Romans, was invoked by a college of priestesses in a rite strikingly like Brigit's. The ancient writer Solinus said that in Sul's shrine "the fire burns continually, and its coals never turn to ash." Variations of Sul's name are found as titles of Brigit, so it is likely they were the same goddess, one invoked by vestals pledged to a divinity embodied in the fire they tended.

※※※※※※

Many cultures connect heat and fire with female power. The sun is a goddess on almost every continent. Fiery mountains, too, are usually female:

the volcanoes of the Pacific Rim, from Fuji in Japan to Kilauea in Hawaii to Washington's Mount Saint Helens, were envisioned as fierce strong women. Among the Celts, the archetype of the fiery woman was connected with a belief that virginity intensified feminine power. But what, exactly, virginity meant is a subject of some debate. No sexual relations? No sexual relations with men? No sexual relations with men except on ritual occasions? No sexual relations that led to childbearing? Each has been suggested as the Celtic definition of virginity. Since the valuing of the *virgo intacta,* the woman with no experience of sexual penetration, was not found among the Celts, it is possible that these priestesses were mothers past childbearing age, women who loved other women, or barren women, rather than virgins as we now define them.

The fire goddess worshiped by Kildare's virgin priestesses was one of the few pan-Celtic divinities. Each Celtic tribe had its own deities, creating such an enormous pantheon that the generic Celtic oath was "I swear by the gods I swear by." Not only were the Celts utterly decentralized politically, but they were also pantheists par excellence. They saw divinity everywhere, in this well and that stream and on top of that mountain and of course, over there in that great oak tree. Their innumerable specific holy places demanded equally innumerable specific holy names, so that there are scores of Celtic divinities known only in one location, like Aeracura in the Rhine Valley, or Metz of Trier, or Belisima on the shores of England's Mersey River. But Brigit, sometimes called by her Latinized name Brigantia, is found throughout the Celtic world, from Central Europe through France and Spain and over to the islands of Britain and Ireland. She must have been a powerful goddess indeed to have inspired such widespread worship.

In Ireland, Brigit was depicted as a triple goddess or as three sister-goddesses who shared the same name. She ruled transformation: of rock into metal, as goddess of smithcraft; of illness into health, as midwife goddess of healing; of ideas into art, as goddess of poetry. The triple Brigit was daughter of the Dagda, the earth god, with whom she shares certain powers, especially that of promoting abundance. She was connected with a magical cow with an inexhaustible udder; with fire, both in the sun and in the hearth; and with water, especially that found in healing springs.

Although Kildare is believed to have been the center of worship of Brigit as goddess, we have no Celtic records of a pagan temple there. This is not unusual, for the Celts did not privilege written documents, relying instead upon the phenomenal memories of the *filidh,* their bards. Not that the Celts were illiterate, but their ogham alphabet — whose invention is attributed to Brigit — was used only for short inscriptions. The Celts were people of the word, not of the book; indeed, I have heard it argued that the reason for the continuing Irish hegemony in English literature is that it is still an oral culture. Resilient as such a culture may be when undisturbed, its treasures can be destroyed in only one generation; just kill the tellers of stories or otherwise interrupt their transmission to a new generation.

In other Celtic lands, destruction of the ancient bardic orders meant the loss of history and myth as well as of poetry. But not in Ireland — at least, not entirely. There, the melding of the Christian and the pagan began early, during the great period of Celtic monasticism. Irish monks of that period provided most of our written records of Celtic mythology. In continental Europe, evidence of Celtic beliefs is found only in sculpture; in Britain, it is found only in a few verbal shards and the occasional inscribed statue; but in Ireland we find entire epics, whole chants and songs, lengthy narratives. In the curvilinear script for which they are justly famous, Irish monks wrote down the stories, poems, place-names, and other lore of their pagan ancestors before it disappeared in the mists of history. Sometimes they blended pagan with Christian details. Thus we first hear of the ancient fire temple in the writings of monks who, possibly to curry favor at powerful Kildare, chose its abbess as their subject, penning a half dozen Lives of Saint Brigit.

According to these sources, the girl who later became Ireland's matron saint was born to a Christian slave woman of the pagan king Dubthach in approximately 450 C.E. Miracles attended upon her birth, including an unearthly flame that shot toward heaven from her birthplace and a sunlike glow around her infant body. From her earliest years, the girl showed an inclination for sanctity. At the age of nine she sold the jewels from one of her father's swords to feed the poor. Threatened with punishment for theft, Brigit cleverly invoked not only Christian charity but also Celtic hospitality to defend her action. ("Still the Isles of Erin fidget," wrote the American poet Phyllis McGinley, "With generous girls named Bridey or Bridget.")

Her father arranged a suitable marriage. But Brigit, who wished to be a bride of Christ, disfigured herself by causing her eyes to drop out of their sockets until her fiancé, revolted by the dangling orbs, rejected her. (In some versions of the story she popped out his eyes too.) Restoring her own sight as she would later cure others' blindness, Brigit gathered a group of women disciples. Together they set off to establish their convent, stopping at several potential sites before they reached Kildare, where Brigit declared their journey at an end. Because she needed land on which to graze her cattle, the saint asked a local ruler to donate it. Giving land to another *tuath,* especially one composed entirely of Christian women, did not seem politically advantageous to the chieftain, but Celtic hospitality meant one should not refuse a guest. So he gave what he thought was a clever response to Brigit's request. Certainly, he said, she could have land — as much as her mantle could cover. Brigit took off her cloak, shook it out, and laid it on the ground. Instantly, it began to grow and swell, billowing out until it covered the entire Curragh, sometimes still called "Brigit's mantle" in remembrance of this act.

Brigit continued to perform miracles, drawing impossible amounts of milk from her herds, filling several baskets with only one butter-churning, providing for seventeen parishes with just one magical barrel of ale. On the more mundane plane, she assumed the spiritual directorship of all Kildare religious, male and female, as well as becoming head of all the nuns of Ireland. She held more power than any woman in the Roman Church. Like the ancient Celtic goddesses of sovereignty, without whose blessing no king could rule, it was Brigit who designated the male bishop of the region. She may even, according to the eighth-century Hymn of Broccan, have been made a bishop herself through an accidental sacrament bestowed by a "god-intoxicated" Saint Mel who, upon discovering his error, also realized the ordination was irrevocable.

By the time of Saint Brigit's death, Kildare was one of Ireland's preeminent Christian centers, and so it remained for hundreds of years. It boasted a great college of artists who created an illuminated manuscript reputed to be the most beautiful in Ireland, even more gorgeous than the Book of Kells, showing "angelic, not human skill" in its design according to a twelfth-century writer — but, alas, the Book of Kildare is now lost. Kildare's hospitality was also renowned; the growing city was a site for pilgrimage and a center of trade. In the tradition of Brigit, the abbesses who followed her were Ireland's leading religious women, with power almost equal to that of Leinster's bishop. And, during all these splendid years, the eternal flame blazed in the fire temple, with Brigit herself tending it every twentieth day.

But life got harder for Brigit's *tuath* as the first millennium ended. The arrival of the Normans set in motion changes that would ultimately destroy Kildare's monastic power. A woman figures prominently in this sorry tale: Dervorgilla, a Leinster lass, was married off to a warrior from way out in wild Breffni, the western land of the O'Rourkes. A suitor, one Diarmuid, went at her urging to rescue her from her husband's bad temper and Sligo's wild weather. (Or perhaps he kidnapped and raped her. History has never decided.) Things got rough, and Diarmuid invited over some hired soldiery to help him win his cause. The trouble was, he didn't have much to offer in the way of recompense. So he offered what was not his to give: land.

The land belonged to the *tuath,* the people, just as the people belonged to the land. Selling it or giving it away was impossible under Celtic law. Diarmuid knew this, though he apparently thought his foreign help would not. But his Brooklyn Bridge–style swindle didn't take into account armed men intent upon seizing what they'd been promised. The Normans arrived, and they did not go away. When, not long afterward, an English king decided that he would rather be divorced than Catholic, Ireland had ample reason to defile the reputation of Diarmuid na nGall, Dermot of the Foreigners, who had brought strangers to their country and thus laid the groundwork for hundreds of years of warfare.

Diarmuid had never been a friend to Kildare; he sacked the abbey and woefully mistreated the abbess, perhaps even raping her. But the bad behavior of one petty king could have been endured. With the coming of Norman forces, Brigit's spiritual center was greatly diminished in power and prestige. Despite this decline, Kildare held on for another five hundred years as an important focus of Catholic worship. The nuns still tended the fire, and Brigit herself still came each twentieth night to help. Generations were born and died, the ancient oak that gave the town its name grew old and finally fell, and still the flame blazed in the city of Brigit.

In the thirteen century a Catholic bishop, uncomfortable with the pagan overtones of Kildare's famous ritual, ordered the sacred flame doused. A bishop is mortal, however, and upon his passing Brigit's immortal flame was promptly relit. But even the long-lasting sisterhood of the Brigidines finally gave away. In 1632, after twelve hundred years of continual ritual observance, the sacred fire was extinguished by a man who disdained not only its pagan but also its Catholic meaning. The nuns were dispersed, and the long-surviving rituals to Brigit — as goddess and as saint — came to an end in Kildare. Even the location of the fire temple, on whose grounds the Protestant cathedral had been built, was forgotten.

Such are the vicissitudes of fortune that the cathedral itself fell into disrepair not long after. For centuries, it stood roofless and untenanted, home only to rodents and nesting birds. But several decades ago, the Church of Ireland — as the Anglican Church is called in Éire — initiated restoration. It was then that ancient flagstones marking the fire temple were discovered and a square stone wall constructed around the site — the original enclosure probably having been circular, built of wood or wicker. It is now a place of pilgrimage for those on the path of Brigit, whether they honor her as goddess, saint, or both.

Today, as for nearly four hundred years, the ancient temple stands deserted. Brigit's fire is but a flickering ghost there, like the shades of those ancient priestesses I sensed on my first solitary visit. But once each year the ghosts come alive. It happens on Imbolc, which the people of Kildare call Lá Féile Bríde, Brigit's feast day. Annually, on that pivot morning in early February, holy women gather to light a sacred fire on ancient flagstones, to forge anew the link to the Celtic and Christian past. Those rumors I had heard in Connemara proved true. The light of Brigit shines again in Kildare. The ancient sisterhood has returned to its home. The sacred fire, extinguished all those centuries ago, has been relit.

It all sounded so stirring when I first heard of it. In the fervent tones of those who spoke of the Brigit revival, I heard archetypal resonances. Reigniting the symbolic flame of a goddess/saint, in the place linked to her in legend and history — surely, I imagined, this had been done in a suitably dramatic and intentional way, as a visible symbol of the feminine power now reenlivening a world that had long since denied or suppressed it. In my imagination, I saw Brigit's fire relit with defiance and great flourish and steely resolve. In my mind's eye, I pictured the sacred flame as enormous, a mighty blaze indeed.

Thus I was unprepared for the modest scale of the sanctuary of Solas Bhríde, "the sun of Brigit," and of its sacred flame. En route from Connemara I had stopped in some nondescript small town in the midlands, found a phone box, and called directory assistance for the number of the Brigidine sisters. My operator was notably chatty, even for Ireland. Before giving me the number, he provided an inspirational lecturette. "I hear from your accent that you're...not Irish," he offered delicately. "Not many of your type, perhaps I should say your countrymen, perhaps I should say your countrywomen — I find not many are interested in spirituality. But it was our spirituality that held the Irish together during the hard times." He went on for five minutes about the significance of Celtic Christianity before locating the number for me. I dialed up Solas Bhríde, and a friendly voice urged me to come right over when I reached Kildare.

⊠⊠⊠⊠⊠

The address was on Dara Place, whose name appropriately includes the Irish word for oak, the druid's tree. I found the street, a cul-de-sac in what Americans call a subdivision and in Ireland is known as a housing estate, just three blocks from the cathedral. It was easy to distinguish the small white stucco home of the Brigidines, for no other doorway in Kildare boasts a stained-glass depiction of a flame. I knocked, the door was flung open, and I was instantly warmed by the embracing smile of Sister Mary Minihan. Hers is a name related to my own. Like its variants, Monaghan means "child of the little monk" and is said to be the surname given to off-spring of clergy in the early days of the Celtic Church, when priests were still permitted to marry. Brigit's own abbey housed both men and women; given the customs of the time, it is probable that some of them produced families of Monaghans. I like to think that my interest in religion is genetic, that somewhere back there, fifteen centuries ago or so, an Irish ancestor was a man of the spirit and of the cloth, maybe even one of Brigit's followers.

And, although I rarely use it except on legal documents, my first name is Mary. So is my mother's; so was my grandmother's. I was told as a child that it is a Mayo tradition to name eldest daughters for the Mother of God, a tradition that survived in America; I have cousins named Susan Marie, Kathleen Marie, and Mary Agnes, each an uncle's eldest daughter. I was also informed that such girls were destined for the convent; when we took final vows, we could reclaim baptismal names that already included the required name of the Blessed Virgin. The smiling woman who greeted me at Solas Bhríde was thus my near-namesake, and although she knew nothing of me save that I came in search of Brigit, Mary Minihan welcomed me like a sister.

Immediately — having done this innumerable times, as her sweep-ingly efficient manner showed — Sister Mary led me down a hallway to a sparsely furnished room that probably, in neighboring homes, served as the parlor. At Solas Bhríde, the room finds a different use. It is essentially empty, boasting only a dozen straight-backed chairs pushed up against the walls and a few cushions strewn on the floor beneath a long window over-looking the garden. Straw Brigit crosses and artwork depicting Brigit's various symbols provide decoration. A crowded sideboard holds books and tapes and pamphlets and plastic-wrapped candles.

From a corner, a flicker of light caught my eye. It came from the cen-ter of a shrine composed of rocks and plants and brightly colored fabric, before which stood a white bisque statuette of Brigit, her arms wide as though to embrace the world. Atop a little table stood a square metal lantern, within which a fat candle blazed merrily. I had come to Kildare to visit the ancient fire temple and had found only emptiness. Now, in a plain back room of an ordinary estate home, I stood before a simple candle. And, like many another pilgrim before and since, I sank down before Brigit's sacred flame and wept.

The tears that came first at the deserted fire temple now flowed even more freely. Not that the shrine — the ancient temple reborn — was designed to create a dramatically emotional effect: quite the opposite. It was composed of common materials arranged in a direct and homely fash-ion. But it was the very ordinariness, of both the shrine and its sacred flame, that moved me so deeply. It spoke of the way ancient knowledge is truly preserved, in the mundane and often overlooked places of our world, of our souls. It hinted at the way feminine strength is found in each extraordinary ordinary action by which we sustain our lives. It told of the deeply archetypal power to be found in even the simplest object and moment.

Sister Mary, as she does during hundreds of pilgrim visits every year, slipped away, leaving me to my meditation. When I emerged, subdued and thoughtful, she had tea ready. In the cozy front room next to a glowing fire-place, she introduced me to Sister Phyllis O'Shea, the other Brigidine in residence at Solas Bhríde. Together they brought out the convent scrap-books and, refreshing me from a pot of tea as bottomless as Brigit's ale vat, showed photographs and told how they had come back to Kildare and relit the sacred fire of Brigit.

Like the flame itself, the story is curiously undramatic, but all the more powerful for that; it is a story of how profound effects can come of small, apparently insignificant causes. Mary and Phil are Sisters of Saint Brigit, members of the order dispersed when the sacred fire was doused in 1632. For some two hundred years the Brigidines disappear from history, until the Bishop of Kerry reestablished them in 1880, emphasizing that this was not a new foundation but a continuation of the ancient sisterhood. A missionary order for more than a century, the Brigidines returned to Kildare in 1992, eighteen generations after they had been banished from their ancient center.

Mary and Phil, at midlife two of the younger Brigidines, arrived with no mandate except to be of service. Many problems called out to them, for this small town southwest of Dublin has seen more than its share of economic and social upheaval in recent times. Housing estates full of unwed mothers — only 10 percent of unmarried pregnant Irish women now give up children for adoption, compared to only ten years ago when Ireland supplied an international adoption market greedy for healthy white infants — were of concern. So were family violence, unemployment, poverty, and discrimination against the Travelers who come to work on the Kildare horse farms. There was no dearth of opportunities for service.

They did not envision relighting the sacred fire of Brigit or spearheading an international Brigit revival. But spirit works in mysterious ways. Not long after Mary and Phil's arrival in Kildare, when the wheel of the year rolled around to February, it seemed appropriate to host a gathering to honor Brigit's feast day. Another Brigidine was visiting from Texas, and, as part of the service, Sister Mary Theresa Collins lit a candle in commemoration of the sisterhood's ancient sacred fire. Then, with song and poetry, the nuns and their friends celebrated the coming of springtime. When the service was over and the ritual area was being tidied, someone leaned over to blow out the candle. A local man, struck by the import of what had occurred on that Imbolc eve in 1993, cried out in protest.

Brigit's sacred flame had been relit, and it would not be extinguished.

From that point on, the mission of the Brigidines in Kildare has steadily unveiled itself. Cháirde Bhríde, "Friends of Brigit," has been established, an association of laypeople who assist with programs and events. Pilgrims are received from around the world to honor the flame and to celebrate ritual. Adults and children are taught about Brigit as

Peacemaker, Prophetess, and Earth Woman, three names for the saint that echo the ancient goddess trinity. And, once a year, Lá Féile Bríde is held, the festival for which I had come back to Ireland.

⊠⊠⊠⊠

Out of the January mist on that first day of the festival, figures emerged, small clusters of people slogging across wet sheep-shorn grass. The top of the Curragh, surely, though only a local would have noticed the invisible incline from the road. We followed the scraggly procession toward a grove of massive trees — the Foxes' Covert, whose name goes back to a time when Anglo-Irish gentry still rode to hounds in Kildare. Within the grove, foxes had been bred in cages for the hunt, then released to live a brutal few hours of freedom. We fell in step beside a broad-faced blond woman. "When I was a child I used to pray," she beamed with girlish delight, "that this land would be made sacred again, that the spirits of the little foxes would be set free at last. I always knew this would happen. I always knew it."

Once within the grove, we joined a ragged circle of pilgrims around a tall ochre pole that we had come to ritually bless. The Peace Pole was an impressive ten-foot beam of native Irish oak, hewn and carved by Cháirde Bhríde. On each of its three sides, the same words appeared: "May peace prevail on earth," written in English, in Irish, and in the slashing lines of ogham. It had been installed near another symbolic site, a labyrinth cut into the Curragh turf, through which some were ceremonially pacing before the ritual began.

Sister Mary called us to attention through an electronic megaphone. Behind her, children clustered, each bearing a paper flag upon which a country's name was handprinted. I could make out some of the names: Angola, Bosnia, Sudan, Indonesia, East Timor. Names of countries at war. Ireland. Printed roughly, in old Celtic lettering. There would be a peace conference all weekend, its events wrapped around the Imbolc celebration, and this event inaugurated both. Her warm voice distorted slightly by the megaphone, Mary taught us the chant that would punctuate the ritual: "May peace prevail on earth. May peace prevail in me."

It was a simple ceremony. Each child walked — moving just as Sister Phil instructed, *deiseal,* in the sacred sunwise direction that reveals and sustains the order of the universe — three times around the oaken pole. We chanted together, a hundred strong in the misty morning, praying for the countries that the boys and girls represented. "May peace prevail in Kosovo…May peace prevail in Macedonia…May peace prevail in Somalia." Some children were awkward, shy, walking hurriedly, eyes downcast. Others were bolder, flags and heads held high. The last child bore the familiar banner of gold and green, and we chanted even more somberly than before, "May peace prevail in Ireland. May peace prevail in me." Finally Sister Phil circled the post with a lantern — in which we could see flickering the sacred flame from Solas Bhríde — before leading the pilgrims on the long walk back to the heart of Kildare town.

I had never before engaged in public ritual in Ireland. Solitary personal ritual, yes: leaving a stone from Roundstone Bog inside the cairn at Loughcrew with a prayer that the spacious bogland might last as long as those monumental stones. Tying clooties — little offerings of pretty cloth — to the oldest trees I met. Throwing coins into holy wells. But I don't go to Mass, and my Irish friends are mostly Catholic, so I had not previously joined with like-minded others in ritual space in my ancestral land. Imbolc in Kildare more than made up for that deficit. Within the span of a few days we would light a huge lantern in Kildare's square as the great Christy Moore crooned an anthem to peace; we would hear the *scéal féin,* the life stories, of IRA blanket men and Protestant Orangemen, coming together in tortured dialogue; we would see the Eucharist consecrated on a crystal morning at the holy well; we would sing and dance with the Biddy Boys, cartoonish white-clad straw-hatted characters who begged money — symbolic change — from us at the *céilí.* And, most unforgettably, we would hold vigil, on the eve of Lá Féile Bríde, at the holy well of Brigit.

There are actually thirty-two holy wells recorded in the Kildare area, though only two are active sites of ritual today. They bubble up from the great aquifer beneath the Curragh, an underground lake so immense it could supply water to Dublin for a dozen years without additional rainfall. All the wells are sacred to Brigit, who in her Celtic identity was goddess of water as well as fire; rulership passed to the saint after Christianity arrived. The wells are reliable sources of clean water; therefore it had traditionally been deemed vital to keep them accessible to all and uncluttered with debris. Myth and legend supported conservation of the water's purity.

If insulted by bad behavior, such as the washing of cattle viscera in its waters, a holy well might get up and move to another village; legends tell of the candlelike flames that accompanied wells engaged in such disciplinary action. But legend has loosened its grip on modern Ireland, and Kildare's smaller holy wells have suffered as a result. Roads have been built over some; others have been bricked over or filled in for lawns or parking lots.

The two major holy wells, however, have been left relatively undisturbed by progress, and they are increasingly active sites of pilgrimage and ritual. Twenty years ago, folklorist Patrick Logan reported regretfully that many of Ireland's holy wells had fallen into disuse and disrepair, sadly predicting that their ancient healing rituals would be forgotten within a generation. But quite the opposite has happened, for the Brigit revival has encouraged more, rather than less, ritual activity at holy wells. At Liscannor in Galway, I now see more offerings — holy cards, statuettes, feathers, and ribbons — than when I first visited the Brigit Vat decades ago. In Sligo, well-attended patterns are held at the beautiful shaded well of Tobernault. And in Kildare, thousands annually visit the two wells dedicated to Brigit, and the crowd for Imbolc eve strains capacity.

The smaller one, known locally as the "pagan well," is situated at the National Stud, home to some of those thoroughbreds we saw out on the Curragh. The road around it has, just recently, been rerouted. The old dangerous corner in front of the well was probably created when two pathways converged upon the holy well where, for untold generations, people came to gather water and to make offerings. It would have been perfectly safe to cross the road when the only traffic was donkeys and cows and the occasional horse. Later, with no nearby parking space, no shoulder, and unpredictable roaring traffic, it became risky to approach the old well. There was a move in mid-century to pave it over, to eliminate the temptation for children and other pagans to try to reach it, endangering themselves in the process. But the well turned out to be unstoppable. So deep that it draws directly from the Curragh aquifer, it could not be plugged no matter how much asphalt went down its narrow throat. So the pagan well remained undisturbed except by people driving by at desperate speeds (everything in Ireland seems to be either "desperate" or "brilliant") until, spurred by the Brigit revival, the town shifted the road.

A path connects the pagan well with the Christian one. Some forty years ago, concerned for his parishioners' safety, a local priest moved the devotional focus for Imbolc and other Brigit rituals a few hundred yards west to what is now the primary holy well of the Kildare area. There, a tiny wooden bridge leads into the grassy sacred precinct, where miniature standing stones link a deep rock-circled well with its outlet in a stream into which shallow stone steps descend. Brigit, sculpted in an old-fashioned nun's habit, stands in a stone grotto amid coins and flowers and other offerings.

One morning I overheard a fierce argument between two Kildare people about what constituted the "real" well. A bearded man stoutly maintained that the pagan well was Brigit's actual shrine, while a woman contended that once Brigit had converted to Christianity, the pagan well became poison. The man shook his head. No, he argued firmly, Ireland had been Christian for many years before the 1950s, the well was only moved because of increased vehicular traffic, the pagan well was perfectly safe, he'd drunk from it many times himself. But no, the woman countered, she knew what she was talking about, Brigit herself had come to her in a dream to announce that she was perfectly happy not to be a goddess anymore, "because it was finally too much, people always demanding you be right all the time." The man clenched his jaw and shrugged, as though to give up in the face of such devout lunacy, but then muttered under his breath once again, "The pagan well is the real well!"

Whether or not the pagan well is the real one, there is no question that today's pilgrim throngs would find it too small to accommodate their rituals. And rituals to Brigit, especially those that plead for healing, have once again become a major activity in Kildare. Sister Mary, welcoming those of any faith or none, assists in simple ceremonies several times weekly, praying with those who dip water from the well to wash afflicted portions of the body. Holy wells are traditional places of healing in Ireland, as well as in England, Scotland, and Wales, all places where the old Celtic belief in water spirits survives. Because of legendary associations — Brigit pulled out her eyes to avoid marriage; she cured the blindness of another nun with a mere touch — the water is held to be especially efficacious for problems with eyesight. But Brigit places no limits on what she will do for the devout. I have seen a man wearing a chemotherapy infusion pack dipping his hands in the holy well at Kildare. Handwritten prayers for recovery from heart disease are pasted inside the whitewashed shed above the Brigit

Vat at Liscannor. Like that from Lourdes in France, the water from Brigit's holy wells is reputed to heal any disorder of mind, body, or spirit.

People come to the holy wells continually throughout the year, in groups and singly, for the healing rituals. But the greatest crowds arrive for Imbolc, originally the Celtic feast of Brigit the goddess, later the Catholic feast day of the saint. There are at least a dozen Irish rituals for this pagan/Christian feast: making the *brídeog,* a little poppet to represent Brigit and the coming spring; whitewashing the house and doing other spring-cleaning tasks; going door-to-door demanding money for "poor Biddy dressed in rags" (her new clothing will be the grass of springtime); twisting four-armed crosses from fresh reeds to protect the house from fire.

Some customs exist only across a small area, like the Connemara tradition of Brigit's girdle, the *crios Brídghe.* Barbara Callan, whom they call in Connacht "a mighty woman," was instrumental in its revival. The tradition had fallen out of use until it was reintroduced in 1990. A *súgán* rope was plaited from hand-reaped oat straw, joined into a six-foot circle, and decorated with four little Brigit crosses. Barbara and her friends carried the *crios* from house to house, calling out *Ligigí isteach Brighid agus a crios,* "open the way for Brigit and her girdle," to which the household responded, *Céad míle fáilte romhat, a Bhrighid, is roimh do chrios,* "a hundred thousand welcomes to you, Brigit, and to your girdle." Each person stepped through the *crios* three times, then passed it three times around their waists, praying for protection for the coming year. "To watch a family, from old grandmother to youngest child, go through the *crios* was moving beyond words," Barbara remembers.

At Kildare, visitation of the holy wells is the primary ritual for Imbolc. In keeping with that custom, the Brigidines sponsor a vigil at the well each January 31, eve of the feast. Hundreds join in, many coming from other parts of Ireland to attend at Brigit's central shrine for her most important holiday. As we gathered in the late evening, we were greeted by a bonfire of gorse wood, welcome in the still-wintry chill. But that was not the only fire that lit the dark well precinct, for Cháirde Bhríde had placed hundreds of candles on the pathways and stone steps, outlining the well and the spring and the pathways. The rushing waters caught and reflected the candlelight, so that the whole precinct shimmered with light.

But the most important light had not yet arrived. For an hour we drifted from group to group, visiting with friends who had been strangers days before. Finally we were called to attention, as Sister Phil arrived with the lantern carrying the sacred flame of Brigit. We quickly fell in line behind her for the processional. A voice was lifted, a song introduced, and we all joined in. "Holy ground ... we're walking on holy ground ... where the Lady passes, there we stand on holy ground." Men and women, Catholic and Protestant and pagan, Irish and American and neither — all joined voices in a chant to the power of the feminine who, unnamed, became all and everything we wished her to be.

The ritual itself is not utterly clear in my memory. There was song, of course, for this was Ireland: Luka Bloom leading us in a newly composed song about the light within, Nóirín Ní Ríain lifting her rich voice beside me, Father Adrian accompanying Mary and Phil on his guitar. And poetry: Gay Barbazon from Cháirde Bhríde reciting the Dougie MacLean lyric, "It's the land that is our wisdom, it's the land, you cannot own the land, the land owns you." And dance: all of us moving slowly *deiseal* around the standing stones, then a smaller group of women circling in stately fashion beneath an upraised torch. And there were symbolic actions: calling out the names of the year's dead, to bring them to Brigit's attention; laying out the Brat Bhríde, the cloth that represented Brigit's mantle, so that she might walk upon it at dawn; invocations and prayers. But in what order these happened, or how long they lasted, or what else transpired, I cannot say, for I was in an altered state, conscious only of the way culture and season and art and history and spirit and my own body's memories came together in a perfect union.

⊠⊠⊠⊠

I have celebrated Imbolc almost yearly since the early 1970s, when I gathered with my women's circle in Alaska, in winter darkness that gave us a very tangible connection to the symbolism of light. Yearly I have spoken, or heard spoken, words about the festival's meaning, how it marks the beginning of spring, how it is the feast of milk because the ewes are lactating. But spring was always weeks away where I lived, and there were never any sheep nearby. In Kildare, at Imbolc, spring awakens the land. Ewes rest heavy bellies on wet greening grass, crocus buds nod their heavy heads, soft breezes tease the skin with suggestions of warmth. The holiday's symbolism is perfectly appropriate in Ireland, the land where the festival was born.

At other Imbolc ceremonies I've attended, the participants have moved through their symbolic actions with the care and reverence that come of learning something first with the intellect, then with the body. No one, including myself, had memories of celebrating Imbolc as a little girl; we joined as adults creating a sacred space. Some of these rituals have been beautiful, moving, profoundly healing, but they are not Imbolc in Kildare. There I celebrated with people who were not creating or re-creating a ritual from books and dreams and symbols; they were celebrating an age-old festival that many remembered from childhood, tracing patterns that their foremothers had traced on that very day, in that very place, for hundreds, perhaps thousands, of years.

And I was one of them. I have never felt more Irish than I did that night. I felt an atavistic sense of blood connection, an awareness that I was celebrating in ways that had been part of my heritage for generations and generations. I felt as though my body were temporary, almost illusory, existing only to trace ancient sunwise paths around a holy place. As though my body reflected, like well water reflecting countless candles, the bodies of others — women of Irish blood, women like me — who had celebrated at that very place, on that very night, down through the centuries.

And the next day, when I woke to hear the first territorial songs of nesting birds, to see the crocus that overnight had burst into bloom on Moate House's lawn, to feel bright sun drying winter-flooded fields, to watch the first lambs bound toward their protective mothers, I felt the magic rightness of that vigil at the well — felt, indeed, as though we had brought spring to Ireland by our songs and dances and prayers.

In that bright dawn, Paula and I went to the well again. Candles, some of them still guttering, brought back the evening vigil. But bright new snowdrops decorated the banks of the stream. Near the well, trees were covered with clooties: ties, ribbons, a strip of cloth that seemed to have been torn from a garment, a black-and-white peace button. The sun, slanting golden through the wood fence, made the water sparkle and the leafy greens become more vivid and alive. We knelt before a large stone on which a bright blue cloth lay. This was the Brat Bhríde, Brigit's mantle, into which the dew and the rising sun had imbued healing power that could be used throughout the year. I cut a strip for Arlen, my dear friend who lay dying in California. And one for myself, a tiny piece of blue that I carry with me still.

Returning to town, we settled in for tea in a cozy café next to the cathedral, where I read the Dublin paper while Paula wrote postcards home. A radio blared the morning news. Kosovo growing tense. Riots in Indonesia. Genocide in Africa. I thought of the children with their hand-made peace flags, of our prayerful chants of a few days earlier. In the cheery tea shop, the news seemed an interruption from a violent world that could not reach us. But tea shops like this in Ireland had been bombed by people who look no different from me or my cousins.

I am American — meaning that I grew up on land to which I have no hereditary connection, surrounded by people to whom I must explain my folkways as I seek to understand theirs, celebrating ritual with people with whom I am connected by choice rather than blood. The border wars, the apparently endless fighting that rages across this globe, had always been unintelligible to me. Even the Irish conflict — despite my cousins imprisoned for IRA activities — has always seemed senseless to me. Not senseless in a way that all wars are senseless, but more deeply senseless, because it seemed to be about so little, only bits of land. I had never experienced the way that ritual in which you deeply believe, celebrated on land that you deeply love with people who look like family, can bond you to that land and to those people. At the Imbolc ritual in Kildare, I understood — not abstractly, but in my body — how such conflicts can occur. Not that I would now fight for Ireland. But I have had a glimpse of why others do.

My reverie was interrupted by a talk show. "Good morning, and happy Imbolc, everyone," said the chipper announcer in a smooth Dublin accent. "Today's program is devoted to Saint Brigit, whose feast day we are celebrating." An on-air guest discussed Brigit's Celtic background, how the sacred fire was a symbol that united both pagan and Christian, how Imbolc was celebrated in various parts of the country. The announcer interrupted him to take a call from a woman with a rolling Cork accent, who rather nervously reminisced about her childhood and how important Brigit's day was to her. "And what do you think about our studio guest, who says that Brigit was originally a goddess?" asked the show's host, emphasizing the latter syllable as the Irish often do.

"May he burn in hell for all eternity for speaking such sacrilege of our beloved saint," the caller said in a single breath.

Paula and I looked at each other across the tea service. Well, I shrugged, apparently not all have accepted Brigit as a bridge figure.

But we had chosen to be with those who had, people struggling to find a way to articulate spirituality beyond the divisions that can seem so enduring. People visioning past the duality that threatens our world. People finding ways to embrace divergent spiritual visions without losing their own. And it was time to join them once more, to return to the place where our weekend had started: time to go, once again, to the fire temple.

⚔⚔⚔

We found a far smaller group than we had at the earlier rituals. Many attenders at Kildare's Lá Féile Bríde had come down from Dublin for the weekend, and Monday demanded their return. Thus perhaps only thirty people entered the cathedral gates that sparkling spring morning. Once again, Sister Phil led us, carrying the lantern in which Brigit's sacred flame swung. In the brilliant sun, it was far easier to walk over the uneven ground of the graveyard than it had been three days earlier in the wintry fog. We stood casually about in twos and threes, beginning the exchange of promises and thanks that are always a part of farewells.

In the sharp thin shadow of the round tower, we grouped ourselves near the entrance to the fire temple, joined at the last minute by a group of elderly nuns of Saint Brigit from Scandinavia. Gay Barbazon formally welcomed us to the sacred space. She related the legends of the nineteen priestesses, the fire that never turned to ash, the miracle each twentieth night. She talked about the years when the fire temple had been lost, buried beneath soil and rubble, and about the revival of Brigit spirituality that had drawn us together. Then she gave us each a square of turf and a small piece of gorse wood — the latter a symbol of the hopelessness that we would burn away in the fire. Fuel was laid in the center of the ancient flagstones and ceremonially ignited from the fire of Solas Bhríde.

We each then walked down the few shallow steps into the temple and placed our fuel upon the sacred fire. A frail blue-veiled nun, who looked to have eight decades behind her, wept as she fed the flames in the very place where her sisters, for thousands of years, had enacted the same ritual. Pungent smoke stung our eyes, but we were all loathe to move into the fresh air outside the little temple. We clung together, unwilling to leave the sacred place or to release the precious moments to the past.

Sister Mary raised her voice in a chant. I had heard it many times in

America, its few poetic lines written by the ecofeminist witch Starhawk for an Imbolc ritual in California some twenty years earlier:

We will never, never lose the way
to the well of her memory.
And the power of her living flame
it will rise, it will rise again.

Pagan and Christian, Protestant and Catholic, men and women, Irish and American and European, we sang together the haunting melody as the fire surged up, wreathing us with misty smoke. Then Sister Mary called out to Brigit, that she herself come join with us on that day, the last Imbolc before the millennium, just as she had been with her priestesses and her nuns on this very spot for so many centuries.

As she prayed, eyes tightly closed, a late-arriving woman descended the stairs and slipped into the crowded temple. As Mary finished her prayer and opened her eyes, she saw the woman who had belatedly joined us. The Brigidine sister grew suddenly pale. In a voice thin with astonishment she spoke again, barely above a whisper. "Do you see, do you all see?" she said chokingly. "Do you see who has entered our circle?"

Several members of Cháirde Bhríde looked similarly stunned, overwhelmed, bewildered. But most of us did not recognize the latecomer or understand the significance of her entry. The woman in question, too, looked momentarily baffled at Mary's reaction. Sister Mary offered an explanation. "It's Bridey," she said, her voice still quavering. "Bridey Duffy. Come just when we called."

Brigit Dubthach. Bridey Duffy. Saint Brigit. Come just when we called for her.

Like so many miracles — like, indeed, the miracle of the relighting of Brigit's flame in Kildare — this was a tiny thing, an almost invisible occurrence whose significance cannot be explained, only felt in the bones and in the heart. And what I felt, as I stood there with the sharp smoke of turf and gorse wood filling my nostrils, was that something momentous had happened that I would, perhaps, never be able to completely articulate. It had something to do with the power of building bridges between people, between religions, between cultures, between the sexes. Something to do with the way change is initiated by small actions whose consequences cannot be fully predicted. Something to do with rootedness in land and in a land's people that would forever alter the way I lived.

We were to leave Kildare for the West the next morning. That evening, we went one last time to the holy wells, to draw sacred water for the year. The pagan well was first, while it was still light dusk. At the deep round pool, Paula held my arm as she descended on slippery rocks to the water, where she filled a plastic liter bottle while I prayed aloud for peace in our world and in our lives. Then we returned to the well where we had kept vigil the night before. The candles were gone, gathered up by Cháirde Bhríde. There was no trace of the bonfire. A few people wandered in friendly solitude through the still darkness. I prayed, silently this time, as Paula filled another bottle from the gushing spring beneath the statue of Saint Brigit.

From out of the night, a sound arose. Though centered somewhere in the trees along the road, it seemed to come from all directions at once and to wrap us in a sudden mantle of beauty. It was an air, sadly joyous and joyously sad in the way of the oldest Irish melodies. A fiddle gave voice to it, that song given to the night and to the season and to the well and to us, too, celebrants of spring's arrival. The song floated on the air like a dark bird, stopping occasionally and then beginning again, so that finally the silences became a seamless part of the song and there was no difference between the music and the silence of the night. Perhaps we left when the music was still playing, perhaps during a pause, I cannot now remember. Like the pagan and the Christian elements that make up Ireland's spirituality, we could finally neither distinguish, nor did we wish to distinguish, one from the other.

Chapter Seven

Wisdom Galore

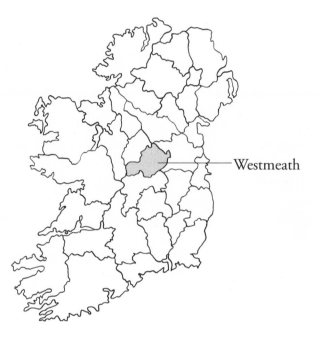

Westmeath

The day I heard the news was raw and wet and wild. A good day to stay indoors, a domestic kind of day. Barbara was bustling about, singing snatches of new songs, reading aloud passages of prose and verse, refilling the teapot whenever it threatened to go dry. Curled up beside the turf fire, I held out my cup so my friend could empty the milk jug into my strong tea. She too looked strong, not gaunt as she had during those fearsome rounds of radiation that had broken her free of cancer's yoke.

There are people with whom you feel an instant kinship, and so it was with Barbara Callan; our first conversation filled most of a day. I was the dogged one, hounding a subject mercilessly, while Barbara was

167

graceful as a cat, playing with meaning until she pounced. Two naively idealistic Aquarians with a passion for Irish myth — how greedily we talked! But similar tastes and opinions alone do not make a friendship. Generous and wise and kind, Barbara could sustain connection over years and miles. I think, in fact, our first conversation never really ended, continuing by post and later e-mail when I was in America, in rambly hours whenever I was in Ireland.

Our best talks always took place at Barbara's house — the old house, her home for a dozen years before the new one was built over in Dawros, on that seaside lot where we paced out imagined walls on stony ground, here's where the computer will go, here's the dining table, won't the view be grand from the fire — but that fine new Dawros house fades in my memory beside the old stone cottage where we sat before the fireplace, dishes bursting from the dresser beyond, books and albums spread around, a disordered sense of an abundant life interrupted right in its midst...

To reach Barbara's old house, you turned off the Cleggan Road and jounced along for a quarter mile to a precipitous drop, at the bottom of which was a tiny turnaround above another sharp cliff. I was never sure what unnerved me more: launching out over the hill and careering down until the moment came to slam on the brakes, or edging in a tight circle until I faced back up the hill and floored the accelerator to the top. That driveway always provided an excuse to have another cup of tea. But even had the drive been less daunting, I would have lingered, for with Barbara there was always one more yarn to spin, one more theory to explore, one more song to sing.

That afternoon, we sat companionably, rain drumming on the roof, Barbara prodding the flame awake every hour or so. A few days before, I had picked snowdrops at Brigit's well in warm Kildare, but winter still held Connemara in its steely trap. We'd planned to assess progress on the Dawros house but sank instead into the comforts of milky tea and talk. My visit to Kildare reminded Barbara that Brigit was often depicted leading a cow. "I wonder, was it a white cow?" pondered Barbara. "Like the one on Inisbofin?"

I knew Inisbofin as the long island, all blue and misty, visible from Barbara's driveway just before the descent. Some claimed it was Hy-Brâzil, the fairy isle named for Brigit's husband Bres, the beautiful ungenerous son of the goddess Ériu. But Inisbofin was fixed in time and space, while Hy-Brâzil rose from the depths only once every seven years and migrated freely about the oceans — at least it did until the Spaniards finally locked it down in South America.

I knew all that, but I knew nothing of cows on Inisbofin.

Barbara laughed, a tinkly sound. "You of all people! Can't you tell from the name?"

Inisbofin? Even with my sparse Irish, I could puzzle out *inis bó finne,* isle of the white cow. But the name's significance escaped me.

Another tinkling laugh. "Bó Finne," Barbara said. "Come on, now, Bó Finne. Think! *Tagan chughainn an Bó Finne, le críonnach is cabhair dár saol.*" Her graceful voice traced ornate patterns in the song. "The White Cow comes to us with wisdom and help for our life."

"Bó Finne? The cow goddess?" Barbara was right: I knew Bó Finne from Lady Wilde's folklore compilation. One primeval May morning, the radiant Bó Finne and her sisters, red Bó Rua and black Bó Dubh, rose from the sea. Each headed off in a different direction: red to the north, black to the south, Bó Finne to the center, there to bear the twin calves from whom all Ireland's cattle descend. Somewhere in a hillside cave, the legend has it, she still lives, ruminating upon the future when she will be queen of the land.

Little else is known of Bó Finne, a divinity of unknown age who, although virtually absent from written texts, we can track across the land she fructified with her passage. Tiny stone monuments mark where she slept, while her name hides in places like Ardbo (cow's height) in Tyrone; Benbo (cow mountain) in Leitrim; Dunboe (fortress of the cow) in Derry; Lough Bofin (white cow lake); and the Boyne (her great milky river). And, I now recognized, Inisbofin, the White Cow's Island.

Barbara's gentle song had been inspired by a tale told on the island. Once, she told me, two fishermen set out in clear weather but were overtaken by a fierce storm near Inisbofin. Realizing they could not make it safely back to the mainland, the men beached their curragh and made a rough camp inside a fairy rath at the end of the island. There they hunkered down, pulling their sweaters up around their ears in a vain attempt to keep dry.

Suddenly, out of the darkness, emerged a stunning apparition: a beautiful young woman leading a white cow. Now, anyone with the dimmest of sense would recognize that beautiful young women, with or without white cows, should be greeted with caution when they appear within raths, for such places are well-known entrances to the Otherworld. But these men were not the sharpest hooks in the creel. They exchanged a wink and a nod, then pounced. One man jumped the girl, the other grabbed the cow.

The mist suddenly grew thicker, until the men could no longer see what they were doing. Undeterred, they clung to their prizes, though both cow and girl struggled valiantly against them. Moments later, the mist cleared. One man found himself hugging a boulder of white quartz, while the other held a slimy handful of seaweed. *"Don duine santach níl fágtha..."* Barbara sang. "For the greedy one, nothing's left but a sea rod in place of the cow's tail." From that time forward, the men's lives were cursed, and they died miserably not long afterward. But the woman and her cow remain free, rising every seven years from the lake in the middle of the island.

Barbara looked at me with bright eager eyes, knowing I too would see the story as "a country conducive to wandering, with plenty of unmarked roads, unexpected vistas, and unforeseen occurrences," in anthropologist Keith Basso's words. Like our best journeys, our best conversations began this way, without maps, with only fragments of lore to guide us, our destination the goal but never the purpose of our wandering.

"Doesn't she remind you of the Glas, the cow of abundance?" I ventured. Like Bó Finne, the green-spotted white Glas is rarely mentioned in written texts but wanders through oral legend, ceaselessly giving milk, increasing her output whenever famine threatens. She filled every bucket, no matter the size, until a wicked soul used a sieve to milk her dry. The Glas turned the milker to stone, then ascended to the heavens to graze on what we call the Milky Way: in Irish, *Bealach na Bó Finne,* the White Cow's Path.

"Well, she would, of course!" Barbara agreed. "They're the same creature. Don't you know there is another Inisbofin, off the northern coast, where the Glas once stopped to graze? And Brigit's cow, the same again. Remember the story of the lepers?" Indeed I did: once Brigit met two lepers begging for alms. She had nothing to give them except her cow, whose milk was so rich that one pail churned enough butter for a province. One leper praised Brigit's generosity, but the other grabbed for the cow, which ambled away, always keeping a few steps ahead of the greedy beggar. They reached the Liffey River, which rose in a sudden flood, drowning both beggar and cow.

"The tales all warn of the consequences of greed," Barbara pointed out.

"All the cows disappear when someone demands too much." I nodded, then frowned. "I wonder, though — can a domesticated animal give willingly?" My friend the ecocritic Joe Meeker employs words like *slavery* and *colonization* to describe herding, for no apparent advantage accrues to animals who fill our walking larder. Whyever do they stay around? Do they not recognize us as predators? For that is what we were, millions of years ago, migrating with the herds, using drums or fire to stampede panicked animals over cliffs or into canyons, gorging ourselves on the rare taste of meat.

"Early human life does seem nasty, brutish and short," Barbara said.

"Nah, that was my old boss." Barbara caught the joke and grinned. "Short — maybe, we don't really know," I returned to the subject of Stone Age economies, "but certainly not nasty or brutish. We worked for a few hours a day and spent the rest hanging out." Anthropologist Marshall Sahlins has called the age of the hunter-gatherer "the original affluent society." For the desert-dwelling !Kung of Africa, still a subsistence culture, four hours a day is enough to gather their hearty meals. In the time it takes agriculturalists to build root cellars, weave storage baskets, and make and sharpen tools, nonagriculturalists cement bonds of kinship through an elaborate system of reciprocal sharing.

I have some sense of that ancient affluence, for I grew up surrounded by wild food. For weeks each Alaskan summer, I gathered berries and herbs and mushrooms. Cranberry bogs stretched out, green streaked with gold, unpickably vast. Raspberries hung luscious and fat in the dappled sunlight. Certainly, there were years when rain demolished the belled blossoms of blueberries, but those might be years of abundant mushrooms. Years when the salmon run was low, we might get a moose. With so many kinds of food available, there is always something to eat.

But bad weather, changes in migratory routes, and competing predators, it was once believed, led to intermittent scarcity that inspired the invention of agriculture. More recent studies disagree, showing that famine and epidemics actually increased with that invention some seven thousand years ago. No one can explain why we stopped following the reliable seasonal cycles of ripening plants and migrating herds. But one thing's for sure: once settled, we had to feed ourselves. Plants had long been our dietary mainstay; campsites from two million years ago reveal tubers baking in ash, looking for all the world like a Girl Scout cookout. Our first agricultural ventures involved dividing and planting such tubers. Seeds and fruits soon followed.

If scholars cannot explain the invention of agriculture, neither can they explain the rise of husbandry over the next thousand years. We had long been hunting partners with dogs; we kept orphaned animals for pets; but herds with horns are different. Historian of domestication Edward Hyams believes cattle made the first contact, seeing our fields as pastures. We killed off the most aggressive, leaving the docile to reproduce. But domestication meant convincing captive animals to breed. Not all animals were up for this; gazelles, ibis, antelope, and hyena died in the corrals of ancient Egyptians in what James Joyce called "pharoaph times." But one animal agreed to breed: Irish geneticists Christopher Troy and David MacHugh have determined that all European cattle, *Bos taurus,* descend from early Egyptian cows.

"And didn't she get to be a god-desh right way," said Barbara, affecting a broad Connemara accent.

"Ah, Hathor," I chimed in. "And wasn't she a white cow herself." Stone Age cave paintings reveal the cow as one of humanity's earliest religious icons; increased proximity only heightened her importance. In Greece she became cow-eyed Hera of the riverine sanctuaries, in Lithuania she was Marsa, Mother of Cows, who gives milk from an inexhaustible well. In Egypt, the great sky-cow's teats rained milk on the earth. In India, too, the clouds were cows, rain pouring from their udders, until a demon stole all their milk and brought worldwide famine.

Such myths reflect the lives of early agriculturalists, to whom a cow was no mere steak-in-waiting but an inexhaustible resource. Her strength was harnessed to plow or wagon. Her dung provided fertilizer and fuel. But her most important use was unimaginable to our hunting ancestors. If domestication is mysterious, milking is unfathomable. Other mammals stop drinking milk in adulthood and never imbibe the milk of other species. Now, I can understand that humans thirst for milk, but why should any animal agree to quench that thirst? And agreement is at the heart of the exchange, for while other foods can be taken, milk must be given. A human drinking a cow's milk requires a cow willing to be milked. It's easy enough to kick the bucket, both literally and figuratively; many animals died in captivity, still untamed.

"In the myth, the Glas offers her milk," offered Barbara.

"Couldn't that just be guilt speaking?" I said into my tea.

"Ah, now, I'd hate to think that," Barbara winced. "Is taking from animals the only way we can relate to them?"

"Relate? Hm. Pass me the dictionary?" I asked. Dimly I remembered an old word, an obsolete plural. Cattle, we learned, is a relatively new word, derived from the same root as *chattel* and *capital.* The original plural of *cow* was *kine,* a word lost except in its derivatives: *kind,* which originally meant any action that sustained the natural order, a usage remembered in the medieval name for Mother Nature, Dame Kind; and words of relationship, *kin* and *kindred* and *kinfolk.*

Having drifted far afield from our starting point, we now doubled back on our trail. Domesticates are social animals, used to reading complex social maps. Cow society, once comprised just of other cows, somehow enlarged to include humans. The stories of the friendly Bó Finne and the generous Glas hinted at an ancient wisdom about animals accepting us as children.

A sudden commotion stopped our explorations. Dave Hogan, Barbara's genial husband, had arrived with their sons, Brian and Kevin. Wouldn't I stay for dinner? Of course, of course. Dave set to work making chicken for the three of us, and vegetables with rice for vegan Barbara. Soon we were eating and drinking, laughing and singing, making music and telling stories.

Then Dave broke the news.

He and Barbara exchanged a significant look and a nod. "I'm working on a project," he began slowly. Knowing of Dave's part in the Brigit revival in Letterfrack and the fight to stop the strip-mining of Croagh Patrick, I leaned forward, curious. "We're lighting the Bealtaine fires for the millennium." He paused dramatically. "At Uisneach."

He went on, talking enthusiastically, describing the project's genesis, work accomplished, website plans — but I heard only a blur of sound.

The Bealtaine fires? On Uisneach hill?

Once all Celtic lands had celebrated Bealtaine — "bright fire" — a festival marking the end of spring's scarcity, often described as a fertility rite with maidenheads merrily lost and marital status conveniently forgotten ("hurrah, it's May, the lusty month of May"). But we have no proof of "orgies of wasteful eating, woeful drinking, rioting and wantonness" that

Puritan demagogues claimed were the norm. Bealtaine sexuality may have been mostly symbolic (phallic Maypoles and beefy Morris dancers), but nonetheless the unrelenting Puritans pushed through a law in 1644 against Bealtaine celebrations that stood until 1975, when the old spring holiday snuck back again as an English bank holiday. But in Ireland not even banks recognize Bealtaine. While other Celtic feasts found safe harbor in Irish Christianity — Lughnasa became Garland Sunday; Samhain, All Saints; Imbolc, Brigit's Day — Bealtaine remained uncontrovertibly pagan, a symbol of the old ways.

And the symbol of their passing. As a girl, I had learned the story of Saint Patrick and the Easter fires. All Ireland's fires had been dowsed, down to the last hearth fire in the lowliest cottage. Beneath Uisneach, the hill where the druid Míde had once kindled a blaze that lasted seven years, a great tribal assembly called the Oenach gathered to await the lighting of twin fires. On nearby Tara stood druids who would light an answering fire, after which the land's remaining fires would spring to life.

In darkness Ireland waited for the fiery signal that the season had turned, that the land would soon bear fruit again. But instead of a fire in the center, there was a blaze from an insignificant corner. Outraged druids stampeded to Slane Hill to find Patrick standing over a fire. He held up a shamrock, discoursed on the Trinity, and converted the druids with his eloquence. (So said the tame version of my girlhood. Ancient texts tell wilder stories involving the saint turning milk curds into stone and setting druids on fire. They also record Patrick's gloating pronouncement: "In this hour all paganism in Ireland has been destroyed." This grandiose verdict was premature: Irish paganism has proven more wily than any serpent.)

It was many years before I realized that pagan Ireland could not have been celebrating Easter. What Patrick lit was a Bealtaine blaze — not only an affront to the king's power but as a threat to the sacred order that assured the land's fertility. No wonder the druids were mad. After Patrick's usurpation, the Church substituted Christ for the milky animal-mother and diverted celebration of life springing from death to Easter. But Bealtaine was not to be extinguished. Lady Wilde remembers Dublin's fires: "The entire population of the district collected round the fire; the elder portion, men and women, bringing with them chairs or stools, to set out the wake of the winter according to the olden usage." In rural areas, says folklorist Kevin Danaher, bonfires remained customary on the eve of May 1. As late as 1740, Irish scholar John Toland described pairs of beacons, "every one in sight of some other," illuminating the springtime land. The day's sanctity was submerged, the tribal assemblies degenerated into cattle markets, but the fires still blazed.

Bealtaine folkways emphasized cattle: garlands of marigolds — the "Bealtaine shrub" — were placed around cow's necks; wells were "milked" with skimmers to gather the first water of May; special dishes like syllabub (fresh milk and whiskey) were concocted. The Irish celebrated, but an undercurrent of caution ran through Bealtaine, for cattle are most at risk of disease in springtime. An ancient Gaelic blessing asked protection for "all kine and crops, all flocks and corn, from Bealtaine eve to Samhain eve, from sea to sea and every river mouth, from wave to wave, and base of waterfall." The twin Bealtaine fires were believed to have a prophylactic effect, so cattle were driven between them with prayers for their safety.

Cattle disease endangered winter-weakened herds, but the fresh sweet grass of Bealtaine soon strengthened them. Even into the twentieth century the rural Irish calendar revolved around the movement of flocks on Samhain and Bealtaine. Every May 1, the herds were booleyed to lush mountain pastures, to remain there until November 1, when they were driven home. Girls tended the cows through the sweet summer days, living in rough huts called shielings, milking each morning, making butter and cheese, packing the produce into churns to bury in chilly bogs for safekeeping. It was a simple life, full of music, because it was believed that cows gave more milk when serenaded.

Such folk traditions long outlasted the religion that inspired them, becoming seasonal traditions rather than religious ones. No one knows what the original festival might have been, but the great scholar of sacred landscapes, Michael Dames, has attempted a reconstruction. He imagines Uisneach, Ireland's magical central hill, as the center of an ancient fire festival in which the mythic hills were set alight. When Uisneach's twin fires were ablaze, royal Tara responded, then passed the torch eastward to Knockawlin and Almu; then the south, the Mother Mountain, went alight; then the western rath of Medb at Cruachain were lit; and finally the north, Ulster, with Emain Macha at the center, until all Ireland was netted in light.

Lighting the Bealtaine fires? The double fires of spring symbolized the eyes of the earth goddess Ériu opening to the new season. And Uisneach hill, site of the greatest ancient gathering, was the spiritual center of Ireland. The rain drummed loudly on the window as though pounding into my mind the significance of Dave's words. Would I be there for the relighting? Of course, I said, of course. I wouldn't miss it.

⨯⨯⨯⨯⨯

The millennial spring seemed almost tangible that February evening as we drew closer to the fire, dreaming aloud, reciting poetry, telling tales. It was Imbolc, day of the triple Brigit, feast of the first milk, spring's awakening. A time of promise. Had I known, that sweet night, what paths we would walk together, would I — would we — have felt such hope, such delight?

One of life's great kindnesses is that we can read its patterns only in retrospect. For life is like a river cutting channels into the landscape of our souls, one day at a time, one drop at a time. Or like a cow, that meandering architect of Irish roads — boreens, they are called, cow trails — tracing indirect routes across the land so that, like Irish conversation, nothing ever goes directly from here to there but veers aside whenever a green pasture calls . . .

In the dim past, unknown druids lit the final Bealtaine blazes on Uisneach hill, never dreaming how many centuries would pass before the fire-eyes of the goddess Ériu opened on a new spring. Ireland stood beneath them, great common pastures opening green amid darker oak and ash. Dotted across those pastures were the herds on which the people's wealth was based, cattle that provided the rich milk — "white meat" — that formed the basis of the Irish diet. "The Irish," said sixteenth-century travel writer John Stevens, "are the greatest lovers of milk I have ever met, which they eat and drink in about twenty different ways," while the poet of the medieval *Vision of Mac Conglinne* praised "very thick milk, milk not too thick, milk of long thickness, milk of medium thickness, yellow bubbling milk, and milk the swallowing of which needs chewing."

Celtic Ireland was a literal land of milk and honey, known throughout the ancient world for the wealth of its lands, herds, and larders. Its people lived in what Russian economist Alexander Chayanov described as a typical peasant economy, providing their own necessities and sharing the occasional surplus in community celebrations. There was no tragedy of the commons, no need for owners to protect Ireland's pastures with fences, for Celtic society assured that one's greed did not destroy the sustenance of all. Ireland's fertile well-manured fields, plus her abundant wild foods — salmon, whortleberries, apples, acorns — provided for her people, who paid a portion of their produce as tribute to chiefs who redistributed that wealth through hospitality. Generosity was Ireland's prime social value, with lowly farmers emulating chiefs by keeping an open door and a spread table for every passing stranger. Folklorist Bríd Mahon notes that "even marauders such as the Vikings were astonished at the unsurpassing hospitality of the Irish" and took home the habit of building houses at crossroads to multiply the possibility of visitors.

Celtic Ireland expressed worth in *cumhals,* each the value of three milking cows. But after the thirteenth century, coin of the realm — the English realm, for Ireland was its neighbor's first experiment in colonization — replaced the ancient system of barter. The institution of working for wages was slow to catch on in Ireland as the economy entered what Karl Marx called the period of "primitive accumulation of capital." Laws were passed denying people the right to provide their sustenance, thus "divorcing the producer from the means of production," as Marx put it. In 1349, King Edward II signed the Ordinance of Laborers, forbidding charity to "sturdy beggars" who refused to work. Then came the poorly named Poor Laws; they should have been called Rich Laws, for their prohibition on gathering, hunting, and fishing steered money into merchants' pockets by forcing rural people into waged work, with threats of amputation of limbs and even execution against those who refused.

With wages came profit for the landowners — Ireland, designated as an agricultural resource by England, was not industrialized — and poverty for an increasing number of the Irish. In 1729, Jonathan Swift was staying with friends in County Cavan, from which he wrote his friend Alexander Pope that "there have been three terrible years' dearth of corn, and every place strewed with beggars...Imagine a nation the two thirds of whose revenues are spent out of it, and who are not permitted to trade with the other third." This poverty inspired Swift's greatest and most savage essay, his "Modest Proposal" in which he reveals his plan to serve up suckling child: "I have been assured by a very knowing American, that a young healthy child well nursed is at a year old a most delicious, nourishing and wholesome food, whether stewed, roasted, baked, or boiled; and I make no doubt that it will equally serve in a fricassee or a ragout. I grant this food will be somewhat dear, and therefore very proper for landlords, who, as

they have already devoured most of the parents, seem to have the best title
to the children."

The Irish well understood the economic stratagems of emerging capitalism. When the eighteenth-century sojourner Nassau Senior — who
found the Irish peculiarly immune to the temptation of "ribands, lace and
velvets" — lectured Connacht children on the need for industry, they reasoned with him that if a person worked four times faster, an employer
would then lay off three-quarters of the workforce. Senior thought their
reply showed them "unaware of the indefinite variety and extent of men's
wants." But various and extensive wants were less important to the economically marginalized Irish than their actual needs, primary among
which was sufficient food.

Despite colonization, Ireland clung to Celtic values until the nineteenth century, when suddenly "customs and traditions that had survived
against all the odds for two thousand years or more were swept away,"
Bríd Mahon says. "Never again would unstinted and prodigal hospitality
be taken for granted." The wrenching change had roots in the late-
seventeenth-century introduction of a South American tuber that grew
spectacularly well in Ireland. Soon potatoes were the only food available
to the rural Irish; on a typical day's fare of ten pounds of potatoes and a
glass of buttermilk, people stayed healthy and strong. Because potatoes
need so little growing space, tenants saw their subsistence land allocations
steadily shrink while pasturelands were extended to supply cheap beef for
the increasingly urban English population.

In 1846, disaster struck: an airborne fungus that turned potatoes into
black slime attacked the Isle of Wight. It spread rapidly through Europe,
forcing people to rely on other foods until the blight passed. But the Irish
had nothing else to eat; without potatoes, they starved. Temperance cru-
sader Father Matthew described the scene: "In July, I saw this doomed
plant blooming in all the luxuriance of an abundant harvest. In early
August I beheld with sorrow one wide waste of putrefying vegetation. The
wretched people were seated on the fences of their decaying gardens,
wringing their hands and wailing bitterly at the destruction."

The destruction of the potato crop was the destruction of the people.
But it need not have been so. As the great economist Amartya Sen has
shown, lack of food does not cause famine: lack of entitlement to food
does. Ireland did not lack food. Vast herds of cattle grazed on grass that

waxed green in the same wet weather that spread the potato blight. The Irish starved while landlords exported these cattle under armed guard. In 1847 — still called "Black 47" in Ireland — a million tubs of butter and almost two million gallons of alcohol distilled from Irish grain sailed for England. Rabbits, honey, salmon, and, in the deepest of ironies, potatoes were all exported on the four thousand ships that left Ireland for England that year, during which four hundred thousand Irish people starved.

The Famine continued for years. "The dreadful reality is beyond yea or nay in this country," a Connacht newspaper reported woefully. "From one end to the other the weal has gone forth that the rot is increasing with fearful rapidity." Observers saw roadsides strewn with "emaciated corpses, partly green from eating docks and nettles," and children of an eerie paleness who looked "as if they had been thawed out of the ice, in which they had been imbedded until their blood had turned to water." Charity, believed to foster indolence, was withheld. The Quakers swam against this current, opening the world's first soup kitchens. Other relief required work for wages that failed to cover the inflated cost of food. Employees on these public projects — the "Famine Roads" that still snake across the land — were starved and worked to death, as economist Pat McGregor has shown. Then there were the workhouses, which offered minimal food, hard work, overcrowded conditions, and a massive mortality rate, but which were mobbed with those who saw no other hope.

Desperate people took desperate measures. They ate anything they could find: weeds, seaweed, even in some dreadful cases the bloating bodies of other victims. They stole blood from the necks of living cattle, which Bob Curran believes gave rise to the vampire legends that Dubliner Bram Stoker made famous not long after. Weakened by hunger, the Irish succumbed to the diseases that run wherever famine walks. Typhus and fever raged; a Dr. Daly reported that from May to May "fever, dysentery and diarrhoea are greatly on the increase, beginning with vomiting, pains, headache very intense."

No one knows how many died. In 1847, English Tory leader Lord George Bentinck accused the government of lying about the number of deaths: "I dare them to inquire what has been the number of those who have died through principles of free trade. Yes, free trade in the lives of Irish people." Perhaps a million and a half died from starvation and disease, their bodies piled into mass graves or thrown into shallow ones by the roadside. Sometimes a cabin was simply pushed in upon a family of victims by neighbors who feared catching fever from the bodies. Anyone who could fled. But emigration held its own dangers, for many died on what came to be called the coffin ships, barely seaworthy vessels with herds of starving passengers crowded into their dim holds. As an American official wrote at the time, "If corpses and tombs could be erected on the water, the whole route of the emigrant vessels would long since have assumed the appearance of a crowded cemetery."

Four years of famine, six more of disease, and the population of Ireland was reduced by one-third. Those who survived faced new losses when Sir William Gregory — later to wed Lady Augusta, whose woods at Coole I know so well — proposed the "congested districts" scheme. Declaring anything less than a quarter acre inefficient, he arranged for the denial of relief to small farmers, who were forced to move or starve. Other farmers lost tenancy because, despite the Famine, landlords expected to be paid. Waiving back rent was unthinkable; in the cruel words of Irish Undersecretary General Buller, "if Paddy once gets regularly to no rent you will require to kill a good many of them before you get him back again." The absentee landlords so bled the people that they became known as "Vampire-Invisibles." Tenants were thrown out on the roads, their houses leveled to prevent them from returning. The *Castlebar Telegraph* reported seeing "wretched creatures endeavoring to root out the timber of their houses, with the intention of constructing some sort of sheds.... The pitiless pelting storm continued, and if they have survived its severity, they must be more than human beings." The milk of human kindness seemed to have run dry.

The evicted farmers were replaced by cattle because, as Kathleen Villiers-Tuthill puts it, "the income from rents was unreliable and troublesome to collect." Within two decades, more than half of Ireland was converted to pasturage; the number of cattle exported to England doubled. Landlords grew wealthier; farmers barely survived, for subsistence allotments were not enlarged. Then, in 1880, a summer of drenching rain caused the potato crop to fail once again. General Gerard Gordon, sent by Prime Minister Gladstone to explore the situation, wrote back that, "The state of our fellow countrymen is worse than that of any people in the world. I believe that these people are made as we are, that they are patient beyond belief, loyal, but at the same time broken spirited and desperate, living on the verge of starvation in places where we would not keep our cattle."

Where storytellers once spoke of the great generous cow, we now find tales of the Hungry Grass, strange patches that remain dangerous even today, for to step there causes death from famished agony. Animals must not eat Hungry Grass, which kills cows as readily as people. Some say Hungry Grass grew under unburied corpses during the Famine, others that it covers grave-yards where victims lie, unmarked, unmourned, unremembered. And the tale of the Hungry Grass was not the only new myth to emerge from An Gorta Mór, the Great Hunger: the beautiful fairy queen, the red-haired girl who stole humans away to her sparkling fairyland, reappeared in a new dreadful guise as *an gcailligh rua,* the red-haired hag who killed without mercy.

※※※※※

My mother's family lived through the Famine. But who they were, and how they survived, we do not know. Historical documents tell me that the average diet consisted of eight meals a month in east Mayo, so I assume my tenant-farmer ancestors endured such privation. Our family history does not begin until the birth of my great-grandmother Honore Dunleavy in 1856 into an empty impoverished land. She married a man named Gordon, whose name is lost; when he died, she married another Gordon. ("No relation," says my family. "In Mayo we were so poor we owned hardly any names.") Honore passed down a legacy of Famine fears. My grandfather, born decades after the Famine, raised us in fear of penury; the slightest squandering brought forth the threat, "Keep that up and you'll end in the poorhouse!" I was in my teens before I discovered that there were no poorhouses in America.

East Mayo, one of the most depopulated areas during the Famine, remains poor even today. In a Swiftian mood, I once conceived a plan to corral money into the local economy: the East Mayo Famine Museum. With heritage tours a thriving industry, Bohola could capitalize on its past by building a village of rude cottages from which rag-clad people would hold out their hands for alms; tourists would read informative plaques beside the historical reenactments. Now here's the genius part: a second-ary business in what the Irish call "slimming," with plump customers pay-ing to enact the parts of Famine victims. Marx articulated the concept of "surplus value": profit as the difference between cost and price. In my plan there is none of the former and plenty of the latter.

Economists tell us that surplus value creates scarcity; primitively accumulated wealth is never equally distributed. The rich get richer, the poor get hungry. Ancient Ireland, by contrast, was a land with food galore. And I mean that in its original intent. The word that now means "excess" is an anglicization of the Irish term for "enough." Once "potatoes galore" meant "sufficient potatoes for our needs." But need is devalued in an economy based on surplus value, which must endlessly fan greed. Our language tells the path we have walked: *stock* is not a herd, *mine* is not a quarry. *Brand* no longer refers to cattle markings, and *share* no longer has anything to do with generosity.

German economist Claudia von Werlhof contends that acquisitiveness creates both want and waste. Nature is naturally abundant, like a nursing mother — "The more the child drinks, the more there is" — but greed is a vampire that sucks everything dry. Through most of human history, we worked to meet our needs: for food, clean water, dry homes. Once needs were met, we turned to satisfying desires: for companionship, sex, laughter, beauty. But there is no profit in a child's smile, none in a true love's touch. Need and desire can be satisfied, but greed is limitless and puts impossible demands on our world. Economist Maria Mies says, "Modern industrial society destroys, with its relentless pursuit of continuous growth of goods and money, the ability of nature to regenerate herself, until she is totally exhausted." In the language of myth, we are milking the great Glas into a sieve.

⊠⊠⊠⊠

A sieve is not a natural object; someone invented it, someone else forged it. Marx said that greed demands technology, whose role is to be "constantly revolutionizing the instruments of production" until "all that is holy is profaned." But Marx wrote of a technology already in the service of capital. The Celts saw things differently. To them, technology was not profane but sacred — indeed, magical. The smelting and working of metals were religious acts, because magicians transformed one thing into another. They were alchemists who made useful tools and beautiful jewelry from apparently useless rock. The intimate technology of the Celtic smith was more art than industry, a form of poetry or of healing.

The god of metalworkers, Goibniu, was symbolized by a cauldron of abundance. It is no surprise then to find him associated with Ireland's primordial deity of generosity, the great Glas. In folklore, Goibniu was humanized into Galvan, a smith from County Cavan who was so busy at the forge that he found a herdsman — sometimes called Cian, sometimes Fin — to follow the Glas as she ranged the countryside. Fin was warned never to get in the cow's way, never to slow her down, never to hinder her passage — and to stay awake, no matter what. For the Glas was endlessly stalked by Balor, fierce Fomorian consort of the land goddess Ériu, whom James Joyce called the "Tortor of Tory Island." From his sea-swept home, Balor plotted to steal the Glas for his daughter Eithne, whose diet consisted solely of sweet fresh milk.

The Glas kept an exhausting pace, covering miles each day in her apparently aimless meanderings. Finally she wore Fin out. Balor caught him napping and stole the Glas, whereupon an enraged Galvan threatened Fin with death if the Glas was not returned. So Fin traveled stealthily to Tory Island. There he noticed a high tower, and in it, a lovely maiden. Druids had once prophesied that Eithne's son would kill her father, so Balor locked his daughter up with a bunch of maidens. But prophecies are not so easily thwarted. Fin draped himself in women's garb and slipped into the tower. There he seduced Eithne and lived as her handmaiden until she bore their child.

There is a reason that Eithne could drink only cow's milk, for she was bovine herself. Her other name is Bóand — a name that, like its variant Bó Finne, means "white cow." These goddesses derive from various mythic traditions, but all converge in the figure of the cow of abundance. To the Celts, an abundant goddess was naturally aquatic, for they saw rivers as the land's fructifying force. Celtic rivers were named for goddesses — Danube for Danu, Seine for Sequana, Clyde for Clutoida. But Celtic rivers were not typically cows. In Ireland, the Celts encountered a primordial cow goddess who meandered across the land like a majestic river, generously feeding her kin as a river feeds the plants of its watershed. Herding folk, the Celts knew rivers were necessary to cows, which unlike sheep cannot survive on the moisture in grass; thus a connection was forged between an immigrant river goddess and an indigenous cow, and Bóand was born.

Bóand's river, the Boyne, bends around the great megalithic shrine where she lived with her husband, the salmon god Elcmar. The Boyne, as "Bouvinda," appears among the earliest Irish river names, recorded in the writings of Egyptian geographer Ptolemy, who also gives Logia, "female calf," as the name of the Ulster river now called the Lagan; the lake near its head, Belfast Lough, is still called in Irish Loch Lóig, "calf lake." The old name of the Blackwater was Bó Guaire, the cow of King Guaire; the nearby Borora derives its name from Bó Finne's sister, Bó Rua. The little river Inny that flows near Uisneach wears the name of Eithne. Ireland's rivers became so associated with the divine cow's nourishing milk that the name of the great Glas herself became a word for a small clear stream.

If the first part of Bóand's name means "cow," the second syllable means "white," a word that in Irish also implies both "shining" and "wise." Thus the white cow was the Wise Cow, for Bóand traveled to the magical well of Connla, named for a prince stolen from Uisneach by a fairy queen. Around the well grew nine hazel trees whose nuts, falling into the water, formed bubbles of inspiration. Otherworldly salmon ate the nuts, developing a red spot on their backs for each nut consumed. Every seven years, uneaten nuts drifted down the river, and anyone who ate them became a great seer.

Within the well swam a one-eyed salmon: Fintan, the oldest living creature in the world. Anyone who caught him could absorb all his wisdom. Only one man ever hooked the salmon, the druid Finnécas, who dedicated seven years to the task. The druid assigned a young helper, Fionn, to oversee the roasting. When a bubble appeared on the fish's skin, the boy pressed it down with his thumb, burning himself. Wisdom passed into the digit, which thereafter Fionn had only to suck to see the future. Immediately he burst into song, praising the month in which he had received his illumination: "Maytime, fair season, perfect is its aspect then; blackbirds sing a full song."

The repetition of "Finn" in the story — the syllable for wisdom that appears in Bó Finne's name — is not accidental. Nor are the other duplications: Bóand's husband, Elcmar, is a salmon; Bóand's other name is Eithne, "sweet nut-meat." Meanings flow together like swollen rivers, the wise cow turning into the nuts of wisdom, the husband playing in his wife's bright waters, Fionn the seer netting Fintan the salmon, the boy gaining wisdom from his fish-self. Where such shape-shifting is found, we stand at the limits of expression, a place beyond the territory marked on language's maps. As mythographer Michael Dames points out, the mythic mind is able to travel in such places because it does not follow a binary "either/or" code but employs "both/and" terms. Wisdom hides in apparent confusion like a salmon in a secret pool.

Finnécas was not the only seeker of wisdom. Bóand too sought the well, though she had been banned from approaching it — a prohibition whose source the myth does not reveal. As Bóand reached it, a splash blinded her in one eye, making her a double of the one-eyed Fintan. Then the well burst its banks and pursued the goddess out to sea. Texts vary as to what happened next: some say the water drowned Bóand, whose body formed the river; others that Bóand outran the water, which could never thereafter be contained within the well.

Many commentators see Bóand's story as a warning to women against overstepping themselves. According to Celticist James MacKillop, Bóand "defied the magical powers" and "violated taboos"; he describes the goddess as little more than a headstrong, careless girl. But such interpretations miss the point; without Bóand's daring approach, the water would have stayed within its pool, never fructifying the land. Like the Glas, who needed to wander freely, rivers provide most abundance when un-restrained. At worst, Bóand's story is one of a *felix culpa,* a happy fault. More deeply, the story is a creation myth in which woman's search for wisdom creates the world anew.

A minor figure in Bóand's myth — the goddess's little lapdog who drowned along with her — expands its meaning. Little lapdogs do not appear often in Irish myth. Indeed, only one other is known, in the tale of Lí Ban, found in the great Book of the Dun Cow. Once an unnamed woman failed to replace the lid on a well, whose water rose in a great flood. The guilty woman escaped, but the family of Lí Ban was killed, including her sister, Ariu (no relation, apparently, to Ériu), leaving Lí Ban alone with her lapdog in a house beneath the waves.

Watching the speckled salmon swim by, Lí Ban prayed for freedom. Her prayer was answered: Lí Ban became a fish with the head of a woman, while her little dog was turned into an otter. After three centuries, the two were hauled up in a net. A row ensued as to their owner, an argument settled when cows came forth from the grave of Lí Ban's sister, Ariu, and carried them away. The inclusion of the dog in the stories may seem inconsequential, but in Celtic iconography, dogs served as guardians of water goddesses in their healing aspect; the source of a river was a depository for tiny emblems of limbs, breasts, eyes, left as silent prayers for miraculous return to health. Dogs are also psychopomps who lead the dead into the Otherworld. Prayers to the river were always answered, but whether by healing or death was left up to the wisdom of the goddess.

❈❈❈❈

My friend Fiona Marron once painted the river that runs through the town of Clane, where she was raised and still lives. It is the Liffey, which despite its smallness is one of Ireland's most famous rivers, the river that inspired James Joyce to create his heroine Anna Livia Plurabelle: "Annah the Allmaziful, the Everliving, the Bringer of Plurabilities, haloed be her eve, her singtime sung, her rill be run, unhemmed as it is uneven!" Anna Livia snakes her way through *Finnegans Wake* as the Liffey does through the countryside around Dublin, as generous a presence as the great Glas — "She must have been a gadabout in her day, so she must, more than most" — becoming goddess, woman, river all at once in Joyce's visionary prose.

The river is just such a muse to Fiona. "I love its Irish name, *An Life,* such a wonderful pun on the English word," she told me as we ate dinner at a Chinese restaurant in Clane. She tried, in her huge blue-green paintings, to capture the feminine power of the water as it fructified the land, what Joyce described in my favorite passage: "first of all, worst of all, the wiggly livvly, she sideslipped out by a gap in the Devil's glen while Sally her nurse was sound asleep in a sloot and, feefee fiefie, fell over a slipway before she found her stride and lay and wriggled in all the stagnant black pools of rain under a fallow coo and she laughed innocefree with her limbs aloft and a whole drove of maiden hawthorns blushing and looking askance upon her."

To paint the river, Fiona walked its entire length, including slogging out to its source in the center of a great raised bog at the base of the mountains of Kippure, where Joyce says "she was just a young thin pale soft slim slip of a thing." The Liffey streams forth from black peat, to run its course and end in the Black Pool of Dublin. "It was magical," Fiona said, "really magical, a pool of water so small, so intimate, you could fit it in the palm of your hand." At such sources, the river's power was believed most condensed; it was there that the river's wisdom swam.

Inspired by Fiona, I decided to find the source of the Boyne. The wavery blue line on my map stopped somewhere near the old Quaker town of Edenderry, so I made inquiries there. Irish directions being notoriously unclear, I've long since learned to stop and ask for help even when I think I know where I'm going. Once with a set of written directions in hand, I arrived at Rooney's, a pub where I was to turn. Cautiously, I stopped to ask directions. And it's a good thing I did. "Now, this is a narrow little town that stretches some ways," a helpful farmer said, pointing up the road, "and there at the exact other end is another pub, also called Rooney's. It's there that you turn." He leaned forward confidentially. "Same family," he assured me.

What with asking at each crossroad, it took most of a day to find the Boyne's source. And I had chosen a desperate time to try, for this was no soft day of misty rain and fog. Rain poured down in a hundred-year storm. The river was swollen to three times its usual size. The unapproachable source was all marsh and drowned trees. Was this how it looked when Bóand bravely approached?

If there were magical hazels at the Boyne's source, they were lost in the flood. No salmon leapt from the reedy waters. Ah, well, I thought, why not follow Bóand's path out to sea, some seventy miles away at Drogheda? But the boreens were impassable. On the radio, a scientist explained that the river plains should have absorbed the water, had not new suburban housing estates been built over them, throttling the river's natural course.

Near the river's mouth, I stopped at a bridge and walked to its center. Below me, turgid water roiled. Bits of debris floated by. Fog erased the boundaries of sky and land. I stood in a gray wet world. Staring down into the water, I tried to imagine it as sacred. I could not.

A motorist stopped and rolled down his window.

"Are you jumping then," he called out, "or just daft?"

Undeterred by my failure with the Boyne, I decided to seek the source of the Shannon, the river that waters one-fifth of Ireland, the navigable artery to its heartland. From its mountainy source, the Shannon swells steadily into the lakes where the mythic cow-sisters once swam: Lough Bofin (white cow's lake) and Lough Boderg (black cow's lake). It's easy enough to find in myth, but myth tells more than maps. I tried for several years to find the Shannon's source. Most maps of Ireland fail to mark it. I have two that do, but each puts it in a different place. I followed one to

Keshcorrigan, where people apologetically shook their heads. The source was not there, despite the little red star on the map I held. Then I found Michael Dames's citation of "a field near Dowra," a little town on the borders of Leitrim and Cavan, as the Shannon Pot's location. It was enough to launch another expedition.

"Dowra?" my Connemara friends said when I announced my plans. "Whyever do ye want to go to Dowra?"

The day before I set off, I ran into Roundstone's maker of Irish drums (*bódhrans*) who so identifies with his work that he answers to the name of Malachy Bódhran. Like everyone else, his response to my planned excursion was, "Whyever do ye want to go to Dowra?" But unlike anyone else he added, "I just bought a farm there." He scribbled down the cell phone number of his estate agent. If anyone knew his way around Dowra, it was surely Tony. Thus prepared — no need for rod and creel, I would be content just to see the salmon leap — I set off one spring morning in search of the source.

I traveled the familiar road north from Connemara into even more familiar terrain near Bohola. East of Sligo, I turned onto roads I had never traveled. I told myself to relax, to enjoy the scenery, that this could be another wild-goose chase, there was no guarantee I would reach Tony, much less that he would know the way to the Shannon Pot. The towns shrank, the stretches of wild land grew, my heart expanded.

At Drumkeoran, I found a phone at the community center. After one ring, an answer. Perhaps luck was with me, perhaps this time I would indeed find the mythic Pot. "Hello," I shouted into the bad connection, "Malachy told me to call, he said you'd know how to find the source of the Shannon." Tony did not know, but he knew who would: "Go into the town, cross the bridge to McGrail's, ask for Oliver."

I thanked Tony profusely. But my hand was still on the receiver when I thought: Oh, no. Should I have asked for more details? I recalled wandering back and forth on a road in Cork, looking for the Maxol station where I was to turn. Finally I stopped at the only station I could find, an Exxon — which had a few years earlier been the Maxol in question. Or how about that hour I spent in Galway looking for the "green house," the one painted blue decades before? Was I once again approaching Rooneyville?

A decade ago, such problems drove me distracted. But Irish directions no longer distress me. They are like coded spiritual messages reminding us that the journey is more important than the destination, that not all places are meant to be found, that not all times are right for the finding. That sometimes what you find will not be what you sought, that sometimes you will find what cannot be sought.

But this time there was no problem: Tony's directions brought me straight to a bridge, across which I saw a dry goods store called McGrail's. Eternal hope sprang. But the store was closed, shuttered tight. I peered into the windows and peeked behind the building. A fine new house stood beside the store, not physically attached but close enough to seem a unit. I rang, and Oliver appeared. He regretted that his brother, the teacher, was not around, he would know so much more. But Oliver could direct me, indeed he could, I was near enough, just follow the road toward Cuilcagh Mountain, I would see the signs for the Shannon Pot soon enough, I would indeed.

I set off again, this time confidently. I had directions, didn't I? But no matter how far I drove on that road, every sign showed that I was seven kilometers from Dowra, and every sign to Glengalvan spelled the town's name differently. Was I going in circles? It was a perfect spring day, with sweet sunlight and fragrant air, white maybush and greening grass. Ah, well, I said to myself, at worst I would have a lovely drive. Then, suddenly, a sign. A few turns, the road narrowing with each one, then a cattle gate, a small hill, an empty parking lot. There was no interpretive center — what Connemara mapmaker Tim Robinson calls an "interruptive center" — just a path.

Would there really be a bubbling pool, or was that just a metaphor? Had I driven all day to see a sodden marsh? Not knowing what to expect, I started down the path. A bit of a stream ran beside me. Was that the Shannon, the river that flows past sacred Uisneach and ends at Hy-Brâzil? I followed the streamlet downhill.

A cow lowed. Insects buzzed. The creek bubbled.

At the bottom of the hill was a little bridge. A tiny river flowed under it, perhaps three feet wide: the Shannon, soon joined by the stream I had been following. Close to the source, the Shannon was already acting like a river, pulling tributaries into itself. Across the bridge, I turned left and took a few steps, then stopped dead in my tracks.

Before me was the most archetypal landscape I had ever seen. A round mountain belly rose above me. Two long flanks of hills reached out to the sides. Where they joined was an almost perfectly circular pool, the life source of the goddess. The water moved constantly, bubbling from springs fed by rain from swallow holes in the white chalk hill above. The pool's sloping sides were green and slick. At the one place I could approach, bright primroses bloomed beneath the surface.

I leaned down, holding my breath. Was it there, the *bradán beatha,* the salmon of life?

Of the Shannon, the same story is told as of the Boyne. The maiden Síonann — called by Ptolemy Senos, "the ancient one" — was determined to become wise by capturing the salmon who lived in the pool. Building a fire so that everything would be ready, she began fishing. Her patience paid off, for she netted the fish and set about cooking it. So far, so good. The moment Síonann tasted the salmon's flesh, wisdom rushed into her soul. But at the same moment, the waters of the pool burst forth and carried her out to sea.

🏵🏵🏵🏵

I understand why the ancient Irish saw wisdom as a salmon. As a girl I watched them in the shadows of the riverbanks, waiting for the tide, great looming urgent presences, their gills bloody, their skin torn into shreds by their headlong migration. My father fed us on salmon he caught in the churning Kenai River or the placid gray waters of Lake Louise. Later I fished Prince William Sound for red-fleshed kings and bargained with Native fishermen on the Yukon for pale dog salmon. Alaska's salmon are a different species than Ireland's, but they share a homing instinct that leads them from the salt ocean, where they lived amid whales and dolphins, back to the river mouth they exited as fry, to the exact spot they hatched years earlier, there to spawn, there to die. Who is wiser than one who knows the way home?

Amazing, too, is their sheer abundance, rivers boiling with fish like the Shannon Pot with rainwater. Even a hillside of dusky blueberries is not, to me, as perfect an image of natural abundance as a run of salmon. I have seen people step into arctic streams and giddily catch spawned-out salmon with their bare hands, heard fish wheels flop, flop, flop fish after silver fish for hour after hour, pulled nets so laden with salmon our fingers tore into red shreds with the effort. A salmon run is a delirium of earth's generosity.

In Ireland, the salmon run begins just as the mayflies — their Latin name, Ephemeroptera, captures the brevity of their lives — hatch, mate, and die, all within hours. It was spring; scores of mayflies added agitation to the Shannon Pot. I watched as they struck the water surface. In the valley beyond, the cow lowed again.

Were those silver fins beneath the water?

I had come without a map to a place where slant light gleamed on the undersides of slim willow leaves. To a round pool that bubbled softly. To an opening beneath a mountain belly from which wisdom might be born. I had failed in my first attempts to find the source. Might it not take several visits to win the eye of the salmon of wisdom? But after all, I reasoned, this was no longer the age of myth; anything I saw would just be a fish, a migrating fish that had swum up from Limerick, past Killaloe and Portumna, through Lough Ree and Lough Bofin, past Carrick-on-Shannon — just a fish, no mythic being with the power to impart wisdom, just a fish after all.

Still I stared at the pool and waited.

Sitting on the green slope, I pondered the persistence of my search. I was not from the region; I had no special devotion to the river's tutelary goddess, Síonann; yet the image of a circular pool from which a great river rises held some compelling power to which I responded. And the Shannon Pot had repaid my persistence, for on that splendid day in May it was uncannily beautiful, a place I could credit with nurturing wisdom.

The Apache people of the American Southwest say that "wisdom sits in places" and tell their children to "drink from places." Apache sage Dudley Patterson once described wisdom as "water that never dries up." He articulated the connection of place and soul this way: "You need to drink water to stay alive, don't you? Well, you also need to drink from places. You must learn their names. You must remember what happened at them long ago." The Apache are a desert people, but their idea of wisdom strangely echoes that of rainy Ireland. It is important, both say, to repeat the names of places, for in doing so we evoke their stories. *That* happened *there:* place and story are deeply tied in both wisdom traditions.

I remembered being stuck in a Chicago traffic jam once, listening to novelist Salman Rushdie on the radio praising the postmodern world as one in which place has become unnecessary. "The roots of the self are no longer in places," he said. The City is our place now, he proclaimed, not separate place-bound cities but that exciting multicultural global City where we will find our stories from now on. But must a denationalized world, I wondered, be denaturalized as well? Where is there a place for storied places of the past, places created by nature but filled with wisdom by humans?

Things do not just happen *there;* they also happen *then.* A story makes then and there into here and now. Past, whether mythic or historical, connects to future in the momentary present. Story revivifies place, brings it alive with people and events, with tears and blood, with tragedy and hope. And some places, like the Shannon Pot, draw to themselves more powerful stories than do other places. Philosopher Mikhail Bakhtin called such places "chronotopes," "where time takes on flesh and becomes visible for human contemplation; space becomes charged and responsible to the movements of history and the enduring character of a people." At such places, the beauty of land and the mystery of myth come together so precisely that it is impossible to tell where one begins and the other ends.

Place stories — from myth, history, rumor, gossip — have been told and retold for millennia in Ireland, where there is a story for each name on the map. The *dindshenchas,* wherein we find the tale of Síonann, is devoted to such narratives. In such stories, wisdom lived like a salmon in a secret pool, for narrative is an ancient way of preserving human knowledge. Great places, argued Yeats, are like great books, but even more lasting; they are "the only hieroglyphs that cannot be forgotten."

But I wonder. So much of what anthropologist Clifford Geertz calls "local knowledge" is being lost, in Ireland as elsewhere, and with it, a certain kind of wisdom. Not a universal, abstract wisdom, the same no matter where you stand, but wisdom expressed and embodied in specific places. We still say we "come from" a place, as though we were birthed by the earth at a specific spot. Yet who among us knows that mother place? Who could, like the salmon, find the way back? And without that knowledge, how can we remember to be wise? "What is the preserving shrine?" asks the great compilation of Irish law called the *Senchas Mór.* "Not hard: the preserving shrine is memory and what is preserved in it. What is the preserving shrine? Not hard; the preserving shrine is nature and what is preserved in it."

I sat there, pondering the place of place. What is the preserving shrine? The pool bubbled. The willows swayed.

Then, a flash of silver.

And gone.

Just like that.

A stillness inhabits extraordinary moments in our lives, moments outside temporality. Eternity, remember, is not a long time; it is beyond time. Barbara once wrote that such moments — "the first meeting with a lover, the dawning flash of an insight, moments that come like the touch of a butterfly's wing" — never left us, nor we them. And indeed, even now, miles and years from that moment, I still sit on the banks of the Shannon Pot as the ancient one-eyed salmon flicks its speckled tail at me.

I would like to claim that the salmon dowered me with wisdom. But does wisdom sit in questions? I received no answers that day. I only saw a fish, leaping into spring sunlight, only a fish that had swum up from Limerick, past Killaloe and Portumna, through Lough Ree and Lough Bofin, past Carrick-on-Shannon. Only a fish...

Once we knew our home places as salmon do, physically, viscerally, by sight and sound and smell. We recognized our kin the same way. But is blood truly thicker than water? The desert-dwelling !Kung claim as kin anyone who shares the same water source. Theirs may be the wisdom of the future, for we increasingly share a world in which the old categories grow elusive, a world for which we have no maps, no *dindshenchas* that tells the stories of its sites. It is a place of incalculable abundance, flooded with wisdom, a place no less real for being virtual. It is a place where new tribes are being formed and new home places declared.

My grandparents came from a preglobal village. When economic exile drove them from Bohola, they left brothers and parents, cousins and friends. My grandmother never returned; my grandfather only once. Occasional letters carried vital news across the great water, but everyday news went unexpressed. Did the old dog die? How was the weather? What color was the shed painted? We might dismiss such matters as trivial, but in doing so we would be deaf to the word's meaning, for Trivia was the Roman goddess of crossroads. Every trivial exchange leads us toward or away from deeper relationship. Without witnessing the trivia of each other's days, even kinfolk become strangers.

Unlike my grandparents, I am in daily touch with a dozen distant people, weekly with scores. I hear about Dawn's accident in Iowa and the bad weather down Maggie's way in Florida. I hear about Fiona's art opening in Laois, my cousin Mike's dog trials in Australia, the marching season in Bob's Ulster town. My siblings send around jokes (invariably groaners), reminders of birthdays, grievances and peeves, song lyrics. I love this ever-widening pool of relationships and wonder how, just a few years ago, I lived in a narrower, more constricted world.

Over in Connemara, Barbara resisted e-mail at first, complaining she couldn't feel the person behind the words without "the swirl of the s, the loop of the h," but finally she succumbed to the medium's immediacy and ease. Many mornings thereafter I sat with my tea, chatting with her as though we were seated beside her fire. The kinship we had felt upon first meeting was deepened by the ordinary chat we shared, Connemara to Chicago. I told her about my garden, my endless household projects; she detailed the ups and downs of the new house in Dawros, her plans for a garden facing the sea. We shared stories and dreams, poems and songs. And plans for the fire lighting on Uisneach hill wound through our messages like a fertile river.

But then, one morning, I found myself reading that Barbara had embarked on a new healing regime. She said she had much to live for, much to give. She was surrounded by love and hope. "Malachy gave me a Claddagh pin, saying 'If a bódhran-maker gives you a Claddagh, it's a sign of good luck.' Coming home across the bog in the full moonlight, we were happy indeed, for just the other side of Clifden we were met by a heart-stopping moonbow, a full arc from ground to ground, a magic moment."

The letters swam on the screen. Recurrence? Tumor? Checked and confirmed? No. Not Barbara. No.

What is the wisdom of this village where we are intimate with people whose faces we cannot see, whose hands we cannot stroke, whose tears we cannot dry? It would be easy to deny that the virtual world can be sacred as the Shannon's source. Easy to demand that we return to a simpler time when only the tangible was real. But our connection has always transcended the physical. We have always touched even when our bodies are separate. How many stories have I heard of mothers who have known the instant a distant child was hurt? Is not the original virtual reality the soul?

I made plans to come over, but that could not be for months. I was frightened, but Barbara's words cheered me. Had she not fought off breast cancer once before? Could she not do it again? I wrote regularly, called, sent books. Her responses grew shorter, less frequent, but invariably hopeful.

Then, one evening, I received a brief message: "It is with great sadness and sense of loss that I tell you that Barbara passed away today at 1 P.M. Irish time. She slid away in her sleep with the dignity and serenity that we have all come to associate with her. Sorry for the brevity DAVE."

I stared at the screen for a long time.

No. Not Barbara. No.

Grief is a strange journey. Each time we embark upon it, it is as though we have never taken its roads before. No, I have that wrong: each grief brings us through a familiar landscape carved into unrecognizable contours. For we do not only lose another person; we lose the person we were with the one we lost. Never again would I be the American friend sitting by an Irish hearth, drinking milky tea, swapping stories. Never again the private audience to Barbara's lilting songs. Never again the astrological twin with a shared passion for the goddess and the land.

Where absence is already part of the story, the road of grief takes especially curious turns. My grandfather did not hear of his mother's death until he received her obituary in the mail. Honore died, it says, "after a comparatively short illness which she bore with the greatest patience and resignation. Deceased was a member of one of the most respected families in the district and the news of her death which was not altogether unexpected, came as a shock to many. She was a good, kind mother, and affectionate wife, and a charitable excellent neighbor. The cortege was one of the largest seen in the district for years, and was representative of all the villages for miles around." What did my grandfather feel as he read those words, forty years and an ocean away from Bohola? Had he known his mother's death was "not altogether unexpected"? Did he look at his four children who would never know their grandmother? Did he try to remember Honore's voice, her face? Did his throat close when he could not?

Because I could not get to Barbara's funeral, Dave described it for me: "The house was packed all day, full of music as we played and sang and celebrated our great, lovely, musical Barbara." She was buried on Omey, one of those bits of Connemara that is sometimes island, sometimes peninsula, depending on the tide. "While her grave was being filled, the sandy grave-yard was alive with dance music as we covered the plot with flowers and a net. Then the mob adjourned to Oliver's, where a hot meal revived every-one's physical (if not spiritual) being. But that is not the end of the story. Out came the musical instruments and a mighty three-hour session ensued. The music, the weather, the glorious crossing of Omey strand, all were mightily appropriate for Barbara — we gave her a good send-off."

In the virtual village, we are confusingly both distant and close, some-where and elsewhere all at once. How do we grieve in such a world? Not long after the funeral I found myself inexplicably furious. Some lost paper-work, a mere inconvenience, but I shook with anger, used words like *unfair* and *unreasonable*. Trying to calm down, I felt my eyes fill. I closed my office door and wept.

Anger, a wise friend once told me, is a form of grief. It was not the lost paperwork that enraged me: it was Barbara's death. It *was* unfair. It *was* unreasonable. Just as it was unfair and unreasonable for Françoise Kelly, my friend Frank's kind young wife, to die just days later of the same disease. Unfair, unreasonable, that women in the prime of life are being struck down, in Ireland, at an unprecedented rate. Cancer is epidemic there; it is predicted that a quarter of the Irish population will suffer from it. Ireland has the fourth highest incidence of breast cancer in the world. More Irishwomen die of it than of any other disease — some 45 percent of those diagnosed.

No one knows for certain what causes this epidemic, but like the proverbial canary in the coal mine, the human breast is an early warning signal for environmental contamination, especially from xenoestrogens — false female hormones — found in pesticides. DDT was long used on Irish farmland; Poland, where 100 percent of human and animal milk shows traces of DDT, has seen a tenfold increase in breast cancer in thirty years. Those who blame the victim — she smoked, ate butter, drank milk — must ignore the fact that 40 percent of the fish in the North Sea have tumors. Was my dear friend a melodious canary, warning against what we are doing to our world?

❋❋❋❋

Sometimes tragedy seems to flood over us like a river over its banks, and so it was that spring, for the months that followed piled tragedy on tragedy.

As Barbara lay dying, swill from a Chinese restaurant was being fed to pigs in England. This not-uncommon practice would have caused no remark except that those animals developed lesions about the mouth — symptoms of a disease so feared that a wholesale slaughter began.

Even now, writing at a distance of time and space, I cannot grasp the scope of what ensued. Within weeks, thousands of cattle had been killed; within months, millions. Foot-and-mouth disease must be horrific, I thought at first, and killing — "culling" — some animals necessary to forestall herds dying of the virus. I soon learned otherwise. FMD causes painful blisters in — yes — feet and mouths, as well as teats. But only 1 percent of the infected animals die, usually the young or the sick. Why, then, the bloody response? Because English herds have no natural immunity to FMD, the virus having been kept offshore for almost forty years. So why not let the animals get sick and recover to develop immunity? Because weight lost during the illness makes stricken animals less profitable at market.

Other European countries turned to vaccination, which is both cheap and effective. But England chose the gun over the syringe, for vaccination would jeopardize the country's favored status in American and Japanese markets. And so entire herds, mostly cows and calves, were slaughtered in an attempt to build a firebreak against FMD, even when owners preferred to nurse them back to health. Week after week, month after month, what journalist Jonathan Miller called an "orgy of killing driven by greed" continued. That year, nearly a hundred farmers committed suicide after losing their herds. That year, almost five million animals — almost all healthy — were slaughtered and burned. That year, their carbonized flesh released enough dioxin to give one-third of the world's population cancer.

Animal plagues have been known throughout history. The *dindshenchas* tell us that "there fell a sickness — sad the news — on the kine of wide-stretching Banba; it killed them, without exception or survivor, all but the bull of the glen and his heifer." In 700, the Fragmentary Annals say, "herds of cattle throughout Ireland were almost destroyed; in the next year there was a human plague for three consecutive years; afterward came the greatest Famine, in which men were reduced to eating unmentionable foods." The Annals of Clonmacnoise say that an unknown illness called *máelgarb* decimated Ireland's cows and sheep in 770; a similar epidemic killed most of the pigs and cattle in 1129.

But it was government policy, not disease, that decimated England's herds. Transformed from kin to commodity, millions of animals could be killed with minimal protest, for industrial agriculture throughout the world views a cow not, as Goethe described her, as "a small world, existing for its own sake," but as a small factory, existing for its owner. "You can judge the moral stature of a nation by the way it treats its animals," Gandhi said. If so, the world is in trouble. Industrial agriculture places cows in densely crowded barns. She is fed, our animal mother, on fish food and chicken manure; her double stomach cannot handle the protein and releases methane, which increases global warming. A cow in pasture can live twenty years, giving a gallon of milk daily in season; agribusiness cows give up to seven gallons of milk each day. This unhealthy life is, perhaps mercifully, short. Milked dry by the age of five, they are then ground up into dog food.

Ireland stands on the brink of industrializing its agriculture; for now, cows still ramble the boreens and give forth their "miracles of milk," in poet Patrick Galvin's lovely phrase. But the pressure of commerce forces more and more farmers into buying high-protein meal and confining cattle indoors. Such conditions make virulent viruses like FMD more dangerous, for cattle in crowded conditions pass disease more readily; for this, antibiotics are provided, which pass through into milk and into our bodies; pathogen mutation soon makes those antibiotics ineffective for both cows and humans. But what's a farmer, struggling to survive, to do?

Relatively few factory farms favored Ireland in the FMD crisis. But Ireland had much to fear. One of the world's top twenty agricultural exporters, it has twice as many cows as people. One-quarter of the population lives from farming and associated industries, with milk and dairy products sustaining both domestic and export markets. So when FMD was found on the peninsula where the great Brown Bull of Cuailgne once grazed, the papers screamed "Farmaggedon!" and Ireland went on red alert. Saint Patrick's Day was canceled, Gaelic games went forfeit. Animal transport was forbidden, human movement discouraged.

Despite the developing crisis, plans went forward to light the millennial fires on Uisneach. Did I say despite? In fact, the project grew in significance, for Bealtaine was the day on which the Celts offered ritual prayers for the safety of the herds, and Europe's herds direly needed prayers. From Chicago, I wrote website copy and researched folklore. I read British and Irish papers online, often weeping at the photographs of football-field-sized animal graves, at interviews with grieving farmers whose herds had been slaughtered. Daily, I prayed that Ireland would be spared.

When at last I kept my springtime promise and arrived just before Bealtaine, I entered a fearful Ireland, a land of disinfectant mats and immobilized herds, of wary farmers and weary merchants. If quarantines and restrictions kept FMD at bay, the twin fires on Uisneach would be lit. We would not know until the actual hour of the lighting whether or not the hillside would be closed to prevent infection. But we would gather there in the shadow of Uisneach nonetheless.

※※※※

Uisneach is not an especially prepossessing hill; indeed, Joyce called it "that mountainy molehill." The molehill of which the druids made a mythic mountain rises near Ireland's geographical center, and the center, to the Celts, was a microcosm of the whole. Whatever happened there affected all other parts of the land. Thus lighting the fires for protection of the herds on Uisneach hill would have, to them, protected all the cattle of the land.

Uisneach was where the arriving Celts met the third goddess of the land, resplendent, bejeweled Ériu, who lies buried beneath the Catstone, a huge glacial erratic that some observer saw as a cat ready to pounce. Its correct name is Ailt-na-Míreann, "Stone of Divisions," for if Uisneach is Ireland's center, the Catstone maps its four-part division with deep fissures on its granite face. Ériu's headstone is Ireland in miniature.

Barbara wrote me once about the first time she saw Uisneach: "The massive Catstone drew us up — I just couldn't keep myself from going straight into the middle of it, the womb place, and straight away the three women gathered there. I remembered the song I wrote for another full moon, and there couldn't have been a better place to sing it than looking out at that moon from inside that stone." I had a similar experience with Fiona and Maggie when we climbed once at sunset to the Catstone. As the shadows lengthened across the midlands, Fiona was inspired to drum a rhythm on the stone. Soon we were all slapping our hands against it, singing a song that seemed to rise from nowhere: "Rock my soul in the bosom of Ériu, rock my soul in the bosom of Ériu, oh rock my soul" as the sun set in a blaze of fire and night gathered over Ireland's magical center.

"Every generation needs to rediscover Uisneach," Michael Dames has said. At the turn of the twenty-first century, a threatened plague helped us rediscover the connection of Uisneach to the safety of the herds. In groups and singly, people were arriving: from Australia and Munster, Ohio and Ulster, California and Kerry, Colorado and Connemara. They came from Belfast and Dublin and the stricken county of Louth. At the little inn at the crossroads beneath Uisneach, we all gathered in the back room for a simple ritual.

Dave began by reading from the works of the local historian Jeremiah Sheehan, who described how the earliest, and startlingly accurate, map of Ireland was made two millennia ago by Ptolemy, whose informants were traders who had traveled to Uisneach. Sailing up the river Senos — the Shannon — those ancient visitors disembarked near Uisneach and climbed to the great Ailt-na-Míreann, where they feasted and traded and swapped stories with the tribes that had gathered for Bealtaine.

Like those early travelers, we had come to Uisneach for Bealtaine. But those who stood there in the darkened room were not the only celebrants. For a call had gone out across the Internet, asking people to join us by lighting ritual fires for the protection of the herds. Messages had been pouring in ever since. We did not know how many until Maggie stepped forward to read the list of Answering Fires. She started in a strong clear voice: Kildare, Kerry, Galway. Armagh, Waterford, Donegal. Her voice quavered as the realization broke over us of how many fires were being lit in response to our own.

Twenty counties across Ireland. Iowa, California, Minnesota, Wisconsin. Maggie's voice cracked again. She stopped to gather her composure. Hawaii, Virginia, West Virginia, Florida. Thirty-eight states. The list went on and on. New Mexico, New York. A nursing home in Washington. Chartres Cathedral. Macchu Picchu. The Irish peacekeepers on the Iraqi frontier.

Across the world, small fires and large ones blazed. Fires lit by families and groups and individuals, by schools and churches, by Christians and pagans and Shintoists and Buddhists. Across the world, people were praying to heal the herds and our relationship to them. Maggie read on and on. And in that moment beside the crossroad beneath the mountain that marks Ireland's mystic center, we entered the Fifth Province. Four of Ireland's provinces are tangible places, places with borders and capitals and coastlines. But Míde, the center, is a spiritual place, able to move, like Hy-Brâzil, on the currents of time and spirit. And that night, Míde expanded until it was everywhere, until each of us, wherever we were, stood at the center.

Suddenly someone grabbed my arm. I was pulled outside. The spring sun was setting. We had waited all day to hear whether we would be permitted to light the fires on Uisneach. Now four of us were trundled into a pickup truck. Moments later, we tumbled out at the top of the sacred hill.

I felt dazed, not only from the abruptness of our ascent but from the vista that lay beneath us. However nondescript it may seem from the base, from its summit Uisneach is extraordinary. Twenty counties lay in a great blue bowl, its rim brimming with fire. Darkening plains swept up to black seaside mountains. A cloudless sky glowed above the rich land.

The sun reddened the mountain ranges to the southwest. The fires would be lit just as night fell, a ritual promise that no darkness is ever total. Flint was struck over hemp in the traditional way, once, twice, a dozen times. The sparks grew brighter and brighter in the gloaming. Finally flames blazed out. We threw the hemp on a pile of brush that towered over us.

The brush caught in a crackling, crashing sound, then a roar.

From below, we heard shrieks and calls. A chant welled up from the darkening valley below. É-r-i-u, É-r-i-u: the name of the goddess, chanted over and over by hundreds of voices. Then there was a staccato eruption of drums.

We moved to the second fire and set it alight. The fires, the fires, I thought. The Bealtaine fires. On Uisneach hill.

Below us, celebration, cheering, singing. On the hill, silence.

I tried to open my mind to the other fires that blazed that night, to the women bearing candles at Chartres, the aged woman striking a match in a nursing home, the couple beside a campfire on the New Mexico desert. But I could not. Instead I saw other fires: England alight with burning carcasses of millions of napalmed animals; Brazil alight with pyres of rainforest trees cleared for pastureland. What were our small fires to those greater ones?

The crescent moon rose over the fires on Uisneach hill. I wanted to believe the Bealtaine fires were an answer, but instead I was flooded with questions.

※░※░※

The Shannon's broad waters caught the silver moonlight. "If the waters could speak as they flow!" Joyce once wished. But they were silent. It was spring, and salmon should have been breasting the current. But where the "health of the salmon" once predicted a long strong life, now salmon return erratically to the Shannon's bubbling pot. The Atlantic salmon have declined 99 percent over the last fifteen years; some Irish rivers see virtually no salmon. The Pacific salmon is also in steep decline, although whether from overfishing or global warming is unknown; the year I stood on Uisneach hill, western Alaska was declared a disaster zone when fewer than one-third of the expected salmon returned to their spawning grounds.

"Only the rivers remain, / slowly bleeding," Paddy Galvin puts it. I thought of how the great hero Fionn was saved in battle by the maiden Síonann. Fionn might have been killed, but the girl threw him a magical stone that increased his powers. After fighting off his assailant, Fionn threw the stone deep into the river. There it still rests, covered by the shining Shannon waters. But Fionn warned that if that stone were found, the world would end. If greed evaporates the waters, will that stone appear again?

The great Greek goddess, bovine Hera, was honored at riverine sanctuaries; in India, primordial Surabhi's milk fed the gods and was churned to form the universe. Today, almost half the world's fields are devoted to raising grain for cattle; the demand for pasture has led to the destruction of the Brazilian rain forest. Trees that should transpire our air are cut and burned, leaving great cancerous holes in the world's lungs. The cleared fields produce for about five years before being depleted, then the cycle starts again. Rain forest destruction leads to global warming, which in turn creates unpredictable weather as the water cycle — river to ocean to rain to cloud to river — is disrupted. The more we worship the golden calf and milk earth's resources, the more we create the very scarcity we fear.

Today, a battle rages between greed and abundance. As Indian physicist Vandana Shiva warns, a greedy few are attempting to homogenize our world by arguing that "nature is a source of scarcity, and technology a source of abundance," which "leads to the creation of technologies which create new scarcities in nature." Of two thousand possible potato varieties, almost half of America's fields are planted in one: the Russett Burbank, which conveniently fits into french fry machines. Did we learn nothing from Ireland's Famine? Wisdom roots for the side of abundance — true abundance, not the consolidation of wealth in the hands of a few, but abundance for everyone. True wisdom knows that enough is plenty. Instead of stock profits for a few, we could have potatoes and milk galore for everyone.

The Bealtaine flames licked the darkening sky. I thought of Barbara, whose friendship had brought me there. I remembered the last time we had gone to her new house, the house in Dawros she never moved into. At lunch afterward in Letterfrack, I had unaccountably begun to describe how Eskimo women could no longer breast-feed their children because of toxic concentrations of DDT in their milk. After I spoke, we fell into a long silence. Then Barbara, reaching for my hand, said brokenly, "Those women are our sisters — our kin. What are we doing? What are we doing?"

There on Uisneach hill, I could hear her voice. I can hear it still.

I had no answer then for my friend. I have none now. But I know we stand at the crossroads of danger and opportunity, that we are traveling without a map, that we no longer know our place or our kin. Perhaps we will continue to destroy our world. Perhaps we will continue to hear only silence where Joyce heard the leafy Liffey murmuring, "if I go all goes. A hundred cares, a tithe of troubles, and is there one who understands me? One in a thousand of years of the nights?... O bitter ending! I'll slip away before they're up. They'll never see. Nor know. Nor miss me. And it's old and old it's sad and old it's sad and weary."

But there is yet hope. In east Mayo, on a monument to those who saw past the Famine to an Ireland free of vampire landlordism, are these words of the great Mohandas Gandhi: "The earth has enough for everyone's need but not enough for everyone's greed." How true: the great Glas still wanders on the Path of the White Cow, her udders streaming nourishment. We just have to put down the sieve and let her provide.

Chapter Eight

Wildish Things

Kerry

Cork

Between Killarney and Cork winds a road. It travels through wild land around Lash and Clash, through little mountain-shadowed Glenflesk, past the turnoff to Lissivigeen and Cullen. Then the road begins to mount and descend in great sweeping curves through the low sandstone range called the Derrynasaggarts. It's a good road, often more than two lanes wide — a rarity in Ireland — along which traffic surges: cars carrying errand-running mothers, dreamy lovers, local people moving from place to place through familiar scenery, ignoring the lonely heritage sign that points out features of the cloud-hazed landscape.

Few cars carry tourists. Such folks are over west, bumper-to-bumper along the famous Ring of Kerry. An inexplicably named road, neither circular nor inclusive of all County Kerry, the Ring is required of those following exhausting itineraries based on the curse of Diarmuid and Gráinne, "may you not sleep two nights in one place." Later you hear the returned tourists brag, "Of course we *did* the Kerry Ring." Not drive the Kerry Ring? That would be like not kissing the Blarney Stone or not buying crystal at Waterford.

My great-great-grandmother Eliza Casey was from Cahirciveen, on the Ring's western edge, so far be it from me to direct tourists away from any distant cousins who may run pubs or petrol stations. But I avoid such itineraries, preferring either the dartboard method of Irish travel or its simpler variant, the ramble: drive until you feel like stopping, stop, stay stopped. Not long ago, two friends employed the latter method, driving west from Dublin until they found a pretty little town where they spent an unforgettable week exploring historic sites and great pubs. Upon their return, horrified acquaintances squealed, "How *could* you miss the Kerry Ring?" Then one traveler discovered her mother's family hailed from the very town to which the ramble brought her, proving — well, proving *something.* (I can almost hear Tom Hannon's voice, observing that "well, Patricia, after all, didn't you find your way, all those years ago, to Gort?")

With possible Cahirciveen cousins in mind, I hereby acknowledge that Kerry merits its reputation as the "most beautiful place on earth," in *National Geographic*'s words (surely they know). Kerry has the Lakes of Killarney that epitomize romantic beauty; the desolate Skellig Rocks standing sentinel in the gray Atlantic; the country's highest mountains (Na Cruacha Dubha, "The Black Peaks," in Irish, though I would call them blue); the Left-Handed Reaper looming over waterfalls and hidden glens. The Gap of Dunloe, where, hearing a bugler at sunset, Alfred, Lord Tennyson wrote:

> *The long light shakes across the lakes,*
> *And the wild cataract leaps in glory.*
> *Blow, bugle, blow, set the wild echoes flying,*
> *Blow, bugle; answer, echoes, dying, dying, dying.*

Great mossy forests of yew and oak suggest (except for those colonizing rhododendrons) how Ireland looked when the first settlers landed. Sunlight splashes off sea and lakes, shatters in the mists of waterfalls and the spume of rocky inlets. No question about it: Munster, Ireland's mountainy south-western province, is beautiful, and Kerry its most beautiful county.

Especially in summer, when Munster is deranged with flowers. In gardens, hydrangeas droop, sweet peas clamber, roses twine, great spidery dahlias nod. Wildflowers press in madly upon the gardens: yellow gorse, orange montbretias, magenta loosestrife, mauve willow herb I knew as fireweed in Alaska. The flowers shine in what Munster novelist Elizabeth Bowen called "the surrounding, disturbing light," that slant light John Millington Synge called "wonderfully tender and searching." Soft light and blossoms: is anything more sensuous than a summer evening in Munster?

Every town land, every parish, every barony in Ireland is beautiful, each in its own way. But everyone knows Kerry is the most beautiful. And so its valleys become tourist-loud glades each summer, crowded beyond bearing. Once I missed a meeting in Dingle because, after a half hour on one quarter mile of Goat Street, I spied an open lane and fled. Kerry is beautiful, no question. But sometimes in summer, it looks like Chicago with scenery.

That road through the Derrynasaggarts is a different story. It offers no fabulous vistas, no midnight peaks beside a sapphire sea, no mirror lakes under a changeful sky. If you pass that way just once, odds are you will see only an unremarkable stretch of road. But north of Ballyvourney, if the wind lifts the clouds for just a moment — there where the road curves sharply to the east before beginning a steep rise to the southeast — there, I promise you, if you stop by that lonely heritage sight and look back to the northeast, you will see something you will never forget.

On the map, two tiny triangles mark "the Paps." The word, no longer in general use, once indicated paired mountains: Scotland's Paps of Jura, the Paps of the Mórrígan near Newgrange. It's a baby word of untraceable ancestry, supposedly evolved from the lip-smacking sounds (what my mother used to call "blowing bubbles") of hungry infants, a word that in the singular means a mild baby-pleasing porridge. In Irish, the hills marked by those wee triangles are called Dhá Chíoche Dhanann, Danu's Two Breasts. The Irish word for "breasts" is, not surprisingly, related to "hungry" (*ciocrach*) and "craving" (*ciocras*), but not to any other Indo-European word for mammaries. Those languages share words for many things — for "sister" and "birch," for instance — but not for breasts. Our

English word births daughters ("breastless" and "breastfeeding") but is of unclear parentage. It is easy, by contrast, to trace the heritage of those abundant euphemisms: *bosom,* like its relative *fathom,* is a measurement word that indicates how much your arms can embrace; *bust* descends from the vocabulary of sculpture; *chest,* a storage unit, comes from the language of furniture.

But none of those apparent synonyms captures the meaning of *paps,* which describes not the whole breast but just the nipple (another untraceable word, related to *nip* and *nibble*). While the Irish word draws attention to the hills' shape, their English name emphasizes a different endowment. For lest some fine day when wind lifts the cloud veil, you fail to note the hills' breasty roundness, the ancient Irish offered a visual aid: from earth and rock they erected mounds and cairns, positioned as anatomically correct aureoles and nipples. In the process, they transformed the wild landscape into a gigantic sculpture of a woman's body, immobile under the moving sky.

Munster has other such mountains: Knockainy with a naval-cairn on its pregnant belly, one-teated Mother Mountain. That line of nippled hills near Ballyferriter called the Three Sisters, the ones Fiona painted while eight months pregnant, the ones she calls "perfect renditions of our Mother's body." With or without cairns, Munster mountains bear goddess names: Slieve Mish, for the wild woman Mis; Dunmore Head for Mór, daughter of the sun; Slievenamon, "Mountain of the Women"; Cnoc Gréine, "Hill of the Bright Goddess."

And the Paps of Danu, rising so splendidly beside the Killarney-Cork road, named for a goddess both famous and obscure. Famous, because her name appears in so many place-names and texts. Obscure, because not even its form is definite. Danu is a reconstructed word, derived backward from the Irish *Danann,* presumably meaning "of Danu." Indo-Europeanist Miriam Dexter has traced Danu to an even older hypothesized "Donu" shared by all Indo-European cultures. The name, which also appears as Dana and Dôn and Danand, has been linked to the Old Celtic *dan,* "knowledge," and to a goddess who gave her name to England's Dane Hills and Europe's great river Danube.

Obscure, for despite frequent references, few narratives are told of Danu, daughter of a sorceress, granddaughter of the god of poetry, herself a poet. *The Book of Invasions* describes Danu as one of a trinity of sisters —

although her siblings' names vary from manuscript to manuscript. Danu was the mate either of Bile, an equally obscure god, or of Bres, whose spouse usually is Eithne or Brigit. Her children are better known: the Tuatha Dé Danann, tribe of the goddess Danu, those magical divinities long ago banished to fairy hills. "She nursed the gods well," says Cormac the glossarist, emphasizing Danu's maternity without telling us much more about her.

Sometimes the hills are called the Paps of Anu, after a goddess named by the ninth-century *Coir Anmnan* as the mother of Munster's wealth. Some scholars see the names as variants of each other, while others claim that Anu (Ana, Anand, Áine) is not Danu at all, not at all. Further complicating the question is the fact that six millennia have passed since a stone-enchanted people trained the sun's eye into the cairn at Newgrange, carved spirals on Loughcrew's granite, and erected the Paps' paps. We do not even know who lived in Ireland then, much less what they called their goddess.

Whoever they were, whatever they called her, she is beautiful. Photographs do not do justice to her loveliness: the way the Paps rise from the Derrynasaggarts, slightly separated from the ridge that curves up to them like a belly; those breasts pointing skyward, the breasts of a woman in her prime, not the tender buds of youth or the soft breasts of age, but full and firm, sensual and motherly at once. The breasts separate slightly, so you know the woman is languidly stretched out. There is no head nor arms nor legs, only breasts and a belly, but it is enough. Enough to suggest that somewhere there is a head we might cradle, somewhere arms that might embrace us, somewhere a womb from which we might emerge, children of earth.

Did the sculptors of Danu intend for us to imagine nature as our mother? Or might this gigantic earthwork mean something else entirely? We can scour archaeological texts for clues, but archaeologists, happy to list heights and weights, are slow to explain why people might employ such heights and weights, instead emitting lectures on how ruins do not reveal what their builders believed. Infrequently ventured explanations even more rarely begin from a woman's point of view. And while debate surrounds Newgrange and similar complex sites, a deafening silence shrouds the eloquently simple monument that crowns the Derrynasaggarts.

In that silence, I find myself imagining how the Paps came to be. I envision, in a valley east of the blue peaks, rude huts clustering beside a sweet-water stream. It is one of those rare days when the clouds hiding the Paps have briefly lifted. Our primal Mick considers the scene. "Now, Mary," says he, pointing, "don't those hills resemble breasts, so?" Our primal Mary looks up, nods, then returns to whatever Irishwomen did before they learned to knit: gnawing hides into leather, maybe, or inventing poetry.

All that is easy enough to imagine. But now imagine Mick gathering up the lads. "Boyos," says he, "let's run over to those breasty hills and cut down all the trees with our stone axes!" Huh? say the lads, taking a pull of primal porter, unconvinced of the necessity for such exertion. "And then," continues himself, "once the trees are gone, we'll heap up great mounds o' earth! Then we can haul big rocks up to the top and build nipples!"

Whyever would the lads agree?

And how did they get the nipples sited just so? Did someone stand at the bottom and yell, "over a bit to the right, Séamus"? Or was there a good deal of huffing and puffing up and down and rearranging of stones? How did they make the cairns stand so solidly? My garden terraces, erected a decade ago, already slump in places, yet the ancient Irish knew how to keep mortarless stone aloft. Why did they bother? What do Danu's Paps mean?

Our fantasies about the past reflect our personal biases. Note that I did not presume a breast-fixated Amazon culture. Nor, come to think of it, did I envision off-planet architects. History, too, limits us, so that most interpreters travel identical routes, seeing in the past reflections of their own known world. But — and this is why I love Ireland so — ancient silent monuments like Danu's Paps drive us beyond the familiar. Trying to imagine their origin encourages us to envision other ways of being human, other ways of living on this earth, than those we take for granted.

Egyptians built pyramids; Americans, skyscrapers; the megalithic Irish, mountaintop cairns. And while I admit it is impossible to be certain what Danu's people believed, the obsessive topping of Munster hills with navels and nipples suggests they saw the land as a woman's body, the earth as feminine. And if so, what then? Did they imagine the earth acting like a woman, laughing, singing, weeping, taking a lover, nursing a child?

* * *

I call the Paps silent, yet they are not, for they gather myths and legends like a veil of cloud. Although dating to four thousand years after the erection of the Paps' paps, these tales may encode the builders' wisdom, passed down generation to generation, or they may have emerged, like my own fantasy, from the imagination of *seanachies,* storytellers confronting a splendid puzzle. While we do not know their ultimate source, these stories point toward the meaning of the Paps.

The stories do not center on Danu — obscure, maternal, divine Danu — but on other heroines. The first, Cred, was like Danu a poet. Eager for a mate, Cred announced she would marry any man who could describe her palace on the Paps. Now here's the tricky part: no man had ever entered it. That should be no obstacle to a poet, for inner vision penetrates the stoniest wall. Many came; many tried; many failed. Finally came Cael, who described Cred's house thus: "Fairy birds sing above her bower's bright leaves, so gently even wounded men fall into restful sleep at the sound." Happy Cred, for she had found her mate. Sorrowful Cred, for he was soon killed in battle, inspiring the poet to write a famous lament for *an laech ro laiged liom:* "the warrior who was my lover."

Cred then married an elderly king, Marcán. But along came another poet, this time a Scotsman. Cred fell hard for Cano. "Love-arrows slay my sleep, love-arrows in the bitter night, pangs for the man who took my bloom," she sings in a seventh-century poem. Love-stricken Cred administered a sleeping potion to everyone but Cano, to whom she revealed her desire. He responded in kind, presenting Cred with a stone containing his soul. But a rival tormented Cred until she threw herself off a mountain, crushing Cano's soul-stone, killing her beloved as well as herself.

Cred's story is a variant of the tale of Tristan and Isolde and King Mark, and that of Guinevere and Lancelot and King Arthur. In each, a woman follows her heart, leaving an old and powerful man for a younger one. Today such tales are usually read psychologically, as though the triangulated actors are mere mortals. But the ancient Irish would have recognized reflections of a larger drama, that of the goddess abandoning an aging king in favor of his more virile successor, her actions not fickleness but immutable fact: if the land is a woman, then one generation after another will know her great body, which outlives us all.

The most familiar Irish version of the myth involves another of Cred's lovers, Fionn mac Cumhaill, who, according to a ninth-century poem, composed poems for her and slept with her "in bed-espousal prepared by willing hands." Fionn had many lovers, for he was Ireland's greatest hero (save perhaps Cúchulainn, favorite of black-winged Mórrígan), but like

any man, he began to age, and his powers to wane. At this point he encountered the glorious Gráinne, a fair-haired buxom willful lass. Their story
opens with all Ireland's women crazy with desire for Fionn. (Note to
tourism planners: mythic reenactment prospect follows.) A footrace was
organized, with Slievenamon's nipple-cairn its goal. It was an appropriate
setting, for the Tipperary mountain got its name, which means "mountain
of the women," from lusty lady fairies who seduced Fionn's warriors,
singing sweet songs until the men mounted, in turn, hill and singers.

Some say that Fionn, waiting on a stone seat for the winner, had organized the race. But given Gráinne's later behavior, I incline toward the version in which the women take the initiative. The princess was fleet and
fierce and used to being on top. Fair Gráinne took off like an arrow. Soon
her strong lungs and sturdy legs left the rest of the women in a cloud of
dust. Gráinne claimed her prize, and the wedding date was set.

But on that festive occasion, a breeze lifted the bangs off a warrior's
forehead. Now this warrior was a handsome man — "a champion with fair,
freckled skin, raven-black curls, a gentle manly countenance, and a soft
voice," says the Book of Leinster. Beyond that, Diarmuid was the foster
son of Oengus, god of poetry, and he was a Kerryman to boot. Were that
not enough, he had a *ball seirc,* a love spot, on his forehead. Any woman
who saw it became insane with lust — which is why our hero modestly
wore bangs.

The moment Gráinne saw the love spot on Diarmuid's forehead, her
heart was lost. (I wonder did she need the excuse; our Gráinne's libido
seemed to need no spur.) Undeterred by the nuptials in progress, Gráinne
drugged her wedding party — all but the bewildered Diarmuid, whom she
placed under a *geasa,* a sacred vow, to elope with her. Diarmuid hesitated,
fearing that Fionn would purse them: "There is not in Ireland a wilderness,
however remote, that could shelter us from Fionn's revenge." Besides,
Diarmuid was already under a *geasa* that he would not run off with any
woman who came to him clothed or unclothed, in daylight or at night,
walking or on horseback. Determined Gráinne came for him at dusk, clad
in fairy cloth, riding a mule. And so Gráinne got her way.

For the next several years they galloped around the country at the
speed of American tourists, always staying a wee bit ahead of Gráinne's
abandoned husband. They slept each night on dolmens, those ancient rock
altars still called "beds of Diarmuid and Gráinne" (until recently, inviting

someone to visit a dolmen constituted a sexual invitation). A medieval verse imagines Gráinne admiring her lover as he slept:

Rest there now, my Glory of the Western World,
While I marvel at your beauty, at your hair's sweet curl.

After seven years, Gráinne conceived a lust for ripe berries on a wild Munster hill; when the couple paused to harvest them, Fionn sprang out of the underbrush. You would imagine — Diarmuid had — that Ireland's greatest hero would wreak a horrible revenge, but all Fionn did was ship the pair off to Leitrim, where they settled down and raised a family.

It's the same story as Tristan and Isolde, Lancelot and Guinevere, but with an Irish twist: Isolde was helpless to undo the magic that bound her to Tristan, Guinevere helpless to resist Lancelot's love, but fair fleet Gráinne was herself irresistible when, as Yeats would have it, "proud and stiff / on love intent." And that makes all the difference. Gráinne becomes subject, not object; active, not passive; protagonist, not prize. And she is not the only passionate woman in Celtic myth, for in the category of tales called *aithed,* or elopements, it is the woman who initiates the affair. Doomed Deirdre pursues raven-haired Naoise; Moriath of Munster drugs her watchful mother to pursue handsome Móen; and Medb brags that she never has "one man without another in his shadow."

Scholars debate what, if anything, the adventures of such willful heroines tell us about the lives of real women. Celticist Lisa Bitel cautions against reading too much into the existence of "stern and gorgeous" goddesses in a land where real women were treated as "stay-at-home legal incompetents." But historian Peter Berresford Ellis believes myth and reality were closer in Ireland than, say, in Greece, where women were household prisoners in cities named for goddesses. Gráinne may be a myth, but real women could be just as forthright, just as bold.

They could be so because the law stood on their side, as we find in legal tracts from early Christian times. It was not Church law the monks transcribed, but Irish law that had, until then, been transmitted orally. For like poetry and history, the law was a spiritual practice and thus in the domain of the druids. Specialists called brehons memorized and recited law and precedent, but they neither judged cases nor assigned penalties. There was no police force, no imprisonment, no capital punishment;

anyone guilty of a crime paid fines to the victim or, in cases of murder, to the bereaved.

The only crime as iniquitous as murder was rape, whether by violence or by assault on an intoxicated or sleeping woman; enormous fines were due the victim. If a raped woman conceived, her rapist bore all financial responsibility for the child. Woe to a man whose victim died in childbirth; fines could bankrupt his family. And rape was not the only sexual crime; penalties were levied for inappropriate touching or "shaming by stroking under the robe"; for verbal harassment; for mocking a woman's appearance; and for shaving off a woman's pubic hair in an attempt to seduce her. (Say what?)

Brehon law provided for women's economic support before, during, and after marriage; divorce was easy if unions failed. Marriage was broadly defined to include even brief relationships, if they resulted in pregnancy; the law did not conceive of illegitimacy, for *saer brú beiris breith do thabairt clí:* "fertile wombs are free to bear." Sexual satisfaction was assumed as women's right, for which reason they were discouraged from wedding an "unarmed" (impotent) man, an extremely obese man (who might find sex difficult), or a *claenain* ("perverted little wretch") who gossiped about women's preferred sexual positions. A woman could leave her husband without penalty if deprived of sexual intercourse, especially if he preferred servant boys to women. Fidelity was expected; if a woman discovered her man had committed secret adultery, she had three days during which anything she did to husband or mistress, up to and including murder, carried no penalty.

For a thousand years, Ireland lived under brehon law. But in the twelfth century a petty king named Diarmuid (no relation) eloped with fair Dervorgilla O'Rourke, then invited the Normans to get him out of the resultant trouble. His guests brought along their own laws — and more trouble. For under English law land was a possession, while the brehons saw it as a trust, held by a king for his people, who elected a new leader upon his death. Here was Diarmuid, promising his allies land that (unless he was a world-class swindler) he believed would revert to Irish control at their deaths; and here were his allies, thinking they had a lock on the land for good and all. You see the problem.

The extent of the problem did not become apparent for almost four centuries. Within the Pale of English influence, their law ruled; beyond the

Pale, brehon law prevailed. Then Henry VIII, believing that brehon law prevented complete subjugation of the Irish, cagily initiated the "surrender and regrant" policy whereby Irish chiefs exchanged hereditary ranks for English titles (whence such curiosities as earls in Munster). It is unclear how many of the agreeable chiefs understood the difference between Irish and English law; some apparently thought death would terminate their titles and with it, the subject status of their people and land, which Henry intended to make irrevocably English.

Henry died before extirpating brehon law, so daughter Elizabeth renewed the assault. Among her fiercest supporters were the Undertakers, aptly nicknamed Englishmen living on (and off) land forcibly taken from Irish chiefs who declined to surrender. The Undertakers naturally opposed the old legal system under which they could not sell or entail their properties. Especially shrill was poet Edmund Spenser, who from his thousands of stolen Munster acres called brehon law "repugning quite to God's law and man's," apparently confusing "man" with "Englishman."

⊠⁛⊠⁛⊠

"Man's law" would win, and women lose. But not immediately. In the dying days of brehon law, a woman was born who lived its possibilities to the fullest. Sometime around 1530, the O'Malley clan of Connacht welcomed a daughter, Gráinne, who grew up as willful as her mythic namesake. Gráinne's family was renowned for seafaring, so much so that it was said *gearr míle ar muir díbh Máille:* "a mile by sea is but an inch to an O'Malley." Gráinne succeeded her father as leader of family enterprises that included — indeed centered on — what the English called piracy because they refused to acknowledge the O'Malleys' traditional right to levy taxes on those who used their sea routes. Gráinne took over as chief of the clan, becoming so successful that she was described to England's Elizabeth as "chief director and commander of thieves and murderers at sea" and "notorious in all the coasts of Ireland."

Gráinne was nicknamed Granuaile, an anglicization of her name in Irish, Gráinne ní Mhaille. Folklore claims the name means "Gráinne the Bald," because the bold young woman shaved her head before going to sea. Shaven or no, Granuaile never neutered herself like England's Virgin Queen, who, believing it impossible to be both woman and leader, chose the latter. By contrast, Granuaile married for the first time at sixteen; Dónal Ó Flaherty, *tánaiste* or leader-in-waiting of a powerful Connemara clan, fathered her first three children. When Dónal turned out to be a blackguard, Granuaile took to the deep blue sea, enduring long weeks aboard ship in pelting rain and high winds, reveling in the loyalty of two hundred men.

When her husband finally died — under suspicious circumstances appropriate to his character — Granuaile did not haste to a re-wedding. Neither did she remain celibate. Indeed, "her sexual exploits were as notorious as those of the men she led," says biographer Anne Chambers. When her young lover, Hugh de Lacy, was murdered, she avenged him in a brutal ambush. When Granuaile found a man whose status equaled hers, the *tánaiste* Richard Bourke, she married him in the old Celtic Teltown way, for a year. At year's end Granuaile locked Bourke out of his castle and, from its ramparts, proclaimed, "I dismiss you" — keeping the castle as a spoil of marriage. (Note to potential husbands: always be cautious when marrying pirates.) The couple later reconciled and had a son, born during a storm on the high seas. The next day, Granuaile's galley was attacked by Algerian pirates and she led the defense, wrapped in a bloody blanket, screaming curses.

For forty years, Granuaile consolidated her power as "nurse to all rebellions in the province," according to an Elizabethan enemy. But in 1593 Granuaile's son — the one born at sea — was imprisoned for sedition against England. What's a pirate queen to do? Granuaile captained a ship to London to sue Elizabeth for her son's release. The meeting of the two queens is the stuff of legend. Did Granuaile really appear barefoot? Did she really converse in Latin? Did she toss Elizabeth's lacy handkerchief into the fire, explaining that the Irish, being "more cleanly" than the English, would never reuse such a rag? Did Granuaile refuse Elizabeth's offer to elevate her to countess because, as equals, neither could make the other such an offer? Whatever happened, Granuaile's son was freed.

Not long after their meeting, both queens died. History, so kind to the Virgin Queen, so thoroughly erased the Pirate Queen that for almost four hundred years she was believed just a legend. Being a woman, and Irish, and a pirate to boot, Granuaile might not have been a fit subject for historians, but the people of Ireland never forgot her. For if history is written by the victors, oral history is the domain of the dispossessed, those from whom land and reputation and dignity have been stolen. Of Granuaile,

songs were sung and stories told — and in the last century, documents surfaced proving their truth. Today we know more about Granuaile than at
any time since her death.

⊠⊠⊠⊠⊠

During those shadowed years, Irish women's rights were inexorably
eroded. Where brehon law assured women economic freedom, English law
stripped them of property rights. Irish women did not go quietly into that
legal night. A pamphlet from Munster circulated through the land in 1703;
Párliament na mBan, the Women's Parliament, described a congress
agreeing that "if women had control of all affairs it is certain that things
would be more settled and peaceful than they are now." Then came *An
Appeal of One Half of the Human Race, Women, against the Pretensions
of the Other Half, Men* — one of the world's earliest feminist tracts —
again from Munster, the province traditionally most associated with
women.

The degradation of women paralleled a decline in the status of poets.
In Celtic Ireland, poets were druids and thus priests, historians, magicians.
That was bad enough, but there was more: the line between poet and brehon was notably hazy. After Diarmuid's deal with the Normans, poets had
attached themselves to noble families, becoming hereditary bards maintained in style and leisure; the Ó Daillaighs, my reputed ancestors, were
such a family. But the dismantlement of brehon law meant the shredding
of social networks that supported poetry. Where poets — and their often
numerous students and servants — once lodged in the homes of kings, they
were now homeless and destitute. English law provided no protection;
indeed the 1366 Statutes of Kilkenny forbade Englishmen even to speak to
poets, while later, under the Munster Articles of Plantation, Undertakers
were forbidden to "retain or lodge any Irish rhymers, bards, harpers or
such idle persons."

A poetic form based on the *caoineadh,* or funeral keening, emerged to
suit the times. Where earlier poets had lamented the deaths of their noble
patrons, the dislodged rhymers and bards sang sorrowfully of the death of
poetry itself and of the Celtic culture that had sustained it. *Ní thuig mé an
lucht so ag labhra / gá dtá ar tteanga mháthardha,* one said: "I don't
understand my own native tongue, I don't know my own people."

Poets eked out a living as teachers and wandering minstrels and farmers. "It's hard," lamented Dáibhí Ó Bruadair, "and thirsty work, plowing a furrow alone." To slake their various thirsts, poets established Courts of Poetry, a grand name that disguises the reality: rude shacks and home brew in place of grand halls and mead. Despite meager surroundings, the spirit of poetry lived on in these Courts, where one could hear the great ancient poems recited in Irish and new ones extemporized.

Munster boasted more Courts than any other province. In the shadow of Danu's Paps, the Courts of Sliabh Luchra and Ballyvourney met. At Glenflesk was the Court of Geoffrey O'Donoghue, whose poetry was almost as good as his drink; further north, near Croom in Limerick, comedy reigned at the School of Merriment. These Munster Courts birthed a new form of *aisling,* a traditional poem full of wild dreamy imagery.

On a road in colonized Ireland, the poet meets a *spéir-bhean,* a woman of the sky, more beautiful than any earthly woman. Literary historian Daniel Corkery describes her this way: "In her cheeks the flushing of red berries contends with the whiteness of a gentle lily. Her throat and brow are as white as the foam on a wild lake. Her face is like the glowing sun seen through crystal. Her breasts are sharp-rounded and inviolate." The great Aodhagán Ó Rathaille called her "brightness of brightness whom I met in the path of loneliness." The sky-woman reveals her name as Roisín Dubh, Aiobheal, or Cathleen ní Houlihan; she weeps over her degraded state; she prophesies a grand future when her lover returns. Slowly, the poet realizes her identity. For the *spéir-bhean* is no woman at all, but Ériu, the land itself.

Hearing the voice of the land was the Irish poet's primary job, for when she suffered, fault lay with the ruler. In ancient times, a poet's satire could sting an ineffectual king's face into boils, a defect that made him unfit to rule; it was the poet's task to clear the way for a better king. But in colonized Ireland, poets became impotent. The smooth faces of the Undertakers remained unblemished by satires in Irish, and the *spéir-bhean* wandered the lonely roads seeking futilely for a champion.

All surviving *aisling* poems were composed by men; the same is true of virtually all Irish poems. Irish poetry was an oral art, but scribblers found women poets, like women pirates, easy to ignore. (Indeed, they find that true of women in general. As poet Brendan Kennelly says, "The history, or herstory, of Irish women is rather like that of the Irish language — much talked about but little heard.") Nonetheless there is evidence of a distaff literary tradition, beginning with the keen, or lament, invented by no less a poet than the goddess Brigit.

In Munster, especially renowned for its woman poets, it was said that daughters inherited the poet's tongue, while sons inherited only the ability to tell stories. It was from Munster that Liadan hailed, the legendary seventh-century poet whom Máire Cruise O'Brien believes was a local version of the goddess of poetry. While making a poet's circuit around Ireland — what Padraic Colum described as "giving recitals, meeting distinguished members of the guild, looking in on bardic schools" — she met another poet, Cuirithir. Instantly smitten, he begged Liadan to become his lover because "any son of ours would be a fine one." Unwilling to interrupt her circuit, Liadan invited Cuirithir down to Kerry, promising him a warm reception.

History does not record how long Cuirithir delayed before leaving, but when he arrived, to his horror, Liadan was wearing a nun's habit. But to his relief she was still drawn to him. Torn between vows and desire, Liadan took Cuirithir to her spiritual director, who offered the lovers a choice: they could either see each other or hear each other's words. Some choice for poets! Through a veil, unable to gaze into each other's eyes, Liadan and Cuirithir shared tender words. Then the monk changed his mind. The couple could sleep together as long as another person slept between them. This they did.

The near-intimacy broke Cuirithir's heart. He fled. Liadan followed, belatedly realizing that holiness was not compromised by bodily love. Sorrowful Liadan, for she was unable to reach Cuirithir, who sailed for parts unknown. At the shore, Liadan spoke a famous lament: "I am Liadan; I loved Cuirithir. The forest sang to me when I was with him, and the great blue sea. Why hide my love, why hide my desire? My heart melts in the furnace of his love." Then she died.

Beautiful as Liadan's lament is, it is not the most brilliant example of the form. That was composed by the Kerrywoman Eibhlín Dhubh Ní Chonaill — black-haired Eileen O'Connell — upon the murder of her husband, Art Ó Laoghaire — Arthur Leary. Her harrowing lament, recited in Munster for generations before being written down, begins with Eibhlín meeting Art in a little market town near the Paps in 1767:

When I first saw you
beside the market-house

I had eyes for nothing else,
heart for no one else.
And I never regretted it.

Eibhlín and Art's happy marriage brought them three children. Then, tragedy: soldiers offered Art five pounds for his handsome bay horse. English law forbade Catholics to own a horse worth more than that pittance, but proud Art refused the offer. So the soldiers cut him down, leaving him by the roadside in a thicket of gorse. The horse returned home, riderless, "trailing her reins, your blood on her shoulders and on the tooled saddle that had cradled you," as Eibhlín describes the scene. Leaping into the saddle, Eibhlín galloped to her husband's side. She was too late: he was dead, but just barely, his blood still flowing. "I did not wipe it," Eibhlín says, "but dipped my hands in it and drank."

Even those who dismiss Irish women's achievements acknowledge Eibhlín Dhubh Ní Chonaill's lament as a masterpiece of Irish literature, as the greatest example of the keening invented by the goddess Brigit and later kidnapped by the *aisling* poets. With its "strange effusion of deep feeling and utter technical control, of powerful utterance dramatically controlled" — the words are those of critic Declan Kiberd — Eibhlín's widow's song for Art, *cara* (friend) and *grá* (lover), may be part of a women's tradition now lost because it was never written down.

Black-haired Eibhlín's lament offers insight into the private life of a seventeenth-century Irishwoman. More than two hundred years after brehon law had been vanquished, Eibhlín was as bold about her desires as Gráinne or Granuaile — "a masterful woman," Kiberd calls her, "in the Gaelic tradition." She describes the pleasure she got from the body of her "soul's darling" and calls Art "a fine bed-mate" whose death drove her almost mad: "What Irishwoman could stretch out her body beside him, bear him three sucklings, and not run wild from losing him?"

Eibhlín had married Art despite her family's objections; she came of Irish nobility (her mother was a distinguished poet, her father a wealthy merchant), while Art was a mere soldier. But in women's diminishing arena of freedom, marriage remained a surprising domain of choice. A simple promise sufficed, often made in the heat of passion and with no witnesses; it was not until 1827 that the Council of Trent's 1563 decree requiring a priest at marriages was enforced in rural Ireland. Irish women were eager partners, marrying in their teens and then, often, again in midlife. Some marriages were "matches," connecting families of similar property, but others were love matches like Eibhlín's. The great Kerry storyteller Peig Sayers recalled a woman who turned down a well-off smith for a poor but handsome man, and another who refused a likely prospect because "I gave the love of my breast and soul to a stranger."

Poetry shows Irish women to have been far from aloof. Kerry poet Pierce Ferriter begged his lover to be more modest: "Hide your white bosom, cover your blooming breast." Women were men's equal in passion in this poem, translated from the sixteenth-century Irish by Brendan Kennelly:

For your sweet sake, I will ignore
Every girl who takes my eye.
If it's possible, I implore
You to do the same for me.

It is, of course, possible these poems were just the wet dreams of frustrated poets, for no silence is deeper than that shrouding ancient intimacies. But the large size of Irish families in pre-Famine years supports the poets' depiction of women as eager partners in the procreative act.

Then in the 1840s, feminine passion, like everything Irish, was dealt a crushing blow. How does one find joy while wild dogs devour starving children? With hunger for food more urgent than hunger for sex, the Irish marriage and birth rate plummeted. Brendan Kennelly remembers hearing the great Munster writer Frank O'Connor describe a woman bursting into dance on the Kerry shores. She was far from young, over fifty certainly, and she danced with grace and joy and passion. "The woman was the entire people, capable of spontaneous artistic expression," Kennelly says. "Capable of it, that is, before the Famine."

⚅⚅⚅⚅

But the population should then have rebounded as life affirmed itself in the face of death. Instead, Ireland entered a period of sexual repression as rising nationalism became hopelessly entangled with Catholic identity. Ireland's invaders, those who had left the sky-woman destitute on the roadsides, opposed Catholicism; the Irish opposed them by tightening their embrace of it. This left men under vows of celibacy in charge of defining sexual mores. Who could be less appropriate? The priests — for whom following their vows was often hard, very hard — preached a body-hating doctrine derived from fifth-century Africa, where Augustine had inseminated Christianity with philosophical dualism. Augustine liked light, not darkness; reason, not emotion; heaven, not earth. An alternative vision, the "happy heresy" of the Celtic monk Pelagius, urged acceptance of the natural world, arguing that if God created darkness and light, must we not embrace both? For Pelagius, we need only look around us to see how "narrow shafts of divine light pierce the veil separating heaven from earth."

Augustine would have none of that. And Augustine — one of the most brilliant men of his era, perhaps of any — wrote so persuasively that Christianity ever after saw light and dark as enemies. Even worse, on the side of darkness, Augustine placed woman, whom he believed could not be "herself alone the image of God; whereas man alone is the image of God fully and completely." Man was mind and goodness; woman, body and evil. The further from women, the better; Thomas Aquinas believed her just "a necessary object, needed to preserve the species or to provide food and drink." As Freud would later say, celibacy driven by hatred caused priests to behave "towards sexuality as a people does which has subjected another one to its exploitation." The body became a thing to be colonized, subjugated.

Thus did Ireland become the "priest-ridden" country of which James Joyce complained. Even traditional dances were suppressed, a straitjacket placed on the upper body to avoid the suggestion of lewdness. (Although whenever I see a young woman showing her panties in high-stepping kicks, I suspect subversion of clerical intent.) Even more scandalously, "Magdalens" — called after the New Testament's reputed harlot — were enslaved as laundresses for convents and hospitals. Girls, usually poor, were "sent to the laundries" for showing sexual curiosity; unwed pregnancy, even if the result of incest or rape, brought imprisonment for the mother while the father went free. Some children were brought up in orphanages on the same grounds as the mothers they were barred from knowing. Others were sent to America, with their adoptive mothers forced to agree never to work outside the home.

When I first came over, the Magdalen laundries were still open, and Irish women had less freedom than ever in history. For strangely, upon winning its independence, the Irish Republic did not revert to brehon law. English Common Law, American constitutional practice, and the opinions of priests formed the new nation's legal system. Thus Ireland fulfilled the hopeful words of Edmund Spenser, who praised any time that men

> *The liberty of women did repeale,*
> *Which they had long vsurpt; and them restoring*
> *To mens subjiection, did true Iustice deale.*

In mid-twentieth-century Ireland, all marital property was the husband's, leaving women economically dependent. Church influence straitjacketed women's sexuality: there was no divorce; contraception was illegal. When, a few years later, married women were permitted to fill contraceptive prescriptions at authorized pharmacies, many doctors refused to write the prescriptions. Couples who wanted smaller families tried the "red-letter day" method, marking presumably safe days with a red mark on the calendar.

A joke of the time tells of a farmer who, too poor to support more children, asked his parish priest for dispensation to use birth control. The priest reminded him of the one approved method. The farmer nodded. A year later, the family came in for another baptism. Taking the man aside, the priest asked him why the couple wasn't using rhythm. "Ah, Father," said the man hopelessly, "and who can afford a *céilí* band every night?"

Ireland being Ireland, there were ways around the law. In Gort, I quickly learned that contraceptives could be purchased from a certain foreigner (presumably not bound by Irish morality) who drank in a certain bar at a certain time each day. Feminist action in Dublin included giving away condoms — quite illegal — on Saint Stephens Green every Saturday. My American accent made me a useful lookout. When I saw the *gardai* approach, I rushed up to them, trilling, "Oh, OFFICERS, I'm SO GLAD to see you, I am SO VERY lost, I just don't know WHERE I am" — while behind me, condoms were stuffed into handbags as my friends rushed to safety.

Today, less than thirty years later, Irish women — and their men — have greater sexual freedom than they have had in centuries. One no longer need look for Johnny Rubber in a certain bar at a certain hour; Ireland's first woman president, United Nations Commissioner for Human Rights Mary Robinson, led the fight for contraceptive rights while in the

Dáil, the Irish congress. One-fifth of births are outside marriage, and fewer women than in the past offer up children for adoption. But vestiges of priest-ridden Ireland remain. In 1992, the Girl X case — wherein a raped teenager was barred from traveling to England — exposed the huge cross-channel abortion traffic. Although Irish law now permits abortions for women in mortal danger, no doctor in the country will perform the procedure.

The Girl X case inspired Munster novelist Edna O'Brien to write a searing novel of a girl's struggle against a woman-hating, body-hating society. The book opens on an idyllic Irish scene. A father and daughter take a summer walk down a mountain road full of "flowers and flowering weeds in full regalia, a carnival sight." In ancient times, a man and a woman on a remote road would be recognized as a poet meeting the lonely feminine essence of Ireland herself. But this sweet boreen leads to a hidden place where the father rapes his daughter, who becomes not only pregnant but mute, silent as the road itself, "somnolent with a speech of its own." In disturbingly poetic prose, O'Brien paints her "wee Magdalen" who refuses, despite all, to reject her *banulachta,* her womanliness.

Not long ago, such a book would have been banned. Indeed, right up there with the *Irish Family Planning Guide,* the Irish censors listed anything by Edna O'Brien. Invariably described as an "earthy" writer, O'Brien caught the censors' eyes with her first novel, *The Country Girls,* about two teenagers resisting institutional repression. Fearful critics called her creation of curious passionate Kate and Baba "a smear on Irish womanhood," and O'Brien's own parish priest burned the novel. Told that the evil pouring forth from its burning pages caused women to faint, O'Brien retorted, "it was probably the smoke."

Book burnings were common in the bad old days. In 1943 censors became alarmed at *The Tailor and Ansty,* wherein Eric Cross recorded the opinions of an elderly Munster couple who embraced sex as one of life's delights, right up there with gossip and drink. If the Tailor and his wife, Anastasia, viewed sex with happy equanimity, not so the West Cork priest who forced the old man to burn the book in his own hearth fire.

The censors' most famous victim — other than freedom — was what critic Séan Ó Tuama called "the greatest comic poem ever written in Ireland." Brian Merriman's "The Midnight Court" was readily available in Irish, but perhaps the censors believed that a sufficiently modest veil.

When it was translated into English, the classic was forthwith banned. (I was in Dublin the very day censorship was lifted in 1975, and to the best of my memory, nothing changed. Drunken men still felt up convent girls at the National Ballroom, teenagers still petted publicly in doorways, and Irish speech, so astonishingly reliant upon a rude word for intercourse, continued its impressive vulgarity.)

Merriman's censor-shocking poem begins as a traditional *aisling,* but true to his name, the poet makes merry with the form. For the Otherworldly woman who appears was no *spéir-bhean.* Napping beside a pleasant lake, the poet is awakened by an enormous woman, bailiff to the fairy queen Aiobheal, come to set up court to hear women's complaints against men. First a young maiden steps up, furious at the men who "balked me and bilked me and slipped from me ever, spurned me and turned from me and tattered my heart." Other women provide equally damning evidence, including the siring of children by priests who took their pleasure without attending to its outcome. When the other side's turn comes, Merriman had already given away his best lines, so the men just whine about women demanding too much. Queen Aiobheal sides with her sex, permitting women to take lovers and sentencing unmarried men to be summarily "whipped with a stout cord." Oh dear, oh dear, thinks our poet, suddenly recalling his state of disunion. Sure enough, the bailiff raises her whip and applies it to the poet, who feels every "tenderly calibrated pain" until he wakes, ready to mend his puritanical ways.

※※※※※

"The Midnight Court" reminds me of all those jokes about Irish men's lack of sexual prowess. "An Irish queer: a man who prefers a woman to a pint," is the most famous, along with the definition of Irish foreplay as "Bridget, brace yourself." My favorite is about the bachelor, finally marrying in middle life, who asks the lads down at the pub about sex. ("About sex?" another joke has it. "About then, you should sit down and have your tea.") One of the lads offers the following advice: "Place your hand on her belly and tell her you love her." Our blushing bachelor climbs in beside his beaming bride, places hands as instructed, and mutters, "I love you." As predicted, she warms to this approach. "Lower, darling," she murmurs. He clears his throat. "I love you," he repeats in a more manly tone.

The women of Merriman's satire, by contrast, recall those lusty mythic wenches Gráinne, Deirdre, Medb, and, let's not forget, the women who arrived on Cesair's ship at the dawn of time and promptly killed the male crew members by — well, by screwing them to death. And right up there on the most-wanton list is Merriman's own fairy queen, whose other name was Áine and who may be the same as Anu, goddess of the Paps. From Áine's name comes the modern Irish word *áineas*, pleasure, and pleasure was Áine's palpable goal. The long list of her lovers runs from gods like Manannán, ruler of the sea, to humans like Earl Muiris of Desmond.

Áine was so beautiful that anyone who saw her naked went insane, so she always wore a feathered cloak that made her look like a swan. Alas, the cloak also made sexual faithfulness impossible. So Earl Muiris stole it and hid it well away. A subdued Áine extracted from him a promise that, no matter what their children did, he would never express surprise. Muiris agreed, so Áine settled down and bore a son, Gearóid Iarla. Things went smoothly until Gearóid was fully grown, when he accidentally revealed magical powers. Muiris yelped in surprise. Áine and her son instantly departed, he as a goose, she as a swan, he to the waters of Lough Gur, she to the mountain that bears her name, Knockainy.

There really was an Earl Muiris; he really had a descendent, the sixteenth-century Gearóid, or Garrett Fitzgerald, who introduced to Ireland the courtly love poetry popular on the continent. One of his poems describes women as

> *victims of their hearts*
> *who love a sound and slender man,*
> *Ancient persons, stout and grey,*
> *they will not choose for company.*
> *but chose a juicy branch, though poor.*

Gearóid seems to have learned something at Áine's knee.

After fighting Queen Elizabeth, the real Gearóid died in Kerry. But legend says Lough Gur, the enchanted lake beneath Áine's hill, claimed her son. Sissie O'Brien Fogarty, who grew up on the lake and told its legends to Mary Carbery a century ago, said Gearóid reappeared every seven years: "He rides on a milk-white horse, shod with silver shoes, and must ride until the silver shoes are worn out. Then he will be loosed from the enchantment that binds him and will live, a man among men, for he has never died."

Every seventh year, local legend still maintains, someone drowns in Lough Gur. And every seven years, its water disappears, revealing an immense tree on the lake bottom. Beneath sits a woman, knitting with green yarn. Once a horseman was riding by just at the moment the lake emptied. As legend foretold, the man saw the tree, and it covered by a cloth of green. Inspired — or perhaps mad — the man snatched the cloth. As he fled, the knitting woman called out, "Awake! From the Dead Woman's Land a horseman rides, from my head the green cloth snatching." Lough Gur's waters rose, reclaiming the cloth. Some say that if the man had escaped with it, the lake's enchantment would be broken; others, that were the green cloth not safe beneath the lake, the land would grow barren.

Foreign tourists rarely visit Lough Gur; indeed, few people come at all, so I have spent lovely lonely days on its shore, seeing Gearóid in every goose and Áine in every swan. It is a soft sweet landscape, not dramatic like the mountains of the Kerry Ring or, for that matter, like the small but steep Derrynasaggarts. The low limestone hills crowd together, blue upon blue, embracing the little C-shaped lake with its tiny island named for Áine's son. Sissie O'Brien describes Lough Gur "lying in summer sunshine like a bright mirror in which are reflected blue sky, bare hills, precipitous gray rocks and green pastures." Great boulders form cairns and circles on its shores, relics of the past. Crouched on the southern shore, a pair of low thatched huts house interpretive exhibits. But I cannot remain long indoors, for the lake calls me to cast food out to the water birds and my eyes up to the surrounding hills.

None are as dramatically feminine as the Paps, but the ancients saw in them the same womanly form, which they emphasized with the usual mounds and cairns. Knockainy's is offset, making the hill a pregnant woman close to term. Nearby rises nipple-cairned Cnoc Gréine, named for Áine's sister, whose identity is otherwise cloudy. Legend says Gillagrianne, "Lady Grian of the Bright Cheeks," had a human father and a sunbeam mother. When she recognized how strange was her conception, Gillagrianne drowned herself in Lough Graney (where Merriman met the fairy bailiff) and was buried at Tuamgraney (Edna O'Brien's birthplace). This mysterious personage may be fleet-footed Gráinne herself, also said to be buried at Tuamgraney. At Cnoc Gréine's summit is a rock called Seefin, "seat of Fionn," very like the stone atop Slievenamon on which our hero sat while Gráinne made her headlong ascent. As is so often the case in Irish legend, the figures are difficult to distinguish, possibly local manifestations of a single original, possibly multiple originals that share common imagery.

❂❂❂❂❂

That common imagery extends beyond cairned female-bodied hills to include sexuality and its associated season. For where Connacht is autumn and the wisdom that comes with waning years, where Ulster is winter and the battle for life in bitter weather, where Leinster is spring with its richness and energy, so in the great seasonal calendar hidden in Ireland's mythic geography is Munster the province of sensuous summer, of juice tasted on hilltops from the sweet lips of a lover.

The connection between summer and Munster's mountains was discovered, appropriately enough, by a woman from that province who noticed what others failed to see — a cluster of rural fairs and festivals around August 1, the ancient harvest feast called Lughnasa after the god Lugh. Máire MacNeill was an amateur folklorist who in the 1930s helped to catalogue material for the new Irish Folklore Commission. Reading through stories and geographical notes, mostly in Irish, MacNeill methodically set about proving her intuition.

Máire MacNeill is one of my heroines, my luggage to Ireland invariably made heavier by her out-of-print *Festival of Lughnasa*. Tom Hannon, who knew this, once became quite mysterious as we were jaunting about the countryside. Guiding me to a little town in north Munster, he located a fine modern home and knocked gingerly at its door. A nurse, fully garbed in white, greeted us, and when Tom asked for Mrs. Sweeney, responded that she was not receiving visitors.

"Tell her," said Tom, "that a fan from Alaska has come to visit."

I knew no Mrs. Sweeney. I stood behind Tom, quite mystified.

A tiny frail woman appeared at the nurse's elbow. "A fan from Alaska?" she quavered.

"Yes!" proclaimed Tom, stepping aside dramatically. "Patricia Monaghan, meet Máire MacNeill."

(It reminded me of the time, years earlier, when I was staying at Frank Kelly's and a rangy blue-eyed fellow stopped in for morning tea. Still in my nightgown, I enjoyed a friendly chat with the man, who identified him-self as "a sort of artist" and said he'd just returned from Africa. "You must be doing well," I remarked, "if you can afford to go to Africa." After the guest departed, Frank leaned over and said, "so, how did you like Peter O'Toole?" Blood drained from my face. "Don't worry," Frank reassured me, "he didn't recognize you either." Neither did Máire MacNeill.)

My copies of her books were back in Gort, and so I have no autograph, only a treasured memory of a cozy sitting room where Tom and Máire drank tea, debating the exact location of the fairy city at the bottom of Inchiquin Lake and sharing other local legends. Well for me that Tom brought me along, for Máire MacNeill died just months after our visit.

Lughnasa rituals, MacNeill argued, survived in fairs and in mountain ascents. The former she believed derived from ancient *oenachs,* summer festivals where gossip was shared, matches made, and cattle traded. As the Celtic system of land tenure disintegrated, so did the great regional feasts. No longer did tribes select a king, no longer did druids conduct rituals to assure the land's fertility, no longer did girls give their hearts in trial mar-riages. But vague vestigial rites continued at otherwise simple harvest fairs.

Such a rite still occurs on Desmond land, forfeited when Áine's descendents refused to submit to Elizabeth. Annually, the town of Kilorglin conducts what MacNeill called "a strange and apparently sym-bolic custom." It begins on Gathering Day, when a wild goat is captured in the Kerry mountains and brought to the town center. There a girl crowns him King Puck, from *poc,* the Irish for — well, for "goat." He is hoisted onto a platform, where he remains for several days, occasionally nibbling cabbages but mostly looking like he misses the hills. Stalls on the streets beneath King Puck sell T-shirts and firecrackers and fortunes. Beneath him too a dozen pubs serve up drinks in plastic cups, the better to encourage outdoor jollity. Finally Scattering Day comes, and the king is released again into the wild.

No one knows when Puck Fair began, although MacNeill believed it to be Norman in origin. Legend remembers Cromwellian soldiers fright-ening goats that fled for safety to Kilorglin. There was also that summer in 1808, when the Kilorglin landlord found fees for his annual market prohibited and his income thereby diminished. But young Daniel O'Connell, black-haired Eibhlín's nephew, found a way around the law:

a goat was hoisted onto a platform, the market dedicated to his species, and penalties avoided, for the English law proscribed only horse, cattle, and sheep fairs.

Whatever legend and history may say, belief runs deep that Puck Fair is the most ancient and pagan of Ireland's festivals. Margaret Murray, controversial author of *The God of the Witches,* believed it "the only known survival of the deification and crowning of a king" from the animal world. But the original pristine ritual, she bemoaned, was "now irretrievably lost," buried under today's debauched, somewhat jocular event. The same moan goes up from other writers who imagine that once, to the heart-tearing sound of drums, a totem animal was crowned by white-clad druids, around whom circled reverent worshipers who felt in their souls' depths the ritual's transformative meaning. (Note to entrepreneurs: test-market bumper sticker reading, "Put the Lugh back in Lughnasa.")

But I wonder. Perhaps the festival was always pretty much what it is today. After all, a hundred years ago, John Millington Synge described Puck Fair as "a crush of drunken drivers and riders" with nothing especially profound on their minds. Which does not mean it is not deeply symbolic and significant. Augustinian dualism, which demands that something be either sacred or profane, has more difficulty with such an event than a Pelagian like me. Ancient pagan fertility rite on the one hand; raucous jollity and debauchery on the other. Must we choose?

Tens of thousands of people crowd into Kilorglin every year, and despite my dislike of crowds, I have done too. A puritanical Irish friend tried to discourage me from going, calling it all booze and bad behavior. ("A bottle and a fuck, and that makes Puck," goes a local rhyme.) And yes, so it is. And perhaps that is the point.

In a strange unforgettable poem, Muriel Rukeyser sang of Puck Fair:

Winds go west over
Left-handed Reaper
Mountain that gathered me
Out of my old shame —

Your white beard streaming,
Puck of summertime,
At last gave me
My woman's name.

I think she had it right, for despite its casual debauchery, Puck Fair touches something primal, some "tragic penetrating beauty, music and filth, cattle and drunkenness, the gypsies and the goat and the marvelous," as Rukeyser has said. That tragic penetrating beauty, that peculiar marvelousness, rises out of sex, for like any fertility festival Puck Fair brings masculine and feminine into balance as the heartiest he-goat of the mountains — cloven-footed Pan to the Greeks, goat-headed pooka to the Irish, the devil to European Christians — is crowned by a blooming girl. Augustine saw the world's two sides well and clearly; he just got it wrong when he declared them in conflict.

Lughnasa's very name proclaims its potent masculinity. Lugh, foster son of Áine's lover Manannán, was called "many-skilled" because he was a poet-harper-historian-hero-magician, and "long arms" because his weapons reached beyond those of other warriors. Lugh's grandfather Balor felt that reach in battle — a mythic metaphor for the endless contest between growth and death. Harvest myths often involve such fights: on Áine's hill, two gods fought annually; at Tailtiu's assembly, Fionn himself led the fighting. MacNeill theorized that faction fights at Lughnasa originated as ritual contests among neighbors contending for the best harvest.

But feminine must balance masculine, so Lugh is said to have inaugurated the feast in honor of his foster mother, Tailtiu. In the Colloquy of the Ancients, we find an earlier name: Brón Trogain, describing the earth groaning in labor as she births the harvest. As pain precedes birth, the day of ripening was preceded by a pinched season of want; the Month of Shaking Out the Bags ended on Lughnasa when the new potatoes, first fruits of the earth, were dug and gratefully eaten.

Wild food was ripening too. The hilltops were a mosaic of berries: huckleberries, brambles, whortleberries, all ripening in the slant summer sunlight. On Lughnasa, young people raced to the hilltops, allegedly looking for berries, the size and abundance of which was an omen for the harvest. But that was just an excuse; really they were up there to court and make merry, as we see in Brian Friel's famous *Dancing at Lughnasa.* In the past, Teltown marriages, named for Lugh's mother, were contracted then — trial marriages, like Granuaile's with Richard Bourke, that could be terminated by either party within the year without penalty.

An area's most prominent mountain was not necessarily designated for Lughnasa ascents, but rather one was associated with myths of love and sex, as though the flirtatious young people who climbed, laughing and filling their mouths with berries and each other's kisses, brought the very gods alive: Knockainy, where Áine entertained lovers after leaving her husband; Anascaul, site of a legendary love triangle; Meelin's Rock, into which a girl flew to escape an unwanted marriage; Nagle's Mountain with its seat of Fionn; the great Mother Mountain, Máthair-Shliabh, also called the Mountain of Éblenn after a queen who eloped with her stepson; Cnoc Sídhe Úna, named for a lustful fairy queen.

And Slieve Mish, named for a madwoman — Lughnasa is often called the "feast of lunacy," although whether because of a bilingual pun or because harvest and insanity were connected is unknown — named Mis, whose father was overpowered and killed in a battle with Fionn mac Cumhaill. Mis found his fallen body and, wild with sorrow, drank his blood. Then she went mad, roving the Kerry hills, eating grass, speaking no known language, raging in pain and grief. "Fur and hair grew on her, so long it trailed on the ground behind," says a medieval poem.

But a kind harper, Dubh Rois, went up into the hills where Mis lived alone, exposed to the elements. Building a fire, he made soft music. In the soft evening light, he saw her draw near. He kept singing until Mis was close enough to touch.

Then he stopped. She did not move. Softly Dubh Rois asked Mis if she remembered music. She nodded slowly, then spoke for the first time since madness had come upon her. She remembered it, she said, from her father's hall. Then she asked what he was playing. "A harp," he said, and handed it to her. She sat in the deepening blue of the evening, holding the harp in her wild hands.

Then the harper moved his cloak and exposed himself. Mis stared. "What is that?" she asked, pointing. "That is the wand of the deed," said the harper. Mis considered this. "I do not remember that," she said. Dubh Rois offered to show her how it was used.

Mis agreed, and they made love, Dubh Rois playing as eloquently upon her body as he had upon his harp. Mis liked it and shyly asked for more. And so Dubh Rois stayed with Mis for two months, bathing away the dirt that hid her beauty until she stood radiant as the *spéir-bhean* herself. Mis's recovery was complete; when her harper was killed in battle, she did not return to madness but became a poet and lamented his loss.

Few books on Irish mythology mention Mis, concentrating instead on a parallel male figure, Suibne Geilt, Mad Sweeney, driven berserk by violence until he believes he can fly and understand the languages of wild things — Sweeney who acts just like the Kerry mountain goddess Mór, who flies through the wilderness like a bird until a king makes love to her. Why are Mis and Mór erased like this? Why censor feminine wildness? Because to exalt light over darkness, man over woman, requires us to choose intellect over emotion, reason over madness, and to draw a sharp line between. Women are imagined to be emotional while men are rational, and a wild mad bestial woman is such an intolerable intensification of all our culture imagines and fears that we dare not even speak her name.

⊠⊠⊠⊠⊠

I remember, at twelve, our reading list for literature class proclaiming its theme as "man against nature." Even then, I questioned the separation; now I also question the presumptuous generic. Does "man against nature" include "woman against nature," or does the phrase imply a battle of the sexes? I think the latter, for the very word *nature,* linked as it is with *nativity,* both points to and hides earth's maternity. When dualism exalts culture, then nature becomes something to be tamed for immediate use or set aside for later taming, the choice being left up to man. As Ursula Le Guin has said, "Civilized Man says, I am that I am, and the rest is women and the wilderness, to be used as I see fit."

Seeing ourselves as separate from nature takes practice, but we are well schooled in it. Those tourists circling Kerry are not seeing the land; they are scouting for landscapes. Before the Elizabethan era, land was not subjected to aesthetic judgment but known in the intimacy of daily life, known as good land for cows or corn, out of the wind, or near good water. And it was known through stories — here Mis found her father, there Gráinne raced — stories that Kerry poet Nuala Ní Dhomhnaill sees as a way to "possess the land emotionally and imaginatively without any need for titular ownership." But then in the early 1600s, Dutch artists invented landscape painting. Soon aesthetes sought out remote places like Kerry for the sublimity of its scenery. And so they still pass through the land without learning its names or its stories, only recognizing it as beautiful because it looks so much like art.

Ireland is full of beautiful ignored wild artless places. Summer roadsides are mad with bloom, brambles blossoming and bearing fruit and going to seed all at once, fuchsia ringing scarlet bells silently in the wind, the orange-yellow spikes of montbretias, and roses, roses, roses. It is hard to discern what is wild, what has escaped from cultivation, what is trying to escape, what is still relatively tame, in a land where everything is provisional and all borders permeable and a horse, there in an unfenced field, could be wild or tame or both. Ireland escapes the cleaving of the world. I have seen wildness in the midst of a town square, and a perfectly cultivated shrine on wild mountain.

As with land, so with people. Once when dining with Irish friends, I asked them to define wildness. The waitress interrupted. "Wildness," she said, her voice brambly with echoes of Irish, "is something everyone has, even society." (She put it just that way, "society.") "Wildness is a good thing. You want to be called wild, it's not a bad thing at all."

My friend Seán Lucy, the Cork poet, used to talk endlessly about Irish wildness, but he never, alas, wrote down his ideas. Not long after Seán died on a Chicago bus, his student Bill Savage and I lifted a glass to him at the Billy Goat Tavern and tried to reconstruct his theory. It goes something like this: the Irish, labeled "wild" by the English, embraced the definition, which allowed them more expressive freedom than their supposed masters. The Irish, Seán believed, wore wildness like a mantle, hiding behind it when they willed, occasionally forgetting where and why that cloak had been woven.

When culture is superior to nature, the wild must be tamed. The English needed the Irish to be wild; what good was their gift of civilization otherwise? In 1188, Geraldis Cambrensis called the Irish *gens inhospita, gens ex bestiis solum et bestialiter vivens:* "an inhospitable people, entirely descended from beasts and living in a beastly manner." In 1537, the Act for the English Order, Habit and Language labeled Irish life "a certain savage and wild kind and manner of living," while in 1610, Ireland's Attorney General called the Irish more "hurtfull" even than "wilde beastes."

Spenser took up that last theory with enthusiasm, for *The Faerie Queene's* author led a frightening career as apologist for England's apprenticeship in empire. Spenser supported extermination — "Force must be the instrument but famine must be the meanes" — but, he assured us, the Irish were scarcely human and engaged in "beastly behaviour." Thus killing them would be more like, say, running an abattoir than like, say, genocide.

Then again, maybe the Irish *were* human. But descended from Scythians. While this theory may seem curious now — Scythians were Asian, after all — Spenser believed these ancient nomads effeminate, like the men of Ireland. Greek geographer Herodotus claimed Scythian men "live like women, and converse accordingly." Hippocrates described veins on their ears that, when cut, caused them to wear women's clothing. Just like Irish men with their mantles, indistinguishable from women's cloaks, Spenser railed — most amusing from a man in silken hose and high heels — showing how the hateful Amazon Radigund (from the Irish "to bestow women's clothes") oppressed Artegall ("Arthur the Stranger") and his manly men:

> *First she doth them of warlike arms despoile,*
> *And cloth in womens weedes; And then with threat*
> *Doth them compell to worke, to earne their meat.*

This is what happened, Spenser warned, when Irish took over. Forcing the English to wear mantles, the Irish thereby "degendered" them. (Note to Gillagrianne: and you thought you had the lock on strange conceptions?)

Well Spenser might worry. Many of his "wylde Irishe" were, awkwardly enough, English. After Diarmuid called for rescue, his Norman helpers became, as is often said, "more Irish than the Irish themselves." They wore Irish attire, followed Irish customs, and generally fell, in Spenser's view, "to flat licentiousness, more boldly daring to disobey the law than any Irish." And it was not a matter merely of mantles and manners, but an utter transformation: "Lord, how quickly doth that country alter men's natures!"

Worst of all was that the settlers spoke, not English, but sweet Irish. Laws had been passed; a 1366 edict warned that, "If any Englishman, or Irishman dwelling among the English, use Irish speech, he shall be attainted and his lands go to his lord till he undertake to adopt and use English." It did not help. By 1578, the lord chancellor complained that "the English, and the most part with delight, even in Dublin, speak Irish, and are greatly spotted in manners, habit and conditions with Irish stains." Spenser's contemporary Richard Standihurst said "the English pale is more willing to learn Irish than the Irishman is willing to learn English: we must imbrace their language, and they detest ours." Spenser knew where

to lay blame: on women (surprise!). "The child that sucketh the milke of
the nurse, must of necessity learne his first speache of her. The speche
being Irish, the harte must needs be Irish."

⊠⊠⊠⊠

And can the opposite be true? Can the heart be Irish when the speech is
not? My mother's parents spoke Irish, but we never heard it. They felt it
shameful, the mark of poverty. In Ireland, as in Indian schools in America,
children were punished for using their native tongue. John Synge met a
Kerry man who remembered that "when I was a boy they tied a gobban
into my mouth for the whole afternoon because I was heard speaking Irish.
Wasn't that great cruelty?" Poet John Montague imagines the process of
extirpating Irish as having a second tongue physically grafted onto one's
own, the new language "like a hobble on a straying goat."

A few centuries of hobbling are effective; today fewer people speak
Irish as their first language than attend Puck Fair each year. Languages
throughout the world are endangered; more than ten thousand perished
in the last century, and every fortnight, another disappears. But the language that geographer Tim Robinson calls "an emanation of the land of
Ireland, the voice of history, telling how all things fall" hangs on. Partly
this results from a national commitment that requires fluency of teachers
and students. Just as important is the impact of poets who compose in Irish,
for though the Courts of Poetry long ago fell silent, poetry is ever the heart
of Ireland.

In his most memorable poem, Munster poet Michael Hartnett said
farewell to English after meeting his own *spéir-bhean*, a barmaid before
whose "mountainy body" he realized that the "gravel of Anglo-Saxon"
was useless. And so he turned to what Nuala Ní Dhomhnail calls the "language of the Mothers" — not just individual mothers but the mothers of
the race, those goddesses who always greet invaders from their nippled
peaks — and refused to write ever again in the "perfect language to sell
pigs in."

But my grandparents needed that language of pig selling. So we
learned no Irish but the occasional curse word from Pop (I repeated one to
a friend, who paled in horror and refused to translate). I who have just the
gravel of English shyly twist my tongue around unfamiliar sounds. But a

language is not just vocabulary, syntax, grammar; it is embodied memory. No matter how I struggle, I can never know the language like someone who was sung lullabies in Irish, called her kitten by an Irish name, heard her first lover whisper softly in her ear in Irish. My child-self heard Irish only in cursing anger, and that wound will never heal.

Yet I try. I learn place-names and names from myth, bits of greetings, lines of poetry, songs. I am drawn to the language that poet Pearse Hutchinson calls "extremely sensuous, even succulent." Frank O'Connor claims the very language embraces sexuality. Of Ansty, wife of the Kerry tailor, he wrote, "She regarded sexual relations as the most entertaining subject for general conversation; a feature of life in Irish-speaking Ireland even in my youth, but which began to die out the moment English became the accepted language." To know Irish would be, I believe, to reach places the conquerer's grave and gravelly language forbid to me. I ponder the world Irish opens to me: two different words for wildness, one for animals, the other for places and people; the related words for woman, *bean,* and sacred, *beannaithe;* no word for "yes" and none for "no." What would it be like, to live embraced by that world?

⊠⊠⊠⊠

I know the way conquerors hear only silence in the speech of the conquered, for I have seen how, like Undertakers in a stolen land, men fail to hear when women speak. French psychologist Jacques Lacan forgives this deficiency by explaining that we do not truly possess language, which begins when a child, separated from mother, loses his *jouissance,* his joy in the wholeness he experienced at her breast. Forever after the child tries to recapture that prelinguistic state (the Imaginary) now ruptured (become Real). And so man creates language (the Symbolic) to mediate between the mother-haunted world and the one empty of her. For women, this problem is erased; we do not need language because we never left the Mother.

This sort of thing can drive a woman wild. We have language — are you not reading it? — even when no one is listening. Indeed, we know multiple languages; we are subtle code-switchers. Just as my grandparents learned English to survive, women learn the languages of men. Yet we know another language too, one we recognize in stories of wild mad women, in fertile succulent poems, in images of pirate queens and swan maidens. This is the language of our bodies, bodies not less than men's but different, bodies that yearn and crave and bleed and bear in ways that only women know. It is this language Spenser muffled when he praised his Amoret for learning "solft silence and submisse obedience." How telling that he instructed her to learn this silence in the Temple of Venus. Wasn't that great cruelty?

Anthropologists Shirley and Edwin Ardener describe the lives of men and women as two intersecting circles. The vulval shape formed by their joining is our shared known world. The half-moon on the men's side represents nature, into which men venture and return to the homey hearth, bringing stories of the hunt. From these stories culture — men's experience, shared with women — is created. But there is another half-circle, and that is women's reality. Men shake their heads and declare it the realm of the unspeakable. But women can speak of it, if men will listen.

Silence speaks volumes to those who would hear. As an example, let us return to Danu's Paps. Specifically, to Danu's nipples.

I once took a random and totally unscientific survey of friends who had seen the Paps. My male respondents saw nothing notable about the nipples.

"They're stone?" one guessed.

Try again, I said.

They just shook their heads and shrugged.

Women reacted differently. They looked side to side, then peered at me a bit suspiciously. "Well..." they began. Then a pause. "Well..." A long pause.

I finally broke the silence. "They're erect," I suggested.

"Yes!" the women said with relief. "They most certainly are!"

There are doubtless men who noticed Danu's hard stone nipples, but none in my survey or in the hundreds of books on my shelves. Those of us who live with female nipples day in, day out realize that if those ancient builders wanted to simply remark upon the earth's femininity, they could have saved themselves a lot of running up and down. They could have left the mountains as they were; women's breasts look like hills most of the time. But there was something else the ancient builders wanted us to know: that the great earth grows aroused when loving her mate, when nursing her child. How can we grasp the breadth and beauty of that vision?

What do we lose when we silence women's private languages? There is a vast territory that we know, beautiful summer mountains full of berries that fill the mouth with sweetness, soft blue lakes on which light shatters into rainbows, valleys filled with countless blossoms. And storms that blacken brilliant skies, penetrating chill, hungers beyond endurance. Familiar roads, familiar tongues, stop short of those secrets that we know. But we are there, like Danu, to greet the bold ones who will come.

Chapter Nine

The Stone in the Midst of All

"When a stone is thrown into water," wrote Douglas Hyde, Ireland's first president, "the water is moved. Long after its fall the wave that the stone has raised is perceived upon the top. This wave swims out from the center like a great ring until it reaches the bank." Yeats used the same image to describe how ordinary men and women could be changed utterly, their beating hearts — "enchanted to a stone / To trouble the living stream" by a revolutionary vision — altering the currents of history.

The idea of nature's sanctity is such a stone, cast into the philosophical stream that divides humans from nature, nature from god. But wait: I have the metaphor wrong. For the stone has been there all along. In some places, a flood covers it, so only ripples show on the surface. In Ireland, where the stream is shallow, that stone allows us to step from this world into an Other.

A windswept bog in Connemara. Up to the heathery blue mountains, low hills roll like ocean waves. Next to me, a stunted twisted thorn. I lean down to the dark wet earth. In the tree's roots, someone has half buried a handful of bright silver coins.

Ireland is full of places where, as a Celt might say, time and space grow thin, where the Otherworld draws nigh. Some, like Tara and Newgrange, are renowned; some, like Cruachain and Slieve Gullion, notable in legend; others, like the haunted ruin on the Old Bog Road, unknown beyond a mile down the boreen. In almost thirty years of searching, I have not found them all. Even with thirty years more — even with thirty years beyond that — I could not find them all. And that gives me the greatest pleasure.

A soft spring morning in the midlands. Rain jewels the fences and trees near Killeigh. At the Seven Holy Wells, I realize that I have nothing to hang upon the clootie-tree. From my fringed plaid scarf, I pull out seven threads and tie them like prayers on a budding branch.

The impossibility of seeing all of Ireland seems to defy logic. I grew up in America's biggest state, which we brag we could split in half to make Texas third biggest. (We also brag about having the world's tallest mountain; oh, yeah, Everest is higher, but only because it stands atop other mountains.) Alaska could hold Ireland almost sixty times over. Ireland is one-third the size of New Zealand, three-quarters Cuba, half Java. Even Iceland is larger.

Tourists from bigger lands — most of the world — get Ireland all wrong. It looks like you can see everything in a week. Dash across the island — two hundred miles — in a few hours (unless you encounter Major Road Works, that portly fellow, in Loughrea, where he has a permanent residence). Tip to toe, Ireland's 450 miles might take you half a day, except that there's no direct road; angling along the coast, you could make it Derry to Cork in a day.

But, as my Irish friends say, whyever would ye?

We have no difficulty finding, right beside the road, the hill fort from which Rathangan takes its name. Paula and I climb through wet grass to the rath's flat top. We talk in whispers, as though not to disturb the past, then giggle at our instinctive hush. With a grin, Paula lets out a whoop, and a hoodie crow gabbles a sudden answer.

For six thousand years, vaguely threatening superstition has preserved Irish sacred places. So has poverty; the poor do not build holiday homes on raths. But Ireland has recently come hurtling into prosperity, opportunity arriving with its inevitable price tag. There was a murder near Gort that friends tell me was caused by a drug deal gone bad. Construction of a speedy new road could destroy Kildare's holy wells. The specter of gold mining hangs over Croagh Patrick like a toxic cloud. Ireland is not the same as it was when, head stuffed with poetry and myth, I first came over.

But Ireland swallows time as well as space. Driving across the Burren to Jessie's, I was halted by a farmer driving his herd between pastures. An Aer Lingus jet rumbled overhead. I noticed the man gesticulating wildly; after a moment, I noticed his cell phone. The road followed an old cow trail; the pastures to each side had been in use for two thousand years. Ireland is both changing and changeless. People look like their own ancestors. And stories are still everywhere, fertilizing the land with memory.

Hunting for a standing stone in the mountains of Éblinn, I stand near a hedgerow studying my Ordnance Survey map. Around the curve come seven cows herded by a rough-clad mountainy woman. She pays no attention to me as she passes, yelling at the straying black. She is old and strong, and her face is the face of Ireland.

One recent morning I was rereading Máire MacNeill, looking for how Saint Patrick killed the serpent goddess, a story degraded into the one about him driving out the snakes. MacNeill calls the tale-motif "Saint Overcomes Female Fiend," and among its many variations, I found one collected in the mid-twentieth century in the east midlands. The story tells of a cannibal hag confined by Saint Patrick under a stone — a temporary confinement, for she will rise again when enough members of her family step upon her grave. The woman, MacNeill told me, was "young and beautiful, named Gargan." My eyes popped open. On her mother's side, my friend Maggie is a Gargan. I e-mailed her immediately. Within minutes the phone rang. No, Maggie had never heard the story. Within moments it was decided. We would go a-Garganing.

The expedition began on a splendid sunny summer day that followed a week of heavy rain. Fiona, always up for a jaunt, came over from Kildare. We had very little idea of where we were going. The story of the ancestral Gargan appears only in MacNeill's book, but luckily, her entries included geographical details. The hag lived at Tierworker — which, unfortunately, did not appear on our maps. She met her downfall while walking toward Moybologue — which also did not appear on our maps. But one of the storytellers had lived in Baileborough, which our maps showed as a small dot on the road between Kells and Monaghan.

Not much to go on. Though we had all sat upon the great stone seat on Loughcrew, none of us was otherwise familiar with the Cavan-Meath borderland. But we assumed that, once off the main roads, we would find those little black-and-white arrows that point to unmapped places. Expecting success, filled with good cheer and unfounded confidence, we set off.

From the backseat, I read versions of the legend. "Here's my favorite," I announced. " 'Garragh-Maw, or the beautiful woman of the Garraghans, who, unhappily for the neighbourhood, appears to have been carnivorously addicted, and to have ranged up and down the country with the appetite of a cannibal, and the capacity of an Anaconda, devouring men, women, and little boys in corduroy trousers, till a Romish priest threw a sperdish of holy water on her which extinguished her life; and her body is buried in the mound of Moybullagh, and is to remain there until nine hundred of her family have passed over her grave, which no Garraghan would do for a pound of gold; at which event, she is to arise, and recommence her anthropophagical practices and propensities, to the great edification of the neighbourhood &c &c. Such is the wild legend which has currency in the country.' "

The story, recorded by one "B" — MacNeill assumes the initial indicates a member of the Brooke family from the region — was published in 1852 in *Dublin University Magazine.* A hundred years later, versions of the wild legend were still told by storytellers, including an otherwise unidentified "farmer named Gargan." Details differ, but the plot is always the same. A red-haired Gargan woman who lived at Tierworker was fasting one morning as she walked to Mass in nearby Moybologue. Seeing some irresistibly ripe berries, Garravogue broke her fast. Instantly she turned into a ravening monster and devoured everything in sight, starting with her servant boy and horse, then proceeding to cattle and those corduroy-trousered children.

Saint Patrick, who happened to be in the neighborhood on an unspecified errand, climbed a rath and threw his staff at the hag. The instant she was hit, Garravogue split apart. Two parts flew off to each side and splashed down into lakes, one part went up into the sky, and the last burrowed into the ground beneath a stone. Saint Patrick then prophesied that if enough Gargans stepped on the stone — nine generations, or nine hundred, or nine times ninety-nine — Garravogue would be reborn.

"What's with the dismemberment thing?" Fiona wondered.

It might hide a creation legend, I ventured. Scholars claim that Ireland lacks a creation myth, but there are stories of a hag who built the land, dropping stones from her apron to form mountains and carving valleys by urinating plentifully. The hag is not usually ripped apart, but in other lands such myths refer to primeval time. Like Babylonian Tiamat or Korean Grant-Aunt Tiger, Garravogue split into earth, air, water: the whole cosmos.

There is nothing I like better than debating the meaning of obscure myths with bright happy friends while exploring the Irish countryside. But even that fun began to wear thin as the day wore on. Tiny roads twisted about, following the sweet hills. In old-fashioned charming villages, we crawled behind tractors and cows. But we had no luck finding Moybologue, Tierworker, a rath, a hag-hiding stone.

Pixy-led in the mountains of the hag, I have been driving for several hours in rainy darkness, crossing and recrossing the same road over and over, infuriated and weary, exhausted by the maze of roads through the empty hills. I stop once again to study my map. Then I turn off the car and get out. Above me, faint aurora play in the autumn sky. An owl asks me who I am. I have no answer. When I drive away, I find the main road within moments.

At a tiny crossroads near Baileborough, Maggie spied a name. "Wait. Killinkere. Some of my Gargans came from there." At a church beside a graveyard on a little hill, we all tumbled out, hoping it was the cemetery at Moybologue. Impossible: it was Church of Ireland, and the Gargan woman had been going to Mass.

Our shadows were short as we wandered behind the church and climbed the little graveyard hill. In the center stood a rectangle of tall yews, densely planted, almost impenetrable. Fiona fought her way through and pushed back ivy to read the gravestone aloud: a heartbroken dedication to a curate who had died in midlife, leaving a wife and large family.

In the silence that followed, I saw Maggie's eyes fill. As we walked back down the hill, I pressed her hand. "I know," I said. "I miss her too."

Letterfrack on a cold February night. The session has gone long and well, with Connemara dancing and smoky talk and Barbara singing. My hand is on the door, pushing outward, when silence falls. A voice, so sweet it could break your heart, eases into the hush. A young man singing in Irish, an Otherworldly air, a song of loss and hopeless love.

Quiet now, we drove on. Not far away, Killinkere — a bit of a town, just a post office, two churches, a few houses — lay deserted under the noon sun.

"What we need now," I announced, "is an Old Guy in a Cap."

Fiona laughed. "Definitely," she agreed.

"There's got to be one around here somewhere." I gestured toward the post office. "I bet the postmistress can help."

At the post office, we said we were searching for Gargan relations. The postmistress nodded. "Ah, yes, the Gargans," she said to Maggie. "Wasn't there a Gargan woman, red-haired just like you, that turned into a cannibal because she ate a blackberry on the way to Mass, and didn't Saint Patrick put her under a stone — but now," she waved her hand dismissively, "that's just old *pishoguery,* we don't tell such stories anymore."

She did not herself know where the Gargans could be found, but she knew who would. At that moment two boys scampered by. She called out, "Where's your grandpa, so?" They pointed up the street. And there, walking along, leaning heavily on his cane, was your man himself, complete with cap. "There's the man you want," the postmistress said, "he'll know all about it."

The back table at Máire's, midnight. The usual lot at the bar, Sharon barely keeping pace with the pints, and us talking about local place-lore. Tom leans forward across the tiny table and points his finger, already a bit gnarly with arthritis. "I only know one secret of life," he says, "and I'll tell you: life is quicksand. Don't fight against it, or you'll just go down quicker."

The postmistress bustled us outside. "We've a Gargan here, looking for her relations."

"A Gargan, then," came the reply. "And a red-haired one, like the old woman who was walking to Moybologue Cemetery, fasting wasn't she, and then that big blackberry tempted her, before Saint Patrick came along to put her in her place — well now, we don't tell that old story anymore..."

We stood for the next quarter hour, talking aimlessly and smiling at each other. Later I thought how odd it was to hear, from two people within a few moments, a story perhaps two thousand years old. I thought how odd that both tellers ended the story by denying it was told anymore. I wondered for how many generations the story had been told and denied that way. But that was later. At the moment, I noticed only golden sunshine and low talk and twinkling eyes and breathing green hills.

John, our new guide, wanted to show Maggie her ancestors' names in Griffiths' Valuations, the listing of pre-Famine residents. So we drove him home, where he pointed across the road to the home he had built fifty years earlier for his wife — "the first house in the area to have indoor plumbing" — and identified the trees in his hedgerow. He was in no hurry. Nor were we.

We had not spelled out our quest; we only said we were tracing Gargans. John told of other Americans who had come through looking for ancestors and gleefully reported that he was mentioned on a genealogical website. He said nothing more about the berries, Saint Patrick, the stone, the cannibal hag. Nor did we.

Then we were off. John, a retired builder, had a tale for every house we passed, including the ruin of the Sheriden family home in Quilca, where Jonathan Swift often visited Thomas and where his son, Richard Brinsley, had rehearsed his actors on a sloping lawn. Finally John told us to pull into a meager parking space beside a whitewashed cottage and ushered us into the haggard. From the door, a milky-eyed woman called hello. Exchanging baffled glances, we followed John through ruminating cows to an airy overlook.

It was the highest place in many townlands, a good place to orient us to the land. "Look there," John pointed south, "that's Loughcrew; our forebears built that six thousand years ago. And there," pointing west, "that would be where the great *Táin* expedition came through, led by queen Medb from Connacht." The ancient myths were local gossip on his tongue. Towering cumulus clouds cast moving shadows like stories across the green land.

As we passed through the cottage yard again, the mistress came out. "You must see my silver bantams," she said, and herded us — all but one strangers — into her barn, where she showed us chickens with feathers sticking straight up from their heads. "Punk chickens," she grinned.

Then we were off for who-knew-where, crawling behind tractors, scooting between hedgerows, nosing across unmarked crossroads, the sun so hot we opened the windows to let the soft wind cool our skin. John said nothing more about hags, and neither did we, so I thought the day would end with our quest unsatisfied. But any day in the Irish countryside is a good day, so I sat back and enjoyed it.

Then we were on a slight rise and John was saying, "Here's Moybologue."

Maggie started. We passed a stone by the roadside. I nudged Fiona.

Just as the myths said, there was a cemetery around a now-ruined church. A half dozen men were cutting the grass for Visitation Sunday. We wandered among Gargan graves, Maggie wondering aloud if any were relations. I found a sad Famine plaque commemorating those who had died crouched in workhouses or by the side of the road, eaten by dogs or buried under cottages, a gravestone for people who had no graves. Then I heard a low hiss. Fiona and Maggie waved from the shadow of an old chapel wall.

Fiona had found a bullaun. No bigger than two cupped hands, such stones are pre-Christian, possibly pre-Celtic, a hollow formed either naturally or artificially to catch rainwater or to hold libations. A small pool shone darkly in the bullaun's cup. We each touched fingers to it, then moved them to our breasts, our mouths, our foreheads.

As we stood, Fiona pointed. Beside us grew a stunted thorn, a fairy tree.

Then she took off, her long stride carrying her away. Nearby should be the rath from which Saint Patrick threw his staff at Garravogue. Maggie and I headed down the road to look at that stone, to see if it was near a widened place where generations of Gargans would have stepped aside rather than awaken Garravogue. And indeed, there was a widened place beside the stone, just as the stories described.

We heard Fiona call out. From the stone, we could just make out earthworks, green and serpentine and overgrown. The outer walls were easy to climb, but tussocks of heather made walking difficult near the rath, which rose like a miniature mountain above ancient stones. The rath was steep; I could get no foothold on the rain-slickened grass. So I tore off my boots and scampered up barefoot, soles tingling from the sharp blades of wild grass.

From the top, we had an extraordinary view. The sun burned in a bright blue sky above fields of ripening golden hay. We joined hands and closed our eyes, feeling the wind tangle our hair. One of us — I don't remember who — began a soft chant, more a whisper or a breath than a song.

Garravogue. Garravogue. Garravogue.

The name became its own melody. Garravogue, Garravogue, our breath rising and falling like the wind. With my eyes tightly closed and my fingers twisted into those of my friends, I could almost see her rise.

The little farm at Barnacoyle in Wicklow. The nesting rooks have made such a commotion that I am up around dawn, walking the sleep out of my bones. I turn a corner and, amid the soft green, a great brown swath of turned earth confronts me. It is the first time I have felt the presence of the goddess in the land. Ériu, I murmur with surprise, Ériu.

We descended in silence. Back at the road, Maggie leaped up on the stone that marks, MacNeill says, "the point where she was slain." She assumed a yogic posture, a hag reborn from stone, while Fiona and I took photos, all of us laughing. We were still ebullient when we found John sharing neighborhood news with the grave tenders. John said nothing about our lengthy absence but suggested it was time for lunch.

He guided us to a pub a half mile away. As we pulled in, we saw an old roadside sign. Tierworker: where the Gargan started her journey! The day was turning out better than we had dreamed. Over sandwiches and strong tea, whiskey and pints, Fiona and John ascertained that he knew her family. They joked about the definition of Cavan farmers: "so tight they won't give you the steam from their piss." We ordered more tea.

Out of nowhere, John mentioned that a sculpture of the Gargan had once stood in Clannaphillip church. I leaned forward breathlessly. But, John shrugged, that church had been torn down. I let out a disappointed sigh. But, John continued, his sons had saved the head. I leaned forward again. They'd given it to the priest. Ah, well, I thought. But, John said, then they'd found a place for the hag's head, and it could still be seen there.

I have no idea whether our Old Guy knew what we were about. It's not good form to be bold, after all. Our guide had said nothing to suggest an interest in hags. We had not mentioned Moybologue and Tierworker. Or Garravogue. But he had given us all we wanted and more.

After dropping John home with cheerful thanks, we followed his directions to Clannaphillip — and well it was he had guided us, for it was yet another unmapped village. There we found a big new church beside a small old graveyard where a stone grotto to the Blessed Mother was filled with flowers. "Perfect!" said Fiona, "it's the feast of the Assumption, and haven't we been making assumptions all over the country all day!"

Behind the grotto, there she was: a small stone face with a stern expression, hair streaming back as though she was standing in a high wind. We stood in silence for a few moments. What a day, I thought. I would have been happy just to explore and read myths and share a few pints with my friends. But we had seen more than we had dared to hope.

Almost at the same moment, we all had the same idea.

From the Virgin's grotto we liberated some blossoms and placed them on the Gargan like a crown. Then we breathed her name again.

Garravogue. Garravogue. Garravogue.

I, who first went to Ireland because of a man named Rock, once again found myself honoring stones: carved bullaun, hag stone, stony head. The oldest part of nature, bones of the mother, such stones remind us of what it is to be rooted, not in "nature" as an abstract whole, but to a specific place with its specific seasons and to the culture that stems from it. For to know the divinity of a specific place allows us to perceive, by extension, the divinity in all the world.

The Wintu shaman Flora once offered this advice for wholeness: "Whoever has sacred places must wake them up." I have tried to do this, with these memories and stories of Irish places I love. Tried to wake them up, the way the *dindshenchas* poets did when they called out place-names and their myths. And in doing so, I awaken myself to the greatest lesson Ireland offers: that I must wake up to whatever place I find myself, wake up to its seasons and weather, its heritage and special beauties, its ultimate and indisputable holiness.

I have news for you: spring comes everywhere with sweetness and hope. Summer's fullness becomes harvest, then the world sleeps through a dark time. This is the only truth: that just as Ireland is sacred, so all land is sacred, as we are all sacred. This is my news.

PRONUNCIATION GUIDE

I rish intimidates many English speakers because the pronunciation seems so different from the way the words are spelled. But think of it this way: English speakers readily read both *ph* and *gh* (as in "phone" and "laughter") as "f." Irish speakers similarly know that *dh* means "v" and that *sí* is pronounced "shee." To help you get a feel for the language, here are suggested pronunciations of the main mythic figures discussed:

Anu. ANN-new.
Aiobheal. EE-val.
Bóand. BO-ann.
Bó Finne. Bo FINN-a.
Brigit. Breed (goddess).
Cailleach. COLL-yuck.
Cred. Creed.
Danu. DA-new.
Echtghe. OCH-ta.
Eithne. ETH-na.
Ériu. ER-ee-oo.
Étain. Et-TAIN.

Garravogue. GAR-a-vogue.

Grainne. GRAN-ya.

Granuaile. GRAN-you-WAIL.

Leannan Sidhe. LEE-a-nan SHEE.

Lí Ban. Li-BAN.

Macha. MA-ka.

Medb. Maeve.

Mis. Mish.

Mór. More.

Mórrígan. MOR-ee-gan.

Niamh. Neeve.

Sheela-na-gig. SHEE-la na GIG.

Síonann. SHA-non.

Glossary

Ailill mac Mata. Ailill, son of queen Mata, husband of the great queen Medb of Connacht.

Ailt-na-Míreann. "Stone of Divisions," also known as the Catstone; huge boulder left by glaciers on Uisneach, Ireland's central hill; in mythology, believed to be the exact center of Ireland.

Áine. Fairy queen or goddess of Co. Limerick; disguised as a swan, she had many lovers, both human and divine.

Aiobheal. Fairy queen of Munster; possibly the same as Áine.

aisling. Dream-poem, especially one in which Ireland appears as a woman.

Amairgin. The great poet of the Milesians, one of the invading races documented in the *The Book of Invasions;* thought to have been an early Celt.

An Gorta Mór. "The Great Hunger," the Famine that struck Ireland in the mid-1800s when the potato crop failed because of blight.

Anu. *See* Danu.

ard rí. Ireland's high king who ruled at Tara.

Armagh. County and its capital city in Northern Ireland named for the goddess Macha (*ard-Macha*, heights of Macha).

Asseroe. Waterfall in Donegal that figures in many myths.

Ballylee. *See* Thoor Ballylee.

Ballyvaughan. Town on the edge of the Burren in west Co. Clare; site of festival devoted to Brian Merriman.

Balor. Fierce king of the mythic people called the Fomorians; lusted after the cow of abundance, which he stole from its owner, a smith; father of the goddess or heroine Eithne.

banais rí. Inauguration feast of Irish king.

Banba. One of the three great land goddesses of Ireland.

bandrui. Celtic woman druid.

banfíli. Celtic woman poet.

Bealtaine. Beltane. May 1, the Celtic feast of summer's arrival.

Biddy Early. Historical woman called the White Witch of Clare, a renowned healer of the nineteenth century.

Bóand. The goddess of the Boyne River.

Bó Du. "Black Cow," one of three mythic cows who brought abundance to Ireland.

Bó Finne. White cow goddess of abundance; possibly the same as Bóand.

Bohola. Named for the cow hut of the obscure saint Thola, a small town in east Co. Mayo.

Book of Invasions, The. Early text that purports to tell how Ireland was settled; written by Irish monks, it freely mixes history with Christian and Celtic myths.

booley. To move cows to and from seasonal pastures, from the Irish word for cow, *bó.*

boreen. A small rural road, from the Irish *boíthrín,* cow trail.

Bó Rua. "Red Cow," one of three mythic cows who brought abundance to Ireland.

Boyne River. River in eastern Ireland named for the cow goddess Bóand.

Bran. Hero who loved a fairy queen, was taken to her world, and was never able to return.

brehon. Translated as judge and lawyer; member of druidic orders who specialized in memorizing and commenting on the law.

Bres. The stingy son of the goddess of the land, Ériu.

Brídeog. A small doll or poppet made in mid winter to represent the goddess (or saint) Brigit.

Brigit. A Celtic goddess of this name ruled water, fire, and transformation; a later Christian saint connected with the same elemental experiences is believed to have been the goddess transformed.

Brown Bull of Cuailgne. The Bull of Cooley; Donn Cuailgne. One of the two great bulls of Irish epic, the reincarnation of a swineherd whose mortal enemy was reincarnated in the bull White Horn.

Brugh na Bóinne. Megalithic (pre-Celtic) ritual or religious site on the Boyne River north of Dublin; includes three great cairns, Knowth, Dowth, and Newgrange, as well as numerous smaller archeological sites.

Burren. Rocky area in west Co. Clare, connected with the hag goddess.

Cael. Lover of the poet Cred.

Cailleach, the. Hag goddess of great antiquity.

Cano. Lover of the poet Cred.

Carns Hill. Small pair of breast-shaped hills near Sligo, topped with cairns to represent nipples.

Cathleen Ní Houlihan. The name given to Ireland when she appears in poetry and song as a beautiful woman.

céilí. An evening of song, dance, stories, jokes, and flirtation.

Celts. An aggressive people from central Europe who settled Ireland in the early third century B.C.E.; not the builders of the stone circles, who preceded them by four thousand years and whose identity is unknown.

ceo druidechta. "Fog of druidry," a cloud that druids and poets were believed to have the ability to create so that they could pass through a crowd invisibly.

Cesair. The first woman to arrive in Ireland in mythic times.

Cliffs of Moher. In Irish, Ceann na Cailleach, "Head of the Hag." Scenic wonder on the western coast of Co. Clare, named for the hag goddess Mal.

Cluricaun. One of the fairy folk, a drunken sort of fellow.

Cnoc Gréine. Small hill in Co. Limerick; twin of Knockainy.

colleen. From the Irish *caílín,* a young woman.

Conaire. Great king of Tara, grandson of the goddess Étain.

Connacht. One of the four great provinces of Ireland, a division dating from ancient times and still in use today; the western province, connected with wisdom.

Connemara. Wild mountainous part of western Galway.

Coole Park. Demesne of Lady Augusta Gregory, founder of the Abbey Theater, and site of several magical places to which the poet William Butler Yeats alludes.

craic. Good talk, laughter, loads of fun.

Cred. Poet whose home was on the slopes of the Paps of Danu.

crios Brídghe. "Brigit's girdle," a circle of rope woven at Imbolc and used in ritual of renewal.

Croagh Patrick. Pyramidal mountain in west Co. Mayo that has been the site of pilgrimage for several thousand years; ruins show it was holy to the pre-Celtic people of Ireland; it is still the site of a huge Christian pilgrimage every summer.

Cróchan Crogderg. Obscure goddess or heroine who gave birth to the great queen/goddess Medb in the cave at Cruachain, Medb's royal seat, named for Cróchan.

Cruachain. Now Rathcrogan in Co. Roscommon, once one of Ireland's four great regional capitals. More than seventy archaeological sites show that this was an important center; in legend, the seat of queen Medb of Connacht.

Crunnchu mac Agnomain. Human husband of the goddess Macha; he brought down ill fortune on the province of Ulster by bragging that she could outrun the king's horses.

Cúchulainn. Great hero of Ulster; favorite of the goddess Mórrígan.

Cuirithir. Poet who loved Liadan.

Curragh. Huge unfenced pasture in Co. Kildare, last vestige of Celtic system of communal land holding.

"Da Dearga's Hostel." Ancient text that tells of a king who broke his vows (*geasa*) and died as a result.

Dagda. "The good god," a god of prosperity and fertility.

Dahut. Last pagan princess of Celtic Brittany.

Danu. Early goddess of whom little is known; possibly the same as Anu; may be deity of fertility and maternity.

dechetal do chennaib. Druidical means of prognosticating; "composing on one's fingertips."

deiseal. To move clockwise or in a circle with the left shoulder outward; the sacred direction; to move rightly.

demesne. Irish term for an old estate, often wooded.

Dervorgilla. Historical woman who, married to one of the O'Rourkes near Sligo, either was kidnapped or eloped with another man; her lover or kidnapper invited mercenary soldiers from overseas into the conflict, thus beginning the Norman invasion of Ireland.

Diarmuid. Handsome warrior who, on her instigation, eloped with Gráinne, the pledged wife of Fionn mac Cumhaill.

Diarmuid na nGall. "Dermot of the Foreigners," Devorgilla's lover.

dindshenchas. Poems of place lore, collected in medieval times but with sources in earlier times.

dolmen. A prehistoric monument consisting of two or more upright stones supporting a horizontal stone slab; thought to be a tomb.

Dooney Rock. High rocky hill over Lough Gill, near Sligo town, of which Yeats wrote.

Dubh Rois. Harper who tamed the madwoman Mis with love.

Dubthach. Father of Brigit.

dysert. Desert, a hermitage, not necessarily dry or arid but usually lonely and remote.

einm laeghda. Druidical means of prognosticating; "illumination of rhymes."

Eithne. Several goddesses and heroines bear this name, the most significant being Balor's daughter, kept imprisoned in a high tower so that she could not give birth to the hero who was fated to kill her father.

Elcmar. Husband of Bóand.

Ellen. Triple-headed monster, sometimes male, sometimes female, that ushers forth from caves and threatens humans with a fiery breath.

Emain Macha. Archaeological site in Northern Ireland, now called Navan Fort; Emain Macha appears in many myths as the center of the province of Ulster.

Eochaid. Many kings of ancient Ireland have this name, which means "horse"; one married queen Tailtiu and became king at Tara.

Ériu. Goddess after whom Ireland (Éire) is named.

Errisbeg. The mountain that looms over Roundstone Bog in Connemara.

Étaín. Goddess who was turned into a fly, which fell into a glass, which was drunk by a woman, who gave birth to the reborn goddess; later queen of Tara. The story of her love affair with the fairy king Midir is one of the most romantic of Ireland's tales.

eth fiadha. The druidic "art of semblance"; shape-shifting.

Fairy. Otherworldly creature, often a demoted divinity, who lives in a parallel universe to ours.

Fairy blast. A sudden wind that dislodges items and people in time and place.

Fand. A fairy queen of notorious lustfulness.

Feakle. A small town in east Co. Clare, famous as the hometown of the poet Brian Merriman and the "White Witch of Clare," Biddy Early.

feis Temro. "Feast of Tara," the inauguration ceremony and festival for the king of the mythical central hill of Tara.

Ferdia. A warrior killed by his foster brother, the hero Cúchulainn.

Fergus. The well-endowed hero who was the lover of queen/goddess Medb.

Fianna. A troupe of warriors who accompanied the hero Fionn mac Cumhaill.

Fifth Province. *See* Míde.

fili. Lowest of the many ranks of poet; often used as a generic for poet.

Fintan. The oldest being in the world, a one-eyed salmon who swims in a magical pool at the head of a river.

Finvarra. A lustful fairy king.

Fionn mac Cumhaill. The legendary hero who gained the power of prophecy by eating the salmon of wisdom; later the rejected husband of Gráinne.

Fir Bolg. "Men of the Bag," one of the mythical races who lived in Ireland before the coming of the first humans; possibly a folk memory of early settlers.

Flaggy Shore. Beach area with flagstones in west Co. Galway, ancestral home to the Ó Daillaigh poets of antiquity.

Flaith. Goddess of sovereignty.

Fódla. One of the three great land goddesses of Ireland.

Fomorians. Mythical early race, sometimes described as sea monsters; may be a folk memory of early settlers replaced by later invaders.

Gaia. Greek goddess of earth; also scientific theory of planet as a self-regulating system, articulated by the scientist James Lovelock while he was living in Ireland.

Garravogue. Hag after whom the river that flows through Sligo town is named; also found on the borders of Co. Cavan and Co. Meath, where her name is sometimes spelled Garrawog; this latter figure was the ancestor of the Gargan family.

Gearóid. Poet son of the fairy queen or goddess Áine.

geasa **(plural),** *geis* **(singular).** A sacred vow.

Gillagrianne. Obscure mythic or folkloric figure of Co. Limerick.

glamour. A fairy spell that makes one thing look like another.

Glas. Great cow of abundance who wanders Ireland giving milk to anyone who asks; finally died or disappeared when milked into a sieve.

Glen-Car. Valley above Sligo that appears in myth and in the works of W. B. Yeats.

Goibniu. Celtic smith-god; appears in folklore as the smith Galvan, owner of the cow of abundance, the Glas.

Gort. Small market town in Co. Galway, near the border of Co. Clare; nearby to both W. B. Yeats's home at Thoor Ballylee and Lady Gregory's Coole Park, it is the setting for Gregory's play about market gossip, *Spreading the News.*

Gráinne. Willful heroine or goddess who chose her own husband.

Granuaile. Gráinne ní Mhaille, a sixteenth-century chieftain of Co. Galway.

Guaire. Legendary generous king of the area around Gort, Co. Galway.

Hag of Beare. A form of the Cailleach, or hag goddess, from medieval literature.

Hungry Grass. Folkloric tale of grass that drives one mad with hunger; sometimes said to cover the unmarked graves of victims of the Famine.

Hy-Brâzil. Mythical island of plenty that rises every seven years in the western ocean.

imbas forasnai. Druidical means of prognosticating; "light of foresight."

Imbolc. February 1, beginning of spring in Ireland; feast of Brigit the goddess and saint.

imramma. Category of ancient tales that involve journeys.

Inchy Wood. One of the mysterious Seven Woods of Coole.

Inisbofin. "Island of the White Cow"; two exist, one off the Co. Galway coast in Connemara, the other off Donegal.

Inis bó finne. "Island of the White Cow"; *see* Inisbofin.

Innisfree. A small island in Lough Gill, in Sligo, that appears in the works of W. B. Yeats, most notably in his poem "The Lake Isle of Innisfree."

interpretatio Romano. Interpretation of native divinities as identical to Roman ones; both preserved and destroyed native culture throughout Europe.

kami. Japanese conception of indwelling holiness.

Kesh Corran. Cave in Co. Sligo associated with many myths.

Kildare. "Cill-Dara," "Church of the Oak," apparently a Celtic center to the goddess Brigit that became a great abbey and center of arts and commerce in early Christian time; the city of this name is the site of a recent Brigit revival.

Kilmacduagh. Ancient church near Gort, Co. Galway, to which much legend adheres.

Kilnaboy. Village in west Co. Clare where a famous Sheela-na-gig can be seen.

Kilorglin. Small town in Co. Kerry, famed for its annual Puck Fair.

Kiltartan Cross. The crossroads of Kiltartan, near Gort; the area around it gave its name to the town land in which Coole Park, Lady Gregory's demesne, is found.

Knockainy. The hill of Áine, in east Co. Limerick.

Knocknarea. Huge hill above Sligo town; under a cairn on its summit, Queen Medb is said to be buried.

Leanan Sidhe. Fairy mistress who steals men from life.

Leinster. One of the four great provinces of ancient Ireland, still in use as a geographical boundary today; the eastern province, it symbolically represents wealth and commerce.

Liadan. Historical but quasi-legendary woman poet of Munster.

Lia Fáil. Stone of Destiny on Tara that called out when the true king touched it.

Lí Ban. Once a woman, she was turned into a salmon or mermaid.

lios. Like *rath* and *cashel,* a name for a Celtic ruin.

Liscannor. Village near the Cliffs of Moher, site of a famous holy well associated with the festival of Lughnasa.

Lissadell. Originally *lios Ó Daillaigh,* the fort of the Ó Daillaighs, a place near Sligo that later became the home of the Gore-Booths, friends to Yeats and family of the heroine of the 1916 Rising, Constance de Markievicz.

Loughcrew. Also called Sliabh na Cailleach, "Mountain of the Hag"; a mountain in Co. Cavan with a cairn on its summit oriented toward the spring and fall equinoxes.

Lough Erne. Lake in Ulster with many mythic associations.

Lough Gill. Small lake near Sligo town; formed from the body of the drowned maiden Gilla.

Lough Gur. Lake in Co. Limerick connected with the goddess Áine and her son, Gearóid Iarla, or Garret the Earl.

Loughrea. Small town near Gort notable for Celtic sites (the Turoe Stone), Celtic myths (the death of Medb), and contemporary traffic jams.

Lugh. God after whom the Celtic harvest feast is named; he established it in honor of his foster mother, Tailtiu.

Lughnasa. Celtic feast of harvest on August 1.

Macha. Goddess of Ulster; three different Machas are known.

Mag Tuired. The site of great battles between Ireland's mythic races.

Mal. The name of the Cailleach on the Burren.

Marcán. Husband of Cred; parallel to King Arthur.

Medb. Queen and/or goddess connected with Connacht, the western province; her name means "intoxication"; she is a form of the goddess of sovereignty.

Mesca Ulad. "The Intoxication of the Ulstermen," an ancient text.

Míde. The central province (also called the Fifth Province) of Ireland, a nonphysical point between the other four ancient provinces (Connacht, Ulster, Leinster, Munster) that represents the sacred center. Often connected with the hill of Uisneach in Co. Westmeath.

Midir. Fairy king of great renown; lover of the goddess Étain.

Milesians. The last of the mythic invaders into Ireland, the first humans.

Mis. Wild woman of the Dingle peninsula, tamed by sex.

Mór. Land goddess of Munster in southeast Ireland.

Mórrígan. Winged goddess connected with the Otherworld.

Munster. One of the four great provinces of ancient Ireland, Munster is in the southwest corner of the island and is mythically connected with women, poetry, and song.

Nemed. One of the first mythic settlers of Ireland; husband of the goddess Macha.

Newgrange. Great spiral-carved rock cairn north of Dublin, into which the sun's rays penetrate on winter solstice.

New Quay. Small town near which can be found the Flaggy Shore, where the ancient poets, the Ó Daillaighs, held their poetic court.

Niall. Noígiallach, or "Of the Nine Hostages," a famous king of Tara.

Niamh of the Golden Hair. Fairy queen and mistress who stole men from this world, including the poet Oisín.

Nuada. Nuada of the Silver Arm. Celtic god whose arm was cut off in battle; it was magically made to grow back so that he could resume ruling.

Oisín. The poet of the Fianna, lover of the beautiful fairy queen Niamh.

Old Bog Road. There are many roads bearing this name in Ireland, but the one referred to in the text stretches from Toombeola into Clifden in Connemara, crossing over Roundstone Bog.

Otherworld. General term for the place where fairies and divinities dwell; its entrance is often described as an island out to sea, as an ancient mound, or as a bog.

Oweynagat. Uaimh na gCat, the "Cave of Cats," the cave of the Mórrígan at Rathcrogan in Co. Roscommon.

Páirc-na-lee. One of the Seven Woods of Coole.

Paps of Danu. Breast-shaped cairn-topped hills on the Cork-Kerry border.

Partholonians. Mythic race of invaders who were killed by plague and therefore play little role in myth.

Pelagius. Celtic monk who, during early Christian times, articulated a theology that relied upon accepting the entire created world; called the "happy heresy," his theology was opposed by Saint Augustine.

pishoguery. Old superstition; a term of dismissal.

planxty. Strange music said to come from the fairy world.

Puck Fair. Festival held in Kilorglin, Co. Kerry, at harvesttime, starring a white wild he-goat.

rath. Circular Celtic hill fort; also can be called *dún* or *lios.*

Rathcrogan. Village whose name derives from the nearby archaeological site, near Tulsk in Co. Roscommon; *see also* Cruachain.

Roisín Dubh. Name given to Ireland when she appears in poetry and song as a beautiful woman.

Roundstone Bog. Vast blanket bog between Roundstone and Clifden, Co. Galway.

Saint Patrick. Legendary founder of Irish Christianity.

Samhain. Celtic feast of the beginning of winter, November 1; it is still celebrated as Halloween.

seanachies. Storytellers; traditional tale spinners.

Senchán Torpéist. Great poet and satirist of ancient Ireland.

Senchas Mór. Compilation of ancient Irish law.

Seven Woods. The great demesne of Coole had seven woodlands whose legends were used by W. B. Yeats in many of his poems.

Shannon Pot. Source of the Shannon River in Co. Cavan, connected with maiden goddess Síonnan.

Sheela-na-gig. The name given to stone carvings of a hag goddess exposing herself.

sidhe. Fairy; also fairy mound, or hill within which fairies live.

Síonann. Goddess after whom Ireland's largest river is named.

Slieve Echtghe. "Mountains of the Awful One" in east Co. Clare, named for an obscure hag goddess.

Slieve Gullion. Hill in Northern Ireland, named for the smith Cullen, that is the center of many myths; a cairn (artificial cave) on it is penetrated by the sun's rays at sunset on winter solstice.

Slieve Mish. Mountain range in Co. Kerry named for the madwoman Mis.

Slievenamon. "Mountain of the Women," a nipple-cairned mountain in Co. Tipperary.

Sligo. County and town in the northwest, connected with many myths.

Sovereignty. Celtic concept of right relationship between ruler and land, embodied in a goddess.

Spéir-bhean. "Sky woman"; name given to Ireland when she appears in poetry and song as a beautiful woman.

Stray Sod. An enchanted piece of earth; stepping on it results in confusion and hours of wandering.

Suibne. "Mad Sweeney," who has inspired many poets.

Tailtiu. Goddess in whose honor the festivals of Lughnasa were said to be founded; a sovereignty goddess of the land.

Táin bó Cuailgne. "*Cattle Raid of Cuailgne* (Cooley)," the title of the great Irish literary epic that shows queen Medb of Connacht attaining her will.

Tara. Hill in Co. Meath used for kingly inaugurations, sacred to goddess Medb.

tarbfleis. Bull divination; wrapping up a poet in the skin of a newly slaughtered ox to encourage precognitive dreaming.

Thoor Ballylee. "Ballylee Tower," a Norman-era tower near Gort that was bought and restored as a home by W. B. Yeats.

Tír na nÓg. "Land of Youth," a name for the Otherworld.

Tobernault. Famous holy well near Sligo town.

Triads. An ancient form of Celtic poetry, often a source of information about Irish myth.

Tuan. Primal poet; he reincarnated in many forms, so that he knew life in all its aspects.

tuath. People of a territory; also that territory.

Tuatha Dé Danann. "People of the goddess Danu," an early mythical people who had magical powers; upon the arrival of the Milesians, according to Ireland's mythic history, the Tuatha Dé were not killed but convinced to live in an alternative universe; now the fairies.

turlough. A depression flooded each winter, a "winter lake."

Twelve Bens. Also Twelve Pins, a dozen mountain peaks in Connemara.

Uisneach. Low hill in Co. Westmeath sacred to land goddess Ériu.

Ulster. One of the four great ancient divisions of Ireland, still in use today; Ulster signifies the north and battle.

White Horn. The great white bull of Connacht, a reborn swineherd full of enmity for his reincarnated enemy, the Brown Bull of Cuailgne; the reason for Medb's great cattle raid on Ulster.

Wild Hunt. Fairy gangs that rove the night hunting humans.

ΠΟΤΕS

CHAPTER ΟΠΕ: THE SACRED CEΠTER

The medieval poems that inspired this book were out of print for more than forty years; a wonderful five-volume new edition of *The Metrical Dindshenchas: Text, Translation and Commentary* by Edward Gwynn is now available (Dublin: Dublin Institute for Advanced Studies, School of Celtic Studies, 1991).

The life of Howard Rock has been well told by his friend Lael Morgan in *Art and Eskimo Power* (Kenmore, Wash.: Epicenter Press, 1992).

John McGahern, who lives in Carrick-on-Shannon, is the author of many sharply drawn novels, most recently *By the Lake* (New York: Knopf, 2002); see also his *Collected Stories* (New York: Vintage Books, 1994) and the controversial *The Dark* (New York: Penguin, 2002). In prose and in person, John is a wickedly good storyteller.

Edna O'Brien's descriptions of Ireland, especially the east Clare of her childhood, can be found in her many novels, including *A Pagan Place* (New York: Mariner Books, 2001) and in her memoir *Mother Ireland* (New York: Plume, 1999).

Miranda Green's many contributions to Celtic studies include *Celtic Goddesses: Warriors, Virgins and Mothers* (London: British Museum Press, 1995).

Many writers have commented on the works of Augustine, usually in a fervently admiring fashion. However, Martha Ruth Miles in *Augustine on the Body* (Atlanta: Scholars Press, 1979) and Kim Power in *Veiled Desire: Augustine on Women* (New York: Continuum, 1996) show some of the philosophical limitations of Augustine's viewpoint. For more on the Pelagian "happy heresy," see J. Stevenson's *Creeds, Councils and Controversies: Documents Illustrative of the History of the Church AD 337–461* (New York: Seabury Press, 1966).

That first Irish poem, as well as many others in good translations from the Irish, can be found in Brendan Kennelly's *Love of Ireland: Poems from the Irish* (Cork: Mercier Press, 1989). This translation is my own, as are all others unless noted.

Brendan Kennelly, professor of literature at Trinity College, is the author of the intensely moving *Man Made of Rain,* about his near-death experience while undergoing bypass surgery; the controversial *Cromwell;* and *The Book of Judas* (Newcastle, England: Bloodaxe Books).

The poems of William Butler Yeats are available in many editions, most comprehensively in the *Collected Poems* edited by Richard Finneran (New York: Scribner, 1996); his prose works on folklore include *Irish Fairy and Folk Tales* (Los Angeles: Metro Books, 2002), *Irish Myths and Legends* (with Lady Gregory; Philadelphia: Running Press, 1999), *A Treasury of Irish Myth, Legend and Folklore* (edited by Claire Boss; New York: Gramercy, 1986), and *The Celtic Twilight: Myth, Fantasy and Folklore* (Minneapolis: Prism Press, 1990).

Patrick Kavanagh, a farmer from Co. Monaghan, wrote the tormented long poem "The Great Hunger," as well as a ballad still sung in Irish pubs, "On Raglan Road." See his *Collected Poems* (New York: Norton, 1964).

A good source for exploring Shinto is Jean Herbert's *Shinto: At the Fountainhead of Japan* (London: George Allen & Unwin, 1967).

Ireland's first president, Douglas Hyde, translated the works of Raftery in *Abhráin atá Leaghta ar an Rechtúire: Songs Ascribed to Raftery* (New York: Barnes & Noble Books, n.d.).

Eavan Boland now lives part-time in America, teaching at Stanford University; *An Origin like Water* (New York: Norton, 1997), *Outside History* (New York: Norton, 2001), and *Against Love Poetry* (New York: Norton, 2001), show the poet at her peak.

Corkman Greg Delanty, who teaches in Vermont, makes biculturalism an important theme in his works, including *American Wake* (Belfast: Blackstaff Press, 1995) and *The Blind Stitch* (Manchester: Carcanet, 2001).

American Indian scholar Vine Deloria's most famous book is *Custer Died for Your Sins* (Norman, Okla.: University of Oklahoma Press, 1988); his recent *Spirit & Reason: A Vine Deloria Reader* (Golden, Colo.: Fulcrum Publishing, 1999) includes reflections on land from which these passages are drawn.

Bob Curran's numerous works include *Complete Guide to Celtic Mythology* (Belfast: Appletree, 2002) and *Bloody Irish* (Dublin: Merlin Publishing, 2002); television audiences delight in his storytelling abilities, as do participants in his Hands on History tours. He can be reached at DrBob@publications99.freeserve.co.uk.

CHAPTER TWO: MOUNTAINS OF THE HAG

Tom Hannon's stories have been recorded for Irish radio and are available on compact disk from folklorist Maurice O'Keefe, Tralee, Co. Kerry.

A good source for the meanings of Irish place-names is P. W. Joyce's *Irish Local Names Explained* (Dublin: Roberts Wholesale Books, 1923, reprinted 1996).

Tony Hawks got drunk one night and wound up hitchhiking *'Round Ireland with a Fridge* (New York: Griffin Trade, 2001), during which expedition he passed through Gort as quickly as he could.

The stories of Ireland's first settlers can be found in R. A. MacAlister's *Lebor Gabála Érenn: The Book of the Taking of Ireland* (Dublin: Irish Texts Society, 1941).

The Irish Triads have been collected in many versions, including *The Three Best Things: A Collection of Irish Triads,* edited by Fergus Kelly (Belfast: Appletree, 1999).

Some sources for Cailleach lore are Douglas Hyde's *Beside the Fire: A Collection of Irish Gaelic Folk Stories* (London: David Nutt, 1890) and Cheryl Straffon's *The Earth Goddess: Celtic and Pagan Legacy of the Landscape* (London: Blandford, 1997).

Helen Lanigan Wood is the author of the *Survey of Museums in Ireland* (Dublin: Irish Museums Association, 1999).

For more on Biddy Early, consult Eddie Lenihan's *In Search of Biddy Early* (Cork: Mercier Press, 1987) and Meda Ryan's *Biddy Early: The Wise Woman of Clare* (Cork: Mercier Press, 1991).

Thomas Westropp's classic commentary on the Burren has been collected in *Archaeology of the Burren: Prehistoric Forts and Dolmens in North Clare* (Ennis, Ireland: Clasp Press, 1999) and *Folklore of Clare: A Folklore Survey of County Clare and County Clare Folk-Tales and Myths* (Ennis, Ireland: Clasp Press, 2000).

The work of Emily Lawless, once so popular, is now regrettably difficult to find; *Grania: The Story of an Island* (New York: Macmillan, 1892) is worth seeking out.

Nuala O'Faolain's lovely memoir, *Are You Somebody? The Accidental Memoir of a Dublin Woman* (New York: Henry Holt, 1999), became a bestseller on both sides of the pond; her first novel, *My Dream of You* (New York: Riverhead Books, 2001) is a stunning examination of the lasting effects of the Famine on the Irish psyche.

Ann Korff's delightful *Book of the Burren* (Doorus, Ireland: Tír Eolas, 1991) includes consideration of the area's natural as well as mythic history.

The Burren Perfumery, Carron, Co. Clare, is on-line at www.burrenperfumery.com.

You can see Fiona Marron's sheela paintings at www.silenagig.com, or you can write her at Main Street, Clane, Co. Kildare.

One of the best sources for more information on the sheela is Jorgen Anderson's *The Witch on the Wall: Medieval Erotic Sculpture in the British Islands* (London: George Allen & Unwin, n.d).

"The Lament of the Hag of Beare," as well as other poems from the Irish, can be found in *1000 Years of Irish Poetry: The Gaelic and Anglo Poets from Pagan Times to the Present,* edited by Kathleen Hoagland (New York: Welcome Rain, 1999). This translation is by the great Kuno Meyer.

Niall's story can be found in Tom Peete Cross and Clark Harris Slover, eds., *Ancient Irish Tales* (New York: Henry Holt, 1936).

Kevin Danaher's comments on time can be found in "Irish Folk Tradition and the Celtic Calendar," in *The Celtic Consciousness,* ed. Robert O'Driscoll (New York: Braziller, 1981), as well as in *The Year in Ireland* (Cork: Mercier Press, 1922).

Clifford Geertz's work on place includes *Local Knowledge: Further Essays in Interpretive Anthropology* (New York: Basic Books, 1955) and *The Interpretation of Cultures: Selected Essays* (New York: Basic Books, 1973).

John Robinson and Geoffrey Godbey collaborated on *Time for Life: The Surprising*

Ways Americans Use Time (Philadelphia: University of Pennsylvania Press, 1997).
Violet Martin Ross and her partner, Edith Somerville, wrote a number of comic novels about *The Irish R. M.* (London: Longmans Green, 1920), as well as revealing correspondence published as *Letters of Somerville and Ross,* edited by Gifford Lewis (London: Faber and Faber, 1989).
Simone de Beauvoir's comments on aging and women can be found in her stirring *The Coming of Age,* translated by Patrick O'Brien (New York: Norton, 1996).

CHAPTER THREE: THE RED-HAIRED GIRL FROM THE BOG

Irish tales of the Otherworld are collected in the classic works of T. Crofton Croker (*Fairy Legends and Traditions of the South of Ireland* [William Tegg, 1862]) and Jeremiah Curtin (*Tales of the Fairies and of the Ghost World Collected from Oral Tradition in South-West Munster* [New York: Lemma Publishing, 1970]). A recent and compelling addition to the literature is Angela Bourke's *The Burning of Bridget Cleary* (London: Pimlico, 1999). More on the fairy mistress can be found in Katherine Briggs's *The Fairies in Tradition and Literature* (New York: Routledge, 1967) and in Lady Wilde's *Ancient Legends, Mystic Charms and Superstitions of Ireland* (London: Chatto & Windus, 1902).
Niamh Parsons and the Loose Connections can be heard on *Loosen Up* (Green Linnet, 1997) and *Heart's Desire* (Green Linnet, 2002).
Joan McBreen's work includes a comprehensive anthology of Irish women's poetry called *The White Page* (Knockeven, Co. Clare: Salmon Poetry, 2000), as well as *A Walled Garden in Moylough* (Knockeven, Co. Clare: Salmon Poetry, 1995).
One of the great books on Irish and other fairies is W. Y. Evans-Wentz's *The Fairy-Faith in Celtic Countries* (New York: Colin Smythe Humanities Press, 1911).
There are many recordings of O'Carolan's music, especially the heartrending song he reputedly wrote as he was dying, his "Farewell to Music." Derek Bell, the late harper to the Chieftains, recorded some lovely renditions, including *Carolan's Receipt* (Atlantic ASIN, 2000); the American Joemy Wilson performs Carolan's works on dulcimer on *Celtic Dreams* (Dargason Music, 1993).
The band Planxty, which included the now well-known Christy Moore and Andy Irvine, doesn't exist any longer, but you can occasionally find old tapes of their energetic music: *Planxty* (Polydor/Seanachie, 1972) and *The Planxty Collection* (Polydor/Seanachie, 1976), are especially worth the search.
Christopher Bamford, publisher of Lindisfarne Books, comments on wisdom traditions in books such as *The Voice of the Eagle: The Heart of Celtic Christianity* (Herndon, Va.: Lindisfarne Books, 2000).
Seamus Heaney often appears at the great Connemara festival, Clifden Arts Week (www.clifden-arts.ie), which runs for ten days in late September each year; his many books include the recent *Opened Ground: Selected Poems 1966–96* (New York: Farrar, Straus and Giroux, 1999). His bog poems are from *Door into the Dark* (London: Faber and Faber, 1995).
Lady Wilde, Oscar's mum and wife of another folklorist, Sir William, collected folklore that was published as *Ancient Legends, Mystic Charms and Superstitions of Ireland* (London: Chatto & Windus, 1902).

Yeats took part in the folklore revival, not only with his poems but with his own collection, *Fairy and Folk Tales of the Irish Peasantry* (New York: Gramercy Books, 1986).

Dermot MacManus's charming book on fairies is *The Middle Kingdom: The Faerie World of Ireland* (Buckinghamshire, England: Colin Smythe, 1959).

Tom Cowan's pioneering work in Celtic shamanism is documented in his *Fire in the Head: Shamanism and the Celtic Spirit* (San Francisco: HarperCollins, 1993).

Lawrence Durrell's comments on landscape are expanded in his *Spirit of Place: Letters and Essays on Travel,* ed. Alan Thomas (Stony Creek, Conn.: Leete's Island Books, 1984).

Bran's story appears in Kuno Meyer's translation of *The Voyage of Bran Son of Febal to the Land of the Living* (London: David Nutt, 1895).

A lovely illustrated version of Charles Guyot's classic book on Ys is Dierdre Kavanaugh's *The Legend of the City of Ys* (Amherst, Mass.: University of Massachusetts Press, 1979).

Burton's depressing *Anatomy of Melancholy* is available in a replica of its first edition (New York: Dover, 2002).

Philosopher Susan Bordo has written of social constrictions on women in *Unbearable Weight* (Berkeley and Los Angeles: University of California Press, 1993).

Jean Markale's many books on Celtic subjects include *The Epics of Celtic Ireland* (Rochester, Vt.: Inner Traditions, 2000), *The Pagan Mysteries of Halloween: Celebrating the Dark Half of the Year* (Rochester, Vt.: Inner Traditions, 2000), and *Women of the Celts* (Rochester, Vt.: Inner Traditions, 1986).

Stories from the *Colloquy of the Ancients* can be found in Cross and Slover's *Ancient Irish Tales,* as well as in Myles Dillon's *Irish Sagas* (Cork: Mercier Press, 1968).

Eddie Lenihan is one of Ireland's most delightful storytellers. His work has been recorded as *The Good People* (Sounds True, 2001). Summers, you can find him at one of the Burren hotels, performing as a traditional storyteller. Eddie's comments on the fairy tree of Newmarket-on-Fergus can be found in *Irish Spirit: Pagan, Celtic, Christian, Global* (Dublin: Wolfhound Press, 2001).

Martin McDonaugh's *Connemara Trilogy* (*The Beauty Queen of Leenane, Lonesome West, A Skull in Connemara*) (New York: Random House, 1998) includes uproarious depressing images of Irish rural life.

Tim Robinson's maps of the Burren and of Connemara are published by Folding Landscapes, Roundstone, Co. Galway; his essays appear in *Setting Foot on the Shores of Connemara* (Dublin: Lilliput, 1995).

CHAPTER FOUR: ΙΠΤΟΧΙCATΙΟΠ

Tales of Medb appear in many works, including Miriam Robbins Dexter's *Whence the Goddesses: A Sourcebook* (New York: Pergamon Press, 1990) and Rosalind Clark's *The Great Queens: Irish Goddesses from the Mórrígan to Cathleen Ní Houlihan* (Buckinghamshire, England: Colin Smythe, 1991).

The classic modern translation of the greatest Irish epic is Thomas Kinsella's translation of *The Táin* (Dublin: Dolmen Press, 1969).

Eithne Strong's work includes *Sarah, in Passing* (Dublin: Dolmen Press, 1974). Strong's descriptive phrase was used by Ailbhe Smyth in *Wildish Things: An Anthology of New Irish Women's Writing* (Dublin: Attic Press, 1989).

The works of Alaskan wildlife artist Bill Berry, whose death plummeted me into poetry, can be seen in *William D. Berry: Alaskan Field Sketches 1954–56* (Fairbanks, Alaska: University of Alaska Press, 1999).

In childhood, Yeats lived with his mother's family, the Pollixfens, in Sligo; many of his early works feature legends he learned there from the Irish-speaking servants.

Jerome Rothenberg's classic anthology of inspired poetry, *Technicians of the Sacred* (Berkeley and Los Angeles: University of California Press, 1985) introduced generations of American poets to non-Western poetry.

A compelling and comprehensive book on Ireland's holy wells is Walter and Mary Brenneman's *Crossing the Circle at the Holy Wells of Ireland* (Charlottesville, Va.: University Press of Virginia, 1995).

Folklorist Dáithí Ó hÓgain's works include an excellent compendium of Irish myth: *Myth, Legend and Romance: An Encyclopedia of the Irish Folk Tradition* (Englewood Cliffs, N.J.: Prentice-Hall, 1991), as well as the comprehensive *The Sacred Isle: Belief and Religion in Pre-Christian Ireland* (Cork: Collins Press, 1999).

Rhys Carpenter's analysis of epic poetry can be found in *Folktale, Fiction and Saga in the Homeric Epic* (Berkeley and Los Angeles: University of California Press, 1974).

Marie-Louise Sjoestedt's work is not readily available but worth seeking out: try *Gods and Heroes of the Celts* (Berkeley, Calif.: Turtle Island Foundation, 1982).

The great critic Walter Ong wrote extensively on the role of the voice in poetry; see *Orality and Literacy: The Technologizing of the Word* (New York: Routledge, 1988).

Maureen Waters's *The Comic Irishman* (Albany: State University of New York, 1984) is a classic commentary on the subject.

Proinsias MacCana is highly regarded for his work on Irish spirituality, which includes *Celtic Mythology* (London: Hamlyn, 1970).

A prolific writer on Celtic matters is the Cornish scholar Peter Berresford Ellis, whose relevant works include *Celtic Myths and Legends* (New York: Carroll & Graf, 2003) and *Celtic Women: Women in Celtic Society and Literature* (Grand Rapids, Mich.: Eerdmans, 1995).

In addition to her classic textbook, *Whence the Goddesses* (New York: Pergamon Press, 1990), Miriam Dexter has written of Medb in "Queen Medb, Female Automony in Ancient Ireland, and Irish Matrilineal Traditions," in *Proceedings of the Ninth Annual UCLA Indo-European Conference,* Karlene Jones-Bley, Angela della Volpe, Miriam Robbins Dexter, and Martin Huld, eds. (Washington, D.C.: Institute for the Study of Man, 1998).

Elizabeth Cunningham's series on Medb is called *The Magdalen Trilogy,* the first volume of which has been published as *Daughter of the Shining Isles* (Barrytown, N.Y.: Station Hill Publishers, 2000).

Nuala Ní Dhomhnaill's work is available in *The Astrakhan Cloak* (Winston-Salem, N.C.: Wake Forest University Press, 1993) and *Pharaoh's Daughter* (Winston-Salem, N.C.: Wake Forest University Press, 1993).

A resident of the area around Tara, Michael Slavin has written the most comprehensive book on the monument: *The Book of Tara* (Dublin: Wolfhound, 1996).

In addition to leading women's mystery groups, Falcon River is a storyteller and raconteur; she can be reached at www.womensriteswomensmysteries.com.

CHAPTER FIVE: BECOMING ΠΑΤΙVE ΤΟ ΤΗΙS ISLAΠD

Emain Macha (Navan Fort) is not extensively described in the literature, but a good source of information is N. B. Aitchison's *Armagh and the Royal Centres in Early Medieval Ireland: Monuments, Cosmology, and the Past* (Rochester, N.Y.: Boydell & Brewer, 1994) and Gabriel Cooney's *Landscapes of Neolithic Ireland* (New York: Routledge, 2000).

Etymologies in this and other chapters derive from the *Oxford English Dictionary* (New York: Oxford University Press, 1989).

Martin Brennan's best-known but controversial work on Newgrange is *Stars and Stones: Ancient Art and Astronomy in Ireland* (London: Thames & Hudson, 1984).

Macha's story is told in Eleanor Hull's *The Cuchullin Saga in Irish Literature* (London: David Nutt, 1898, reprinted 1972).

An excellent source for Irish natural history is *Nature in Ireland: A Scientific and Cultural History* by John Wilson Foster (Chester Springs, Pa.: Dufour Editions, 1997).

John Hewitt's poems are collected in an edition edited by Ulster poet Frank Ormsby (Belfast: Blackstaff Press, 1991).

CHAPTER SIX: ΤΗΕ WELL OF HER ΜΕΜΟRY

Donations are always welcome to assist the work of the Brigidine sisters of Kildare: send to 14 Dara Place, Kildare, Ireland.

Mary Condren's comments are from her book *The Serpent and the Goddess: Women, Religion and Power in Ancient Ireland* (New York: Harper & Row, 1989).

For David Leroy Miller's commentary on polytheism, see *The New Polytheism* (Dallas, TX: Spring Publications, 1981).

Fifteen years of research in the subject convinced me that the sun is often seen as feminine; see my *O Mother Sun: A New View of the Cosmic Feminine* (Freedom, Calif.: Crossing Press, 1994).

The Irish American poet Phyllis McGinley's work is now unfortunately out of print, despite her great popularity in the mid-twentieth century; this poem is from *Love Letters of Phyllis McGinley* (New York: Viking, 1957).

Christy Moore's work is collected on his self-titled album (Atlantic, 1988).

One of my greatest treasures is Patrick Logan's book *The Holy Wells of Ireland* (Buckinghamshire, England: Colin Smythe, 1980), inscribed by the author to Tom Hannon.

Barbara Callan's memoir of the revival of the *crios Brídghe* can be found in *Irish Spirit: Pagan, Celtic, Christian, Global* (Monaghan, ed; Dublin: Wolfhound Press, 2001).

Luka Bloom's website is www.lukabloom.com; his many albums include *Keeper of the Flame* (Cog Communications, 2000) and *Salty Heaven* (Sony, 1998).

Nóirín Ní Ríain's rich voice can be heard on her many albums, including the recent *Vox de Nube* with the monks of Glenstal Abbey (Gael Linn, 2001) and on *Celtic Soul* (Celtic Music Distribution, 1996).

Dougie MacLean's work includes *The Dougie MacLean Collection* (Putumayo World Music, 1995); see www.dougiemaclean.com.

Starhawk is one of America's most notable ecofeminists; her most recent book is *Webs of Power: Notes from the Global Uprising* (Gabriola Island, B.C., Canada: New Society, 2002).

CHAPTER SEVEN: WISDOM GALORE

Barbara Callan's song "Inis Bó Finne" is available on the compact disk *On the Bright Road* (lynnsaoirse@eircom.net).

The story of Bó Finne appears in *Island of the White Cow,* by Deborah Tall (New York: Atheneum, 1986).

Anna Livia Plurabelle, the poetic embodiment of the Liffey River and a literary version of the river's goddess, winds throughout James Joyce's great *Finnegans Wake* (New York: Viking Press, 1939).

Keith Basso's *Wisdom Sits in Places: Landscape and Language among the Western Apache* (Albuquerque: University of New Mexico Press, 1996) offers a fascinating comparison with Irish sensibility.

Joe Meeker's *The Comedy of Survival: Literary Ecology and a Play Ethic* (Tucson: University of Arizona Press, 1997) is widely regarded as a foundational text in ecocriticism.

Anthropologist Marshall Sahlins has written on the way "native informants" see the anthropologists who study them in *How "Natives" Think: About Captain Cook, For Example* (Chicago: University of Chicago Press, 1995) and *Culture in Practice: Selected Essays* (Cambridge, Mass.: Zone Press, 2000).

Edward Hyams's work includes *Animals in the Service of Man* (Philadelphia: Lippincott, 1972).

The work of Christopher Troy and David MacHugh was reported in the *Economist,* 26 April, 2001.

John Toland is one of those fascinating but little-known Irishmen; he coined the term *pantheist* and wrote *Pantheisticon* as well as his *Memoirs,* both now rarely seen.

Perhaps the best treatment of the connection between Uisneach and Bealtaine is in Michael Dames's *Mythic Ireland* (London: Thames & Hudson, 1992).

See Alexander Chayanov's *Theory of Peasant Cooperatives* (Athens, Ohio: Ohio University Press, 1991).

The best book on Irish folklore and history of food is Bríd Mahon's *Land of Milk and Honey: The Story of Traditional Irish Food and Drink* (Cork: Mercier Press, 1991).

Karl Marx foresaw globalization in *The Communist Manifesto* (New York: Signet Classics, 1998).

Jonathan Swift's "A Modest Proposal" is widely available and searingly relevant to the present.

The works of English economist Nassau Senior have been recently republished as *Collected Works* (Bristol, England: Thoemmes Press, 1999).

Many excellent books on the Famine are available, including the stunning novel *The Hungry Earth* by Sean Kenny (Dublin: Wolfhound Press, 1999), whose work also appears in Tom Hayden's *Irish Hunger* (Dublin: Wolfhound Press, 1997).

Pat McGregor's work on the Famine was reported to the Royal Economic Conference in 1998.

Connemara historian Kathleen Villiers-Tuthill has gathered Famine documents in her *Beyond the Twelve Bens* (Clifden: Connemara Girl Publications, 1997).

Among German feminists working on sustainable economics, see Claudia von Werlhof's *There Is an Alternative: Subsistence and Worldwide Resistance to Corporate Globalization* (London: Zed Books, 2001) and Maria Mies's *The Subsistence Perspective* (London: Zed Books, 2001).

Celticist James MacKillop wrote the *Oxford Encyclopedia of Celtic Mythology* (New York: Oxford University Press, 2000).

Malachy Kearns is readily found at Roundstone Music, IDA Craft Center, Roundstone, Co. Galway, or on the Web at www.bodhran.com.

For more on cities and globalization, see Saskia Sassen, *The Global City: New York, London, Tokyo* (Princeton, N.J.: Princeton University Press, 2001).

Philosopher Mikhail Bakhtin has deeply examined place and language; a good start is *The Dialogic Imagination: Four Essays* (Austin: University of Texas Press, 1981).

Jonathan Miller is the "Mean Fields" columnist for the *Sunday Times* (London).

Paddy Galvin's stirring poems have been collected in *New and Selected Poems* (Cork: Cork University Press, 1996).

Vandana Shiva's organization is the Research Foundation for Science, Technology, and Ecology; with Maria Mies, she wrote *Ecofeminism: Reconnecting a Divided World* (London: Zed Books, 1993).

CHAPŤER EiGHŤ: WiLDiSH ŤHiΠGS

A good source on Irish women and marriage is Art Cosgrove's *Marriage in Ireland* (East Lansing, Mich.: College Press, 1985).

Alfred, Lord Tennyson's poem on Ireland can be found in *Tennyson's Poetry: Authoritative Texts, Contexts, Criticism* (New York: Norton, 1999).

The Munster novelist and short story writer Elizabeth Bowen commented extensively on her native province in her memoir, *Bowen's Court* (New York: Norton, 1979).

Although more associated with the Aran Islands than with Munster, John Millington Synge wrote of his visits to the southwest of Ireland in his *Collected Letters* (New York: Oxford University Press, 1989).

Stories about Lough Gur form a backdrop to the description of rural Irish life in Mary Carbery's *The Farm by Lough Gur: The Story of Mary Fogarty* (London: Longmans, Green and Co., 1937).

Celticist Lisa Bitel describes a bleak life for Irish women in her *Land of Women: Tales of Sex and Gender from Early Ireland* (Ithaca: Cornell University Press, 1996).

An excellent book on Ireland's pirate queen is *Granuaile: The Life and Times of Grace O'Malley* by Anne Chambers (Dublin: Wolfhound Press, 2002).

Kennelly's remembrance of Frank O'Connor's speech appears in the introduction to his *New and Selected Poems* (Loughcrew, Co. Meath: Galley Books, 1976).

Irish literary critic Declan Kiberd's sometimes controversial but always illuminating comments on the Munster poets can be found in his *Irish Classics* (Cambridge, Mass.: Harvard University Press, 2001).

The great Kerry storyteller Peig Sayers found her way into print in two books: *Peig: The Autobiography of Peig Sayers* (Dublin: Talbot, 1974) and *An Old Woman's Reflections* (New York: Oxford University Press, 1993).

Munster writer Frank O'Connor's many works include his *Collected Stories* (New York: Random House, 1982).

Edna O'Brien's novel on the Girl X case is *Down by the River* (New York: Plume, 1998).

The once-scandalous book by Eric Cross, *The Tailor and Ansty* (Dublin: Irish Book Center, 1995), seems unremarkable today.

The great Munster poet John Montague describes the process of de-Irishing children like him in his moving poem, "A Grafted Tongue" in *Contemporary Irish Poetry: An Anthology,* ed. Anthony Bradley (Berkeley: University of California Press, 1980).

Máire MacNeill's life work resulted in a two volume book, *The Festivals of Leyhnasa* (London: Oxford University Press, 1962), now regrettably out of print.

Margaret Murray's *God of the Witches* (New York: Oxford University Press, 1992) remains a controversial vision of the pagan past.

Rukeyser's long out-of-print novel *The Orgy: An Irish Journey of Passion and Transformation* has recently been republished (Ashfield, Mass.: Paris Press, 1997).

Brian Friel's *Dancing at Lughnasa* (London: Faber and Faber, 1992) was made into a film (pronounced as two syllables in Ireland) starring Meryl Streep.

Ursula Le Guin is the author of many widely beloved novels as well as the book of theory, *The Language of the Night* (New York: HarperCollins, 1992).

The late Seán Lucy's work was collected as *Unfinished Sequence* (Dublin: Wolfhound Press, 1984).

Spenser's dreadful comments on the Irish are found in *A View of the State of Ireland* (Malden, Mass.: Blackwell Publishers, 1997).

Michael Hartnett's provocative words can be read in *A Farewell to English and Other Poems* (Loughcrew, Co. Meath: Gallery Press, n.d). He translated Nuala Ní Dhomhnaill's *Selected Poems, Rogha Danta: The Bright Wave* (Chester Springs, Pa.: Dufour, 1997).

Many books explain the theories of Jacques Lacan; for his own words, see *Ecrits: A Selection,* translated by Bruce Fink (New York: Norton, 2002).

Shirley Ardener's theories are articulated in *Women and Space: Ground Rules and Social Maps* (New York: Berg Publishing, 1993).

CHAPTER NINE: THE STONE IN THE MIDST OF ALL

The name Garravogue occurs in various areas around Ireland, especially in Sligo, where the river that bisects the city bears the hag's name. The story of the world-creating hag, the Cailleach, can be found in many sources, but the site-specific tale of Saint Patrick and the Gargan woman has been published only in MacNeill's great work, *The Festival of Lughnasa* (London: Oxford University Press, 1962).

Index

Page numbers of maps appear in italics.

Π

O

P

Acknowledgments

G rateful thanks are due to many people for their support and assistance towards this book. In Ireland, Barbara Callan and Tom Hannon provided not only great stories but inspiration in connecting those stories to the Irish land. In addition, I thank my Irish friends for their hospitality and support: in Clare, Jessie Lendennie, Tim Allen, Síobhan Hutson, Eddie Lenihan; in Galway, Anna Hannon, Frank Kelly, Françoise Kelly, Ann Bercot, Dave Hogan, Carol Anne Joyce, Valerie Joyce, Fidelma Mullane, the O'Neill family; in Mayo, my many cousins including Pat and Nora McHale, and Joe and Catherine Devine McHale; in Ulster, Bob and Mary Curran, and Kevin Morgan; in Dublin, Seamus Cashman, Kay Doyle, Chenile Keogh, Aideen Quigley; in Kildare, Fiona Marron and Brian Dunning, Sr. Mary Minihan, Sr. Phyllis O'Shea; in Waterford, Lynn Saoirse, Michael Coady; in Cork, Paddy Galvin and the crew at the Munster Writers Centre; In America, in Westmeath, the Maxwell family; and in exile in America, Sean Kenny, Liam Heneghan, and the late Séan Lucy.

On the other side of the water, too, friends have supported the research and writing of this book, especially Maggie Courtade, Barbara Flaherty, Ray Olson, Paula Luedtke, Sandi Liss, Kay Thurn, Pamela Castellanos,

Jamie O'Reilly, Deb Trent, Sally Strosahl, Charlene Baumbich, Mimi Hill, Gaye Mack and Etta Worthington. Mary Jo Neitz, Flo Golod, Leslie Van Gelder, Miriam Robbins Dexter, Ethna McKiernan, Elizabeth Cunningham, Liz Davidson, Wendy Griffin, Helene Hulbert, Falcon River and Dawn Work-Makinne read and commented upon this work as it developed. Colleagues at DePaul University have assisted in many ways, especially by providing the interdisciplinary vision necessary for such work; in addition the University Research Council as well as my own college, the School for New Learning, provided funds for some of the travel. The Center for Celtic Spirituality at Old Saint Patrick's Church in Chicago, especially Colleen Grace, offered a venue for trying out some of these ideas, as did the Priestess Gathering of the Re-Formed Congregation of the Goddess in Madison, Wisconsin and the supportive folks at Transitions Bookplace in Chicago. My agent, the sterling Elizabeth Frost-Knappman, offered invaluable and constant support, as did Georgia Hughes and the staff of New World Library. Thanks to all for their part in helping this book through to print.

About the Author

P atricia Monaghan first traveled to Ireland as a graduate student in the early 1970s, studying Irish poetry and mythology. Since that time, she has returned often, especially to the western counties from which her family emigrated; she holds dual Irish and American citizenship. Patricia has published several books in Ireland including a volume of poetry based in science, *Dancing with Chaos* (from Salmon Poetry). She recently edited the anthology of Irish and Irish-American essayists, *Irish Spirit: Pagan, Celtic, Christian, Global* (Wolfhound Press).

On this side of the water, she is also widely published. She is the author of the definitive encyclopedia of the world's female divinities, *The New Book of Goddesses and Heroines* (Llewellyn) and an new encyclopedia of Celtic myth and folklore (forthcoming, Facts on File). She has edited two collections of Irish-American literature, *Unlacing: Ten Irish-American Women Poets* (Fireweed Press) and *The Next Parish Over: Irish-American Writing Today* (New Rivers Press). She is co-author, with Eleanor Viereck, of *Meditation: The Complete Guide,* published by New World Library.

Patricia is a member of the interdisciplinary faculty at DePaul University in Chicago, where she teaches literature and environment. She also lectures widely on goddess mythology and Irish spirituality. Further information is available on her website, www.patriciamonaghan.com.